Mastering Windows Group Policy

Control and secure your Active Directory environment with Group Policy

Jordan Krause

BIRMINGHAM - MUMBAI

Mastering Windows Group Policy

Commissioning Editor: Pavan Ramchandani
Acquisition Editor: Meeta Rajani
Content Development Editor: Arjun Joshi
Technical Editor: Sayali Thanekar
Copy Editor: Safis Editing
Project Coordinator: Jagdish Prabhu
Proofreader: Safis Editing
Indexer: Mariammal Chettiyar
Graphics: Jisha Chirayil
Production Coordinator: Arvindkumar Gupta

First published: November 2018

Production reference: 1291118

Published by Packt Publishing Ltd.
Livery Place
35 Livery Street
Birmingham
B3 2PB, UK.

ISBN 978-1-78934-739-5

www.packtpub.com

Contributors

About the author

Jordan Krause is a six-time Microsoft MVP, currently awarded in the Cloud and Datacenter Management category. He has the unique opportunity to work daily with Microsoft networking and remote access technologies as a senior engineer at IVO Networks. Jordan specializes in Microsoft DirectAccess and Always On VPN. Committed to continuous learning, Jordan holds Microsoft certifications as an MCP, MCTS, MCSA, and MCITP Enterprise Administrator, and regularly writes articles reflecting his experiences with these technologies. Jordan lives in beautiful west Michigan (USA), but works daily with companies around the world.

About the reviewers

Neville Sanford is a Sr System Administrator for a national construction law firm. He has over 20 years' experience of working with Microsoft products. From NT 4 to the latest tech, he has worked on many projects over the years. Neville has worked with Microsoft Group Policy for many years, first implementing it in 2005. Neville is married and has 2 children. In his spare time he and his family run a mobile laser tag company.

Anderson Patricio is a Canadian Microsoft MVP and he is an IT Consultant based in Toronto, his areas of expertise are around Microsoft Exchange, Skype for Business, Azure, System Center and Active Directory. Anderson is an active member of the Exchange Community and he contributes in forums, blogs, articles, and videos. In Portuguese, his website contains thousands of Microsoft Tutorials to help the local community, besides of his speaking engagements at TechED in South America and MVA Academy training courses.

Packt is searching for authors like you

If you're interested in becoming an author for Packt, please visit `authors.packtpub.com` and apply today. We have worked with thousands of developers and tech professionals, just like you, to help them share their insight with the global tech community. You can make a general application, apply for a specific hot topic that we are recruiting an author for, or submit your own idea.

`mapt.io`

Mapt is an online digital library that gives you full access to over 5,000 books and videos, as well as industry leading tools to help you plan your personal development and advance your career. For more information, please visit our website.

Why subscribe?

- Spend less time learning and more time coding with practical eBooks and Videos from over 4,000 industry professionals

- Improve your learning with Skill Plans built especially for you

- Get a free eBook or video every month

- Mapt is fully searchable

- Copy and paste, print, and bookmark content

Packt.com

Did you know that Packt offers eBook versions of every book published, with PDF and ePub files available? You can upgrade to the eBook version at `www.packt.com` and as a print book customer, you are entitled to a discount on the eBook copy. Get in touch with us at `customercare@packtpub.com` for more details.

At `www.packt.com`, you can also read a collection of free technical articles, sign up for a range of free newsletters, and receive exclusive discounts and offers on Packt books and eBooks.

Table of Contents

Preface

Technology is ever-changing. New pieces of technology arrive on our doorsteps almost daily, often replacing old or outdated items. The race is always on for the fastest processors, the highest pixel counts, the safest cars, and smartphones with screens as big as my head. You get the idea. This is as true in the Microsoft-driven data center as it is in consumer electronics. With every new version of the Windows operating system, both client and server, we see parts and pieces come and go. Out with the old, in with the new, as they say. To give you some examples, it wasn't very many years ago that we were talking about things such as IPv6, Network Access Protection (NAP), and Windows Vista as the latest and greatest things since sliced bread. As technology progresses, so does our mentality about what is important. IPv6 is still a thing, obviously, but it's no longer the topic that everyone is telling doom and gloom stories about. Almost nobody uses it inside their networks, because it's simply not as critically important as everyone thought, and IPv4 networks are still working just fine (before you get huffy with me, remember that I said *inside* the network). NAP was a terrific idea, I still think so, but nobody took the time to learn and implement it, and so it is officially dead. And Windows Vista? I don't feel like I need to throw many words around here. Suffice to say that my Vista installer disk is safely tucked away, right next to my installation disc for Windows ME.

Turning things around, what are the topics we drool over today? It seems like marketing teams are still drawn to any and every way to use the word "cloud". In addition to that, we are starting to add some terminology such as software-defined networking and hyperconverged infrastructure. We don't even bother with giving new versions of Windows cool names anymore. Starting with Windows 7, operating system names got ultra boring. Now we're not even progressing beyond Windows 10, but just tagging numbers on the end, like 1709, 1803, and 1809.

Am I ever going to get round to actually making a point? It's possible. My entire thought process here is simply that Microsoft technologies come, and Microsoft technologies go. However, and this is a big however, there are some bits of the Windows Server operating system that have become so commonplace, so essential to the way that we do IT business, that when we think about them, we can't fathom that they would ever disappear or be replaced. These are often referred to as the "core infrastructure" pieces inside a Microsoft-driven data center. You can probably name these as well as I can, and maybe even add a few more. The things I'm talking about here are things like **Active Directory Domain Services (ADDS)**, **Domain Name System (DNS)**, and, you guessed it, **Group Policy**.

This book is all about Group Policy. This means that naturally, this book is also all about Active Directory and the core infrastructure services, because Group Policy is so ingrained in Active Directory that you cannot have one without the other. Group Policy is a management technology that has been around and built into our Windows Servers for a very, very long time. Being one of the core infrastructure technologies and so tightly integrated with AD, I expect that Group Policy is one of those few items in the Server operating system that will outlive our IT careers. I fully expect to see Group Policy continue to be utilized in Microsoft environments 10 or even 20 years down the road.

Group Policy is one of the most important and, at the same time, one of the most under-utilized pieces of Microsoft technology that has ever existed. Perhaps this is not the case for your company, but I have a fairly unique day job that allows me to interact with new IT departments on a daily basis, and I often get a glimpse into how much (or how little) said company is using Group Policy in order to manage their users and devices. The sad truth is that many are hardly scratching the surface of what this technology can do for them, and these folks spend unnecessary time, money, and effort trying to accomplish tasks in a less efficient manner.

Who this book is for

If you are an IT professional working with Windows Servers in an Active Directory domain environment, then this book is for you. Desktop administrators will also benefit from a knowledge of Group Policy, allowing you to centrally manage every aspect of your organization's workstations. A basic knowledge of Microsoft Windows, how Windows Server fits into an enterprise's infrastructure, and some knowledge of an Active Directory domain environment, will aid you in understanding the concepts covered in the book.

What this book covers

Chapter 1, *Group Policy - The Basics*, gets us comfortable with the different types of Group Policy and creates an understanding as to how it works. We will also use this time to build a test lab that will be used throughout the book.

Chapter 2, *Group Policy Management Console (GPMC)*, explores the primary interface for interacting with Group Policy and all of its associated settings.

Chapter 3, *Daily Tasks in Group Policy*, tackles many of the commonplace items that you, as a Group Policy administrator, would need to accomplish on a daily basis.

Chapter 4, *Advanced Filtering of Group Policy Objects*, dives deeper into GPMC to explain the different ways that Group Policy settings can be filtered so that they only apply to users, workstations, or servers of your choosing.

Chapter 5, *Deploying Policy Settings*, takes us into the Group Policy Editor, where we begin crafting GPOs into usable objects inside our domain. Here, we learn how to start making real changes to our workstations by deploying policy packages to them.

Chapter 6, *Group Policy Preferences*, showcases the differences between policies and preferences, and spends time working with the settings available on the preferences side of the house.

Chapter 7, *Group Policy as a Security Mechanism*, portrays numerous ways that Group Policy can be used to enhance your overall security strategy. Security is possibly the greatest benefit of all the services offered by Group Policy.

Chapter 8, *Group Policy Maintenance*, gets into the less exciting, but need-to-know tasks associated with maintaining your Group Policy environment and ensuring that it runs well for years to come.

Chapter 9, *Group Policy Troubleshooting*, helps guide the troubleshooting process whenever diagnosing an issue inside Group Policy. Most troubleshooting involves hunting down improper links or filters, but there is also potential for some under-the-hood issues.

Chapter 10, *PowerShell for Group Policy Administration*, takes what we know about Group Policy and shows us how to accomplish it via PowerShell. This helps to automate tasks, and allows interaction with Group Policy strictly from a command-line interface.

To get the most out of this book

Being familiar with the Microsoft Windows operating systems will put you a step ahead when reading this book. We will be interacting with Windows Server 2016 and Windows 10, but Group Policy has been included with the Windows Server operating system for many years. You do not have to be running the latest and greatest operating systems in order to follow along with this book, though you will learn why it is always best to be using the newest versions of Windows when interacting with the Group Policy management tools.

If you have access to a Windows Server 2008 or newer system, you should be able to easily follow along with everything that we are doing in this book. If you've never seen Windows Server before, it is available as a trial download from Microsoft's website. You'll need a place to install this operating system though, which means you will need either a piece of hardware capable of running Windows Server, or access to a virtualized infrastructure, such as Hyper-V or VMware, in order to spin up a new virtual server.

Download the color images

We also provide a PDF file that has color images of the screenshots/diagrams used in this book. You can download it here: `https://www.packtpub.com/sites/default/files/downloads/9781789347395_ColorImages.pdf`.

Conventions used

There are a number of text conventions used throughout this book.

`CodeInText`: Indicates code words in text, database table names, folder names, filenames, file extensions, pathnames, dummy URLs, user input, and Twitter handles. Here is an example: "Or you can also type `MMC` from a command prompt or PowerShell prompt and open it that way as well."

Any command-line input or output is written as follows:

```
Invoke-GPUpdate -Computer LAPTOP2
```

Bold: Indicates a new term, an important word, or words that you see on screen. For example, words in menus or dialog boxes appear in the text like this. Here is an example: "Probably the easiest and quickest way to open a PowerShell window is to right-click on the **Start** button, which invokes the quick admin menu."

 Warnings or important notes appear like this.

 Tips and tricks appear like this.

Get in touch

Feedback from our readers is always welcome.

General feedback: If you have questions about any aspect of this book, mention the book title in the subject of your message and email us at customercare@packtpub.com.

Errata: Although we have taken every care to ensure the accuracy of our content, mistakes do happen. If you have found a mistake in this book, we would be grateful if you would report this to us. Please visit www.packt.com/submit-errata, selecting your book, clicking on the Errata Submission Form link, and entering the details.

Piracy: If you come across any illegal copies of our works in any form on the internet, we would be grateful if you would provide us with the location address or website name. Please contact us at copyright@packt.com with a link to the material.

If you are interested in becoming an author: If there is a topic that you have expertise in, and you are interested in either writing or contributing to a book, please visit authors.packtpub.com.

Reviews

Please leave a review. Once you have read and used this book, why not leave a review on the site that you purchased it from? Potential readers can then see and use your unbiased opinion to make purchase decisions, we at Packt can understand what you think about our products, and our authors can see your feedback on their book. Thank you!

For more information about Packt, please visit packt.com.

Group Policy - The Basics 1

I mentioned in the preface to this book that **Group Policy** is often underutilized in our corporate environments, and I genuinely believe that to be true. It's not *a* centralized management technology for our servers and workstations—no, it is *the* centralized management technology for our servers and workstations. Group Policy is built right in; there are no extra parts to install or configure, and there are no extra costs or add-ons that are required. When you build an **Active Directory** domain, you automatically build everything that is needed to start using Group Policy to push configuration and security settings to all of the users and devices attached to that domain.

If your day job requires you to touch Domain Controller servers, you should have a working knowledge of Group Policy to do your job well. Even if you work in IT desktop support and never interact with the Windows Server operating system, you can still help your company to build more manageable, more secure computers for your workforce by understanding what is possible with the Group Policy engine. Wouldn't it be great to be able to make intelligent suggestions to the Active Directory team about settings or policies that might be pushed out to those desktop computers that are under your jurisdiction?

Terminology

Let's back the train up a little. Some of you know all of this, and may in fact know everything that we discuss in this first chapter. But some will not, and we need to cover our bases. We have already thrown around some terms that are uber important to know and understand as we progress, and there will be more, so let's take a minute to spell out some of the things we are going to be referencing throughout this book:

- **Active Directory Domain Services (ADDS)**: More commonly referred to as simply AD, this is a directory or a listing of all the users and computers that are part of your organization. It's sort of like a really important Rolodex.

- **Domain Controller (DC)**: A server that is running the ADDS role, and therefore stores the information about your organization's directory, is known as a Domain Controller. Most environments have multiple DCs, each of which stores a copy of the directory data because this Active Directory data is so important, you definitely don't want to lose it!
- **Active Directory Users and Computers**: One of the tools (probably the most common one) that is used to interact with the data that is stored inside AD. Active Directory Users and Computers is a great place to stop for information about, surprise surprise, any user or computer that is joined to your domain.
- **Active Directory Sites and Services**: Businesses like to grow and make money, and often this means that a company will eventually span multiple geographic locations and network subnets. AD Sites and Services is a tool that helps to organize your physical sites as they pertain to the information stored inside Active Directory.
- **Group Policy**: Gives centralized management capabilities of both user and computer settings for the machines and user accounts that are part of your Active Directory domain environment.
- **Group Policy Object (GPO)**: These are objects created and stored inside Active Directory that contain the settings that you are applying to users and computers.
- **Group Policy Management Console (GPMC)**: The primary interface that administrators use to interact with Group Policy settings.
- **Group Policy Management Editor (GPME)**: The interface opened when editing a Group Policy Object. GPME is what you use to place settings into GPOs.
- **Organizational Unit (OU)**: Inside Active Directory, you organize your domain hierarchy by placing device and user objects inside containers known as OUs. Each domain object can only be a member of one OU at any given time. This will be important to remember later.

What is Group Policy?

Group Policy is a toolset inside the **Microsoft Windows Server** operating systems that enables IT administrators to centrally manage many aspects of both their domain user accounts, as well as domain-joined computer accounts. In fact, it can even be used without a domain in the mix, but we'll talk more about that in a few minutes.

Most of the time, Group Policy is used when you need to publish or issue out settings to a wide (or narrow) base of users or client desktop computers within a corporate environment. Group Policy is incredibly useful for these kinds of tasks, and can save IT departments countless man-hours as opposed to putting these same settings into place on all of their computers in a manual fashion. While Group Policy provides desktop administrations with a ton of flexibility and extra free time, it can become even more powerful when you realize that computer accounts inside Active Directory include desktop/laptop computers as well as servers. Most companies have separated roles for Desktop Administrators and Server Administrators, but both can benefit greatly from the powers that are stored inside Group Policy. In today's information-security-focused mindset, where are we most often putting that focus? Certainly, we are somewhat putting that focus on the users and their devices, making sure that those computers aren't influenced in a negative way from outside forces, but I would say that the majority of our network-security provisioning is placed on the server infrastructure side. The servers in your network are the devices that are providing services and storing your data. Keeping that data safe is a big, big deal. Securing your servers is essential in today's world, and there are many ways that Group Policy can be used to enforce that security.

All of this sounds good on paper, but that doesn't mean anything unless you know how to set up, configure, and really use Group Policy. That is the entire purpose of this book. We will be hands-on, as much as possible, as we discuss Group Policy, its management consoles, and the ways that you can use it right now in your network. There will be many step-by-step examples of establishing and distributing common settings that companies are using to secure their environments. We will also cover examples of settings that are not so commonly used, but probably should be. There are many ways to spend money on third-party solutions to have management capabilities of your company devices, but for anyone who really takes some time to dig into Group Policy, I think you will be surprised at how many of those capabilities already exist and are just waiting to be tapped into.

Active Directory Group Policy versus Local Group Policy

So far, I have mentioned Active Directory about a million times, so based on this section heading, you are probably assuming that we are discussing Active Directory Group Policy. That is correct, but it is also important to note and understand that the AD perspective is not the only way to think about Group Policy settings.

Local Group Policy

Every Microsoft Windows operating system (starting with Windows XP) has a grouping of configuration settings that is accessed and structured in a similar way. These configuration settings can be used and tweaked to manage and manipulate the workstation or server to your heart's content. This locally-stored conglomeration of settings that exists individually on each machine is known as **Local Group Policy**, or sometimes simply **Local Policy**. These local settings could certainly be used on a **machine-by-machine** basis to administer your entire workforce, but there is nothing centralized about it. You would be talking about massive man-hours to accomplish all of these changes.

If you're sitting in front of a Windows computer right now, **Local Group Policy** can be accessed by clicking **Start** | **Run**, typing GPEDIT.MSC, and pressing *Enter*:

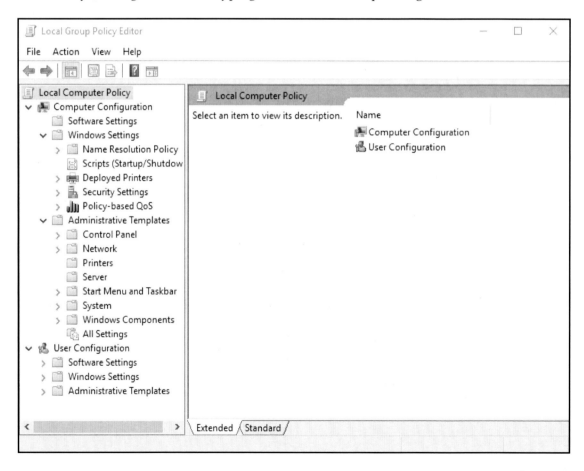

Throughout this book, we will spend much more time in an interface quite like this one so as to explain the text and settings shown here—but for the purposes of explaining Local Group Policy, this **Local Group Policy Editor** console is the place where you could make administrative changes to the workstation. The changes you make here take effect immediately, so don't poke around too much, or at least read over the descriptions of the settings very well!

Active Directory Group Policy

Local Group Policy is great and is a wonderful way to test new settings and to poke around and find out what kind of restrictions you can put into place on your workstations, but running the **Local Group Policy Editor** on every workstation in your environment and configuring all of the same settings sounds like an administrative nightmare. How do we overcome the centralized administration challenge? This is where we up-shift and start talking about Active Directory Group Policy.

Active Directory Group Policy takes all of these local policy settings and makes them available anywhere inside your domain. The interface for editing policies and settings is almost exactly the same as the local policy editor, but an additional layer of technology is introduced by being integrated with Active Directory. Inside AD-based Group Policy, you have the ability to create a policy (or hundreds of different policies) and quite easily choose which users and/or which computers that those policies apply to. In an organization that is making good use of Group Policy, it is very normal to see dozens of different **Group Policy Objects** (**GPOs**) that are being assigned to all sorts of different users, computers, or groups of users or computers. AD Group Policy stores its information on your Domain Controller servers, which is an incredibly nice aspect from an IT perspective because it means you don't need additional servers or infrastructure to utilize Group Policy.

For the rest of this book, we will be focusing on using Group Policy within an Active Directory domain environment.

What does Group Policy look like?

The bulk of interaction between an administrator and Group Policy will be via a **Microsoft Management Console** (**MMC**) called the **Group Policy Management Console** (**GPMC**). Chapter 2, *Group Policy Management Console (GPMC)*, is all about this console so we won't discuss it too much here, but the primary things to remember are that the GPMC is the place you will visit to both configure settings and filter where you want them to apply, and that you will be able to launch and tap into this console from many different places within your environment.

Here is a quick screenshot of the GPMC for your viewing pleasure:

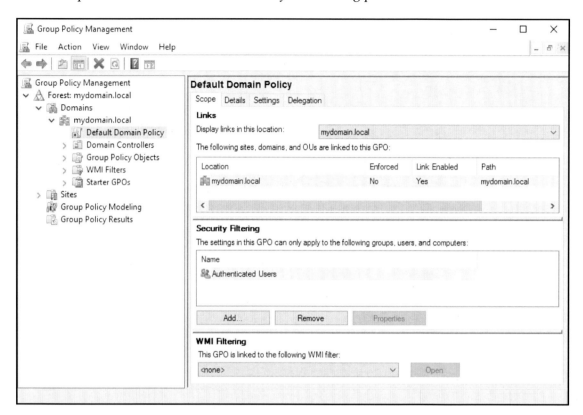

 In addition to GPMC, there are numerous PowerShell cmdlets that can now be used to interact with Group Policy Objects and settings. We will be covering these `cmdlets` later in the book as well.

Another piece of the Group Policy puzzle that is important to understand is the placement and storage of its data. As mentioned, for the remainder of this book, we will be focusing on Active Directory Group Policy. In this setting, the data for Group Policy settings is stored on your Domain Controller server or servers. Small environments may only have one DC, but any SMB or larger will have multiple servers that are hosting this same role. In some cases, an organization may have hundreds of DCs. When multiple DCs are present, the Group Policy settings and data are replicated among all of them, so the failure of one node does not result in the loss of this data. We will dig deeper into the details on what information is stored, and where, in `Chapter 8`, *Group Policy Maintenance*.

Requirements for Group Policy

This really is quite simple: you need to be running a domain. This is almost assuredly already the case for anyone who works for any company that has any servers. The first server in any Microsoft-centric network is almost always a DC, and the act of having a DC implies that you have a domain, and if you have a domain, then you have Group Policy available to you.

If you want your users to receive settings from Group Policy, the user accounts that they use to log into computers need to be domain accounts, and I think it goes without saying that the same is true for computers. If you would like to enforce settings on to computers or servers inside your environment, they must also be domain-joined. A domain is the hub for so many things inside any company network, including Group Policy processing and settings.

While Group Policy hasn't been around since the beginning of time, I also don't think that it is very important to spend too much time hashing out the details of what versions of Windows Server Domain Controllers have Group Policy, or what client-operating systems can take advantage of Group Policy settings. The reason this is not so important these days is because any operating system, both client and server, that Microsoft is still currently supporting does have Group Policy capabilities. In the very near future, we will start losing Microsoft support for Windows 7, and Group Policy has certainly been around for a lot longer than that.

So, the requirements for Group Policy = One Domain Controller.

However, if you want to establish a GPO and put some settings inside it and actually test it, then we'll need another device or user to which we can apply those settings and really test them out—so perhaps a DC plus a workstation.

 One DC is enough to get Group Policy up and running, but multiple DCs are even better and enhance the stability and resiliency of both the domain and Group Policy itself.

Who can use Group Policy?

Any IT administrator who is working within a Microsoft domain environment, or those who are building networks from the ground up can use Group Policy. It benefits everyone involved—the IT administrator as well as the end users. AD and domain administrators will interact with the Group Policy Management Console on a regular basis to establish settings and design the rollout process for those settings to get to their respective users and computers. End users benefit from Group Policy by having preconfigured workstations that they know to be company-appropriate and, most importantly, secure. In fact, in my eyes, the ability to place security settings and requirements on to users and computers is the single biggest reason that every company should be utilizing Group Policy. We will, of course, spend some time securing your devices within this book.

Hierarchy of Group Policy processing

To make use of Group Policy, you don't really have to understand how it works under the hood. You configure GPOs, which contain settings, and then you instruct Active Directory on who or what those GPOs need to apply to. Then, when those computers and users are connected to the corporate network, and therefore connected to Active Directory, they will automatically receive those GPO settings and put them into place on the computers. In other words, Group Policy processes those settings automatically.

What is very important to understand about Group Policy processing is the hierarchy that it follows. As with most Microsoft technologies, Group Policy processing follows a tree-scheme, where the application of settings flow down branches of a tree. There are four levels—also known as tiers or branches—in which Group Policy processing happens.

Levels of GPO processing

The four unique levels of hierarchy for Group Policy processing are called **Local**, **Site**, **Domain**, and **OU**. Let's spend a few minutes going through each one so that you can understand how they are different, and also how they fit together.

Local Policy

We already discussed Local Group Policy and using `gpedit.msc` to reference these settings. This is the Local Policy of a computer, and any settings that are plugged into Local Policy will process first when Windows starts. These settings affect the entire computer—it doesn't matter which users are logged in. It is very rare that companies would make use of Local Policy to push any settings, because it means that you would be manually touching each workstation to put these settings into place. That's not very time-friendly. What is most important to understand about Local Policy is that your settings that are plugged in at the local policy level may not always be in effect. Since Local Policy is first to apply, it means that any levels of the Active Directory Group Policy that we are about to cover in a minute will take priority over Local Policy. In other words, your computer might put your Local Policy settings into place, but milliseconds later during the boot process, those settings could be overwritten by AD policy settings.

Site-level policies

Something that is sort of outside the scope of this book, but is relevant here, is **Active Directory Sites and Services**. Inside any Active Directory environment, your DCs will automatically have this tool installed, called AD Sites and Services. The purpose here is to define your physical locations of the network, sites, if you will. The many small businesses have only a single site, and often they never have to even open this tool. Makes sense, as everything is always connected to the same site. However, as soon as you grow your business and expand to a second location, the network typically gets much more complex, and you now have IP subnets that are different between the two sites. Active Directory Sites are defined by what IP address space, or subnet, a computer is currently residing in. When your computer checks in with AD, it is automatically known what site you are part of based on the IP address of your computer.

Here is a quick picture of **Active Directory Sites and Services**, so you can see the layout and also see that the different sites are defined by which IP addressing spaces they contain:

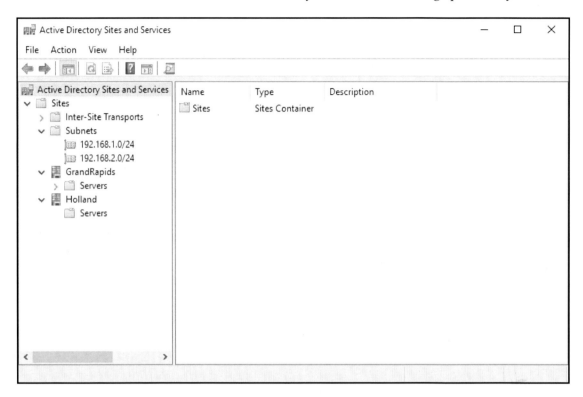

Once your environment is large enough and you have defined your Sites inside this tool, you have now enabled Group Policy to be able to issue settings to computers (and users) based on the site that they reside in. Users follow the computers in this scenario. If a computer account is logging in and Group Policy recognizes it to be in the GrandRapids site, it will apply all GPO settings that are flagged for GrandRapids. The same is true of any users that log into that computer; since the computer is currently sitting in GrandRapids, any user-based policies that are filtered for GrandRapids will also apply.

 Keep in mind that computers only receive site-based Group Policy settings while they physically reside in that site. If a computer moves to a new site, any site-level GPOs that were being applied will stop, and new site-level GPOs from the new site will apply.

Domain-level policies

Some policies and settings are going to be things that you want to apply to all of the machines or users in the entire domain, and the appropriate place for those settings are domain-level GPOs. It's important to point out that the GPOs themselves are not different as we talk about all of these different policy levels—a GPO is a GPO. The level at which the GPO is **linked** is what we are talking about when we discuss these hierarchical levels. So far, we haven't discussed GPO links, and that is because we will spend a lot of time discussing links and linking when we start to cover the bases on filtering these GPO settings, in upcoming chapters. For now, we simply need to understand that some GPOs will contain settings that need to apply to everything in the domain, and these GPOs will be linked at the domain level.

In the following screenshot, the **Default Domain Policy** has been linked at the top level, or root, of the domain:

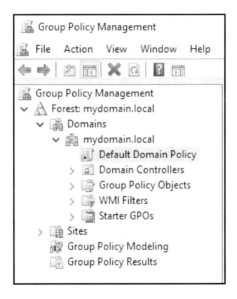

When you link a policy at the top of the domain, that GPO will filter down to each user account and device account that is present inside the domain to where it is linked, theoretically applying to all workstations, servers, and users. I say theoretically because there are a couple of reasons why a domain-level GPO might not actually apply to everything inside the domain. One of those reasons would be that the GPO was filtered to only apply to certain machines or groups (we will discuss this much more in `chapter 4`, *Advanced Filtering of Group Policy Objects*). Another reason is that some locations inside Active Directory may have **inherency blocking** enabled, which would stop GPOs from applying to any objects contained inside those locations. These locations that I am talking about are called OUs, and they are our next level of GPO processing.

OU-level policies

OUs are containing folders for computer and user accounts that are joined to your domain. OUs themselves are managed and manipulated by using the Active Directory Users and Computers tool, and this is the way domain administrators commonly keep all of their objects organized. In a simple environment, you may have an OU for Users and another OU for Computers. Getting a little more advanced may bring you separate OUs for Accounting, Finance, Human Resources, and so on. Taking full advantage of OUs will result in multiple OUs contained within larger-scope OUs. For example, you may have an OU for Accounting user accounts, and a separate OU for Accounting computer accounts. Or you could even create separate OUs for desktop computers versus laptop computers. Maybe one for tablets, one (or many) for your servers... the list goes on and on. If you wanted to get really crazy, you could create a different OU for every single one of your computers! (Please don't do this, as the admin who takes your job after you retire will loathe you because of it.)

Nesting OUs is a very common practice as well. Just like creating folders inside of other folders by using File Explorer, you can use AD Users and Computers to create OUs inside other OUs. This is important for making a clean structure to contain all of your domain objects, but it is also important to the Group Policy processing... er... process.

When you ask any administrator who has worked with Group Policy before, "Where does that GPO apply?" they will almost certainly start thinking in terms of "What OUs does this GPO apply to?" Applying Group Policy at the OU level is our default mentality when working with GPOs, because it is by far the most common tier to which settings are applied. Linking GPOs to particular OUs gives us extreme flexibility in handing different settings to different groups of people or machines. In contrast to the domain-level GPO shown earlier, here is a screenshot of a **GPO** that is being linked to only one OU (**Human Resources**). Even though many other OUs exist and contain objects, the settings inside the **Firewall Settings** GPO will only be applied to those machines that are sitting inside the **Human Resources** OU:

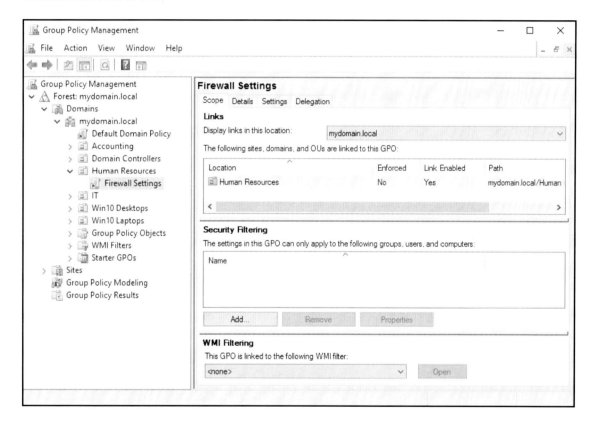

GPO workflow

Now that you know the four tiers of Group Policy processing, let's bring it back to the reason why this is even important. Certainly, you could start creating GPOs and handing out settings willy-nilly without knowing any of this, right? Yes, and you might get away with it for a long time as well, but eventually you'll have to troubleshoot a GPO or figure out where a particular setting is coming from, or perhaps why a setting is not showing up or not working. That is when this information comes into play.

It's also super helpful to know all of this when taking a new job at a new organization where you were not the original creator of the Group Policy infrastructure.

The four types of policy processing are listed in a particular order for a reason. This is the order that the workflow follows when Group Policy does its thing. When a computer boots, it processes the Group Policy settings in this order:

- Local Policy
- Site-level policies
- Domain-level policies
- OU-level policies

The machine flows through these policies from top to bottom, which is a good way to think about it, because when you are looking inside GPMC keeping a top-to-bottom mindset will also help you understand which policies are getting applied first. The settings contained within these policies are applied cumulatively, so they absolutely do have the capability to step on one anothers' toes. If you have conflicting policy settings among two tiers of GPOs, one of them is going to win and one is going to lose. Looking at this list will help you to determine which settings will exist at the end of a GPO processing cycle.

Looking at the processing order list brings to mind a few examples that may be helpful to round out your understanding on this topic:

- Since Local Policy goes first, anything inside any Active Directory Policy has the potential to nullify or change that local policy setting.
- Site-level policies received by a computer will change based on what physical location they are plugged into, so it is important to keep in mind that these settings can be fluid.
- If there is a domain-level policy setting that contradicts a site-level policy setting, the domain-level policy applies last, and therefore wins the day. That setting will be the one that ends up on the client workstation.
- If an OU-level policy applies that conflicts with a site-level or domain-level policy, the OU-linked policy will win every single time.

OUs have even more to consider, because you could easily have multiple GPOs linked to the same OU that could conflict with each other. In this case, one of them is going to win, and in my experience it isn't always the same GPO. This can be a little confusing for sure, so it is critical that you plan the filtering of your GPOs appropriately when creating them.

The capability to have OUs nested inside other OUs also brings some complication to this scenario. Remember the general rule is that Group Policy processes from the top down, so GPOs that are linked to a nested OU will most likely outweigh GPOs that are linked at a higher-level OU.

When a machine receives a GPO setting from a tier that is above the OU where it is sitting, it is known as **inheriting** that GPO. The term inheriting will be important when we later discuss inherency blocking and the reasons why you may want to do that. Here is an example based on previous screenshots. Computers inside the Human Resources OU will be receiving the settings from inside the **Firewall Settings** GPO, because it is linked directly to that OU. Computers inside the Human Resources OU may also be receiving settings from the Default Domain Policy, which is being applied at the domain level, and in this case those computers would be "inheriting" those settings from the Default Domain Policy.

Building a lab to test Group Policy today

Words are great, but getting your hands dirty and jumping into something is the best way to learn. If you don't have an Active Directory environment available to you right now, and if you have never configured a DC before, there is only one place to start—the beginning. Let's walk through a quick and simple lab build-out that will give you everything you need to start testing and working with Group Policy. We will utilize this lab environment throughout the book to showcase the features and settings that we are going to discuss.

For this exercise, we will be building two systems, and I will preface this with the expectation that you have either two pieces of hardware, or a virtualized environment of some sort upon which you will build these two systems. The virtualized environment could be a Windows Server running Hyper-V or VMware, or it could even be a Windows 10 Professional or Enterprise laptop. These specific versions of the operating systems include the ability to add the Hyper-V role to Windows 10, which will give you a fully-capable hypervisor platform that runs right on your laptop, with the ability to spin up two virtual machines that we can use for our lab, as long as your laptop has enough CPU and memory resources to run two VMs at a time.

Domain Controller

As you already know, we need a Domain Controller server to be the host for everything that is stored inside our domain, including the Group Policy settings. For this purpose, I have installed Windows Server 2016 Standard. I won't walk through the installation of the operating system itself, but when we start the process it will be on a very fresh installation that has not yet been configured in any way.

Windows 10 Client

Having a DC fulfills our requirements for being able to use Group Policy, but for practical purposes, we also need a system that we can throw settings at to make sure that our policies are doing what we want them to do. For this, I am installing Windows 10 Enterprise onto a client computer that will be plugged into the same network as our Windows Server 2016 Domain Controller.

If you have the resources available, you could also spin up some additional DCs and join them together to increase the resiliency of your domain, and you could also create some additional testing devices. Perhaps you want to test some settings on Windows 10, but you also have some Windows 7 and Windows 8 clients in your network. Or maybe you have a bunch of Windows Server 2012 R2 servers and you want to test applying settings to those servers from Group Policy. Create as many client or server systems as you want to test with, plug them into the same network, and take the same procedures on those devices that we will be taking on our Windows 10 client in order to increase your testing capabilities.

Configuring the Windows Server 2016 Domain Controller

These are step-by-step instructions to create the first DC in a lab environment, or even an environment which you intend to turn into a production network:

1. Install the Windows Server 2016 operating system onto your server, whether virtual or physical. You can run a DC as a Server Core, but if this is your first Windows Server into an environment, I strongly recommend you choose the option for **Desktop Experience**. Only this option will give you a full point-and-click graphical interface for interacting with your server. The default **Windows Server 2016 Standard** option is for implementing Server Core, which would generally only be used by more experienced administrators:

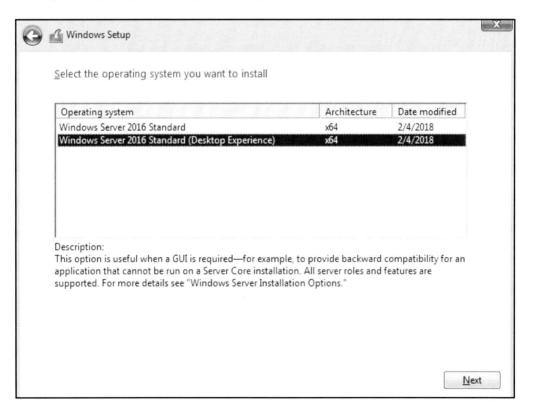

2. Once inside the operating system, configure a static IP address. While it is possible to change the IP address of a DC if you really need to, it is common practice to consider an IP address on a DC to be a permanent fixture, because changing it down the road could result in problems. So, choose your IP wisely. Since basically everyone installs both the Active Directory Domain Services and the DNS roles at the same time on all of their DCs, we will assume that should be the case for you as well and as such, you want to also insert this DC's own IP address as the primary DNS address inside the NIC properties, as shown. Alternatively, you could input 127.0.0.1 as the **Preferred DNS server**, that would work just as well:

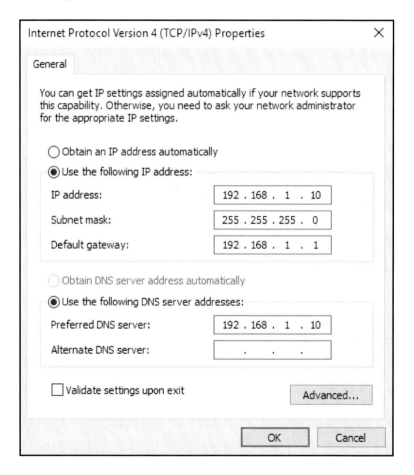

3. Give this server a permanent hostname. You can accomplish this by right-clicking on the **Start** flag, then choosing to open **System properties**. Then click **Change settings** under the **Computer name** section, and press the **Change...** button:

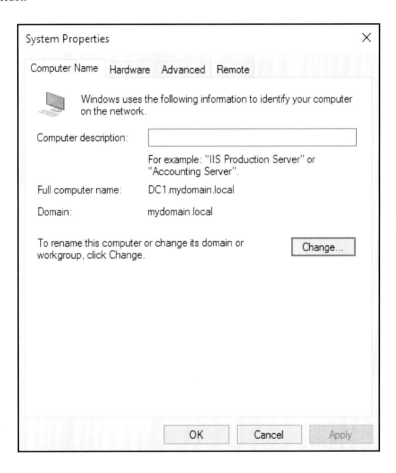

4. Input the name of your DC. This name will not be able to be changed later, so make sure you pick a good one. DC1 always works well for a test lab:

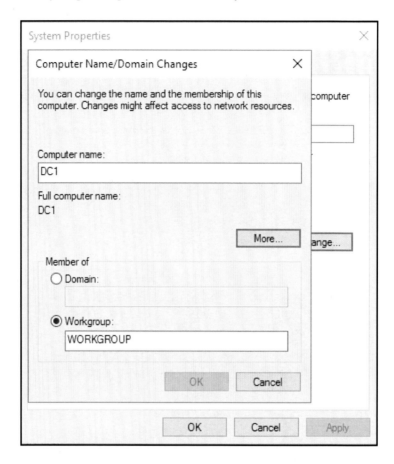

5. After changing the hostname, you will be asked to **Restart** the server. Go ahead and do that now. Once it reboots, you should now be sitting on the desktop, looking at the **Server Manager** tool (it opens automatically).
6. Near the middle of Server Manager, click on **Add roles and features**.
7. Click **Next** three times. You should now be at the **Select server roles** screen. This screen is a list of all the Roles that are available to install on to your Windows Server.

8. Check the box for **Active Directory Domain Services**. When you select this box, you will be asked whether you want to **Add features that are required for Active Directory Domain Services?** Make sure to press the **Add Features** button to agree to add these features:

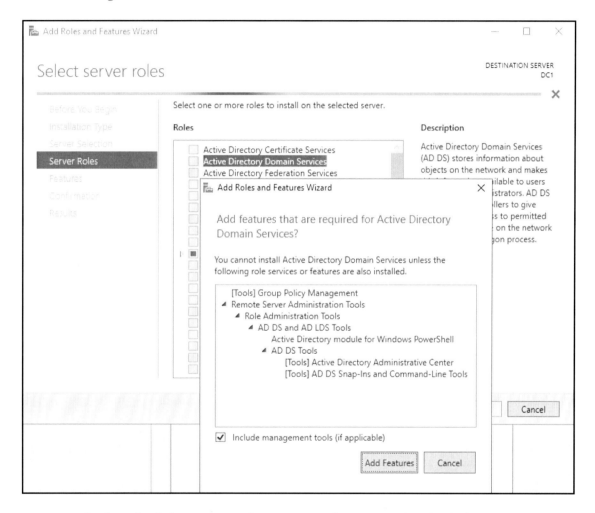

9. Back at the **Select server roles** screen, make sure to also check the box next to **DNS Server**, to make sure those components are installed as well. DCs are almost always DNS servers.

10. Click **Next** and you'll find yourself on the **Select features** screen. You don't have to do anything here, but you'll notice that there is already a checkbox next to **Group Policy Management**. This is your indication that when this role finishes installing, you will have the Group Policy toolset available to you on this new server:

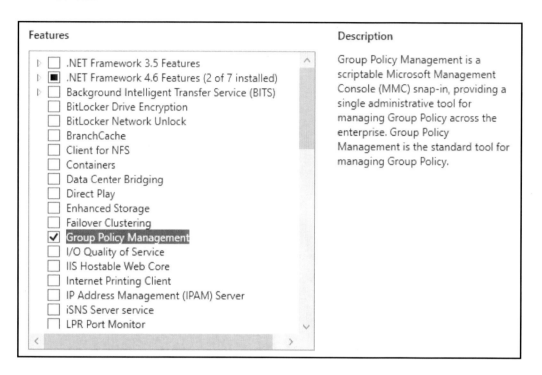

11. Click **Next** three more times, and then click the **Install** button. This will kick off the installation process for Active Directory services on this server:

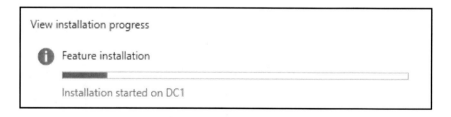

12. When the role installation is complete, you will notice a yellow exclamation mark near the top of Server Manager. Go ahead and click on that, and it will tell you that additional configuration is required for Active Directory Domain Services. Click on the link that says **Promote this server to a domain controller**.

13. Since this is the first DC in our environment, choose the option for **Add a new forest** and then type a name for your domain:

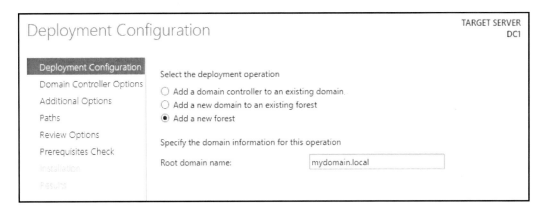

14. This name is even more important than the hostname of your DC, because the name of your domain will be integrated into everything and will be around for a very long time!

15. On the **Domain Controller Options** screen, specify a Directory Services Restore Mode password and click **Next**. When setting up a brand-new domain, the rest of the settings that default on this page are generally the ones that you want to stick with:

16. Unless you have a specific need to change one of the remaining settings, you can simply click **Next** through all the remaining screens of this wizard.

 If you are building this to be a production DC, you may want to make some adjustments on the **Paths** screen. Generally, the file locations for these items should be stored on a volume other than the operating system volume (Drive D instead of drive C, as an example), and if this DC is a virtual server, you should make that new volume an SCSI-based disk rather than an IDE. For the purposes of a test lab, ignore all of this and simply click **Next**.

17. There will be a few expected warnings on the **Prerequisites Check** screen, and these are normal. Go ahead and click **Install**. When finished, the server will reboot automatically. You now have a fully functional domain hosted on this new DC, and you are ready to start playing around with Group Policy!

Configuring the Windows 10 client

Now that we have a DC up and running, we need a device upon which we will apply settings to start testing Group Policy. For this lab, I am going to start with a Windows 10 client computer. You could implement additional devices for testing by following these instructions, whether working with Windows 10 or just about any other Windows operating system, the procedure is going to be the same:

1. Install Windows 10 Enterprise on to a computer. In my case, this is another virtual machine that I am plugging into the same network so that it can communicate with DC1.

2. Assign an IP address to this client. As of this moment, my lab does not contain a DHCP server, and so my client computer will not automatically receive an IP address. Instead of building a DHCP, I am going to simply assign another static IP address to my Windows 10 computer's NIC, as we did with DC1. Since DC1 is hosting DNS for my new domain, I will specify DC1's IP address as the Preferred DNS server on my client computer:

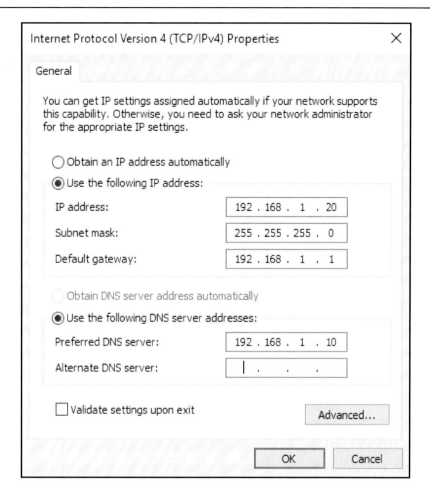

3. Define a hostname for this new device. The process has changed a little bit in the newest versions of Windows 10. As we did on the DC1 server, start by right-clicking on the **Start** flag, and choosing **System**. Once inside the System properties, scroll down until you see the button that says **Rename this PC**, and click on that button.

4. Enter the new name; I am going to call this machine `LAPTOP1`:

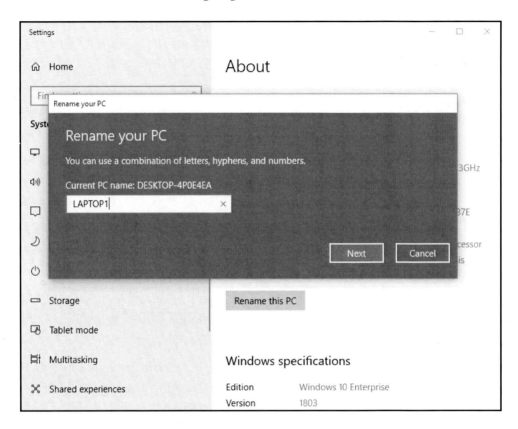

5. Restart when prompted.

In the latest builds of Windows 10, there are now many different ways that you could rename a computer and join it to a domain, as we are about to do. One option that we will not cover here is via PowerShell.

6. We need to join LAPTOP1 to our domain for it to really communicate with DC1 and be able to pull its Group Policy information (as well as everything else from Active Directory). Microsoft has done some revamping of the settings screens in the newest versions of Windows 10, as they migrate settings from the old Control Panel over to the new Settings interface. This makes the domain-join task a little bit more confusing than it used to be. You will find that you cannot join a Windows 10 computer to the domain from the **Rename this PC** screen inside the Settings menu. Thankfully, the fix for this is quite simple. If you open the old Control Panel-based System properties, you can still rename and join the domain, just as you have been able to do in the past. Let's walk through that together, because getting into the old Control Panel is not very straightforward.

7. Click on the **Start** button, and type Control Panel. You will see it appear in the search results. Then simply press *Enter*.

8. Inside the legacy Control Panel, click on **System and Security**, and then click on **System**. This will get you into the old System properties screen, where you can then click on the **Change settings** link to change the name of the computer, or to join it to a domain, which is what we are going to do:

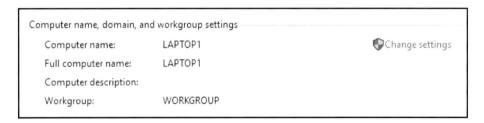

9. Click the **Change...** button.

10. Select the radio button for **Domain**, and then type the name of your domain. If you remember from a few pages ago, I called mine `mydomain.local`:

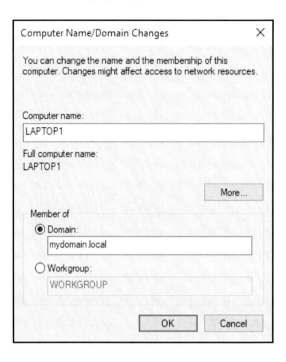

11. You will be prompted to enter a username and password of a domain user account that has permissions to join this computer to the domain. Enter those credentials, and press **OK**. You will now be asked to restart the computer again, and `LAPTOP1` is now fully joined to my domain:

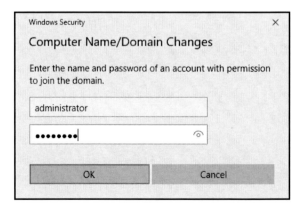

We now have a Domain Controller server and a Windows 10 workstation that are fully prepared to communicate with each other. Very soon, we will begin using `DC1` to create some Group Policy settings, and then jump over to `LAPTOP1` to take a look and see whether our settings were applied without even having to touch that workstation.

Summary

There are certain critical pieces of information for any job that are simply "need to know." When discussing Active Directory Group Policy administration, this chapter is that essential material. Remember, not everyone who handles Group Policy has the advantage of having been the original instigator of the domain at their companies. In fact, I would say the vast majority of IT administrators have come into their roles within an organization long after Active Directory, and therefore Group Policy was already established. In this sense, understanding the basic core capabilities of Group Policy and its behavior could turn out to be completely necessary as you jump into an environment that is already established and running in production, but is completely new to you. You are now equipped to start working with Group Policy, and even able to set it up from scratch in the future, should the need ever arise.

In `Chapter 2`, *Group Policy Management Console (GPMC)*, we will take a closer look at the GPMC, the primary tool you will be interfacing with to create, modify, and control Group Policy.

2
Group Policy Management Console (GPMC)

The **Group Policy Management Console** (**GPMC**) is without a doubt the primary and most common interface that **Active Directory** (**AD**) administrators use to work with anything and everything related to Group Policy. In this chapter, we will explore the functionality inside the GPMC and get a feel for working within this console.

The GPMC is installed by default on all of your **Domain Controller** (**DC**) servers, but in a security-conscious environment it is common practice to limit access and logins to DCs, so we are also going to take a look at some other options for using the GPMC that don't involve the need to touch one of the DCs.

The following topics will be covered in this chapter:

- Technical requirements
- Launching the console locally
- Accessing Group Policy remotely
- Exploring the GPMC

Technical requirements

If you have access to a DC server in your environment, then you already have the toolset needed to work with the GPMC. All DCs have the GPMC installed by default, and this chapter will show you the ways to open it.

We will also cover options for launching the GPMC on a Windows 10 workstation. There are no special requirements for this machine, except that you will want it to be joined to your domain so that it can communicate with the DC. If Windows 10 is not available to you, it is possible to introduce the same level of functionality by using Windows 8 or even Windows 7, but we won't cover those operating systems specifically because, as you will learn, there are advantages to always using the latest and greatest operating system whenever working within the GPMC, to ensure you have all of the newest functionality.

Launching the console locally

The most straightforward approach to opening the GPMC is to launch it right from an Active Directory DC server. If you happen to be logged into a DC anyway, or are even sitting at the console, there are numerous different ways to open this tool. The one that you choose to employ regularly is completely your preference, but knowing various ways to accomplish the same task is always helpful in the Microsoft Windows world, so let's take a minute and cover the different ways that you could go about launching the GPMC from a DC.

Server Manager – the most common way

You have probably noticed (and perhaps been annoyed by it) that when you log into most Windows Server operating systems, there is a tool that likes to automatically open called **Server Manager**. Most IT professionals close Server Manager with a grunt of frustration and then move on to launching whatever administrative tool they intended to use in the first place, but Server Manager can actually be an incredibly useful hub for managing almost any aspect of the server operating system.

Bar none, the most useful and most commonly visited menu inside Server Manager for me personally is the **Tools** menu that is listed in small letters in the top-right corner of the screen. You can see it in the following screenshot, right between **Manage** and **View**:

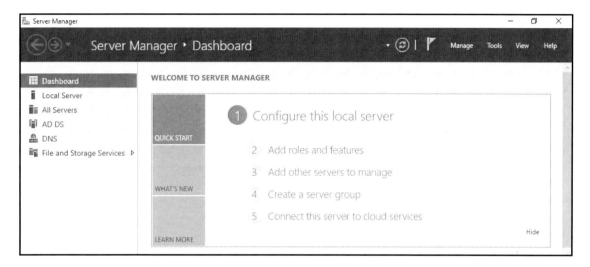

Figure 2.1

Click on **Tools**, and you will get a drop-down list, seen in the following screenshot, of all kinds of goodies. This list grows or shrinks depending on what roles and features are installed upon the server where you are working. Back in the Server 2003 days, we were always opening up a folder called Administrative Tools and finding the consoles that we wanted from there. While Administrative Tools does still exist in Server 2016, it is harder to find, and it is overall much easier and more efficient to launch the admin tools that you need to use right here from the Tools menu inside Server Manager. Inside this list, you can see **Group Policy Management** listed.

Clicking on this is one common way of launching the GPMC:

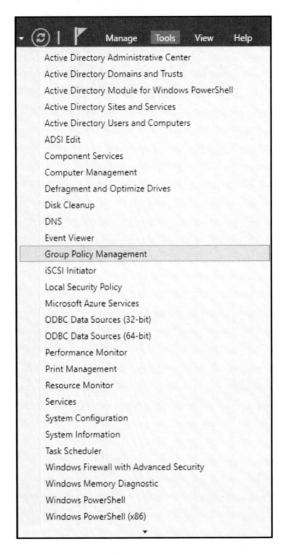

Figure 2.2

 As you can see, **Active Directory Sites and Services** and **Active Directory Users and Computers** are also listed inside the Tools menu, and these are both tools that you will be opening regularly as an AD administrator.

Microsoft Management Console (MMC) snap-in

Opening the GPMC is also accomplishable by using the more traditional, classic **Microsoft Management Console** (**MMC**). The MMC is a general administrative console within which you **snap-in** one or numerous different administrative tools. To open the GPMC this way, you start by opening up the MMC. You can do this by clicking the start flag and typing MMC and pressing **Enter**. Or you can also type MMC from a command prompt or PowerShell prompt and open it that way as well.

Once inside the MMC, click on the **File** menu, and choose **Add/Remove Snap-in...**:

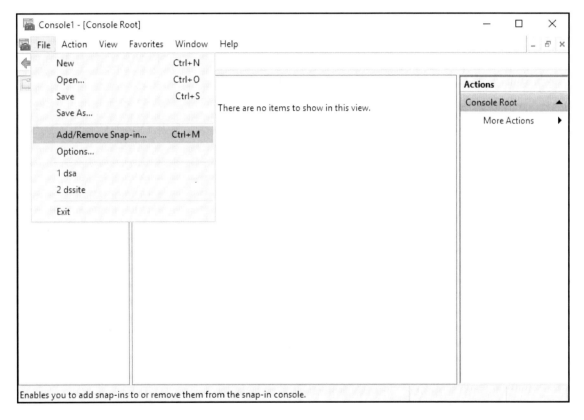

Figure 2.3

You are now presented with a wizard interface from which you choose which administrative tool(s) you would like to snap into the MMC. For our example, we are going to choose **Group Policy Management** and click the **Add >** button in the middle. This moves Group Policy Management over to the right side of the screen, after which you can press **OK**:

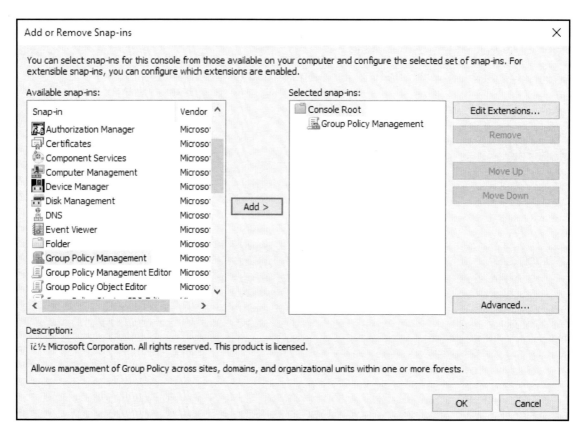

Figure 2.4

You are now looking at the MMC console that has **Group Policy Management** snapped into it. From here, you can create, edit, or modify any **Group Policy Objects** (**GPOs**) just as you would from inside the traditional GPMC launched in any other way:

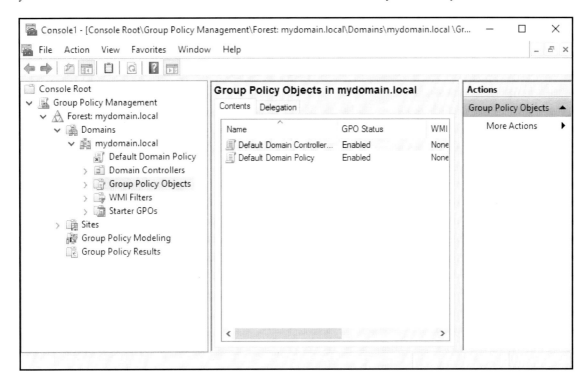

Figure 2.5

As you probably noticed, inside the **Add or Remove Snap-ins** screen, you have the capability to add many different administrative tools into the MMC, and it will allow you to do them all at the same time. This can be an extremely powerful option. For example, AD administrators often work inside Group Policy Management, Active Directory Sites and Services, Active Directory Users and Computers and DNS all at the same time. By opening the MMC and snapping in all of these consoles, you can drive all of your daily administration duties from inside one window pane:

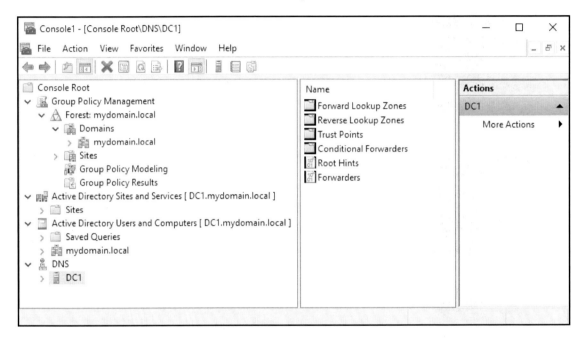

Figure 2.6

Start menu

This one is pretty short and simple, but still worth a mention mostly because I see server administrators struggle all the time to find things inside their **Start** menu. There are two quick places from which you can open the GPMC. Immediately, when clicking on **Start**, you will likely see some live tiles on the right side of the **Start** menu, and one of those is the **Windows Administrative Tools**. Clicking on that tile will open a folder with links to all of the administrative tools, including **Group Policy Management**.

Alternatively, you can open the folder for **Windows Administrative Tools** that is on the left side of the **Start** menu, which will expand all of the tools right there, inside the **Start** menu. From there once again, it's simply a matter of clicking on **Group Policy Management**:

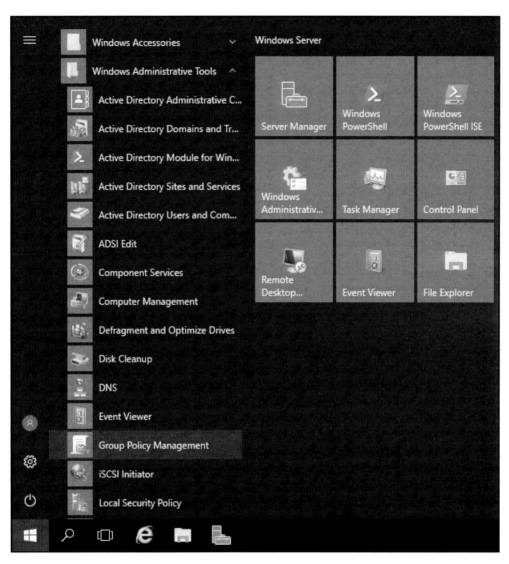

Figure 2.7

As easy as this option seems, in my experience, the new **Start** menu can be a bit of a resource hog and therefore slow to respond on many systems. So, while this seems like the logical place from which to launch applications, I find it to be the least likely candidate for most IT personnel.

GPMC.MSC

I love keyboards. By saying that I love keyboards, what I'm also implying is that I don't really like using a mouse. So, anytime that I can accomplish something without the mouse, I'm all for it. **GPMC.MSC** is a tool that can be used in a myriad of ways. It's not really a tool per se, but rather an MMC shortcut. When you launch GPMC.MSC, it opens the MMC and automatically snaps in **Group Policy Management**. In other words, by issuing a GPMC.MSC command, you are shortcutting your way into the GPMC.

GPMC.MSC can be launched from just about anywhere that you can type it. Certainly, the most common place I type it is inside either a Command Prompt or PowerShell prompt, since I almost always have one or the other open all the time:

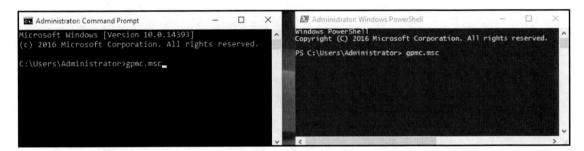

Figure 2.8

It is possible to call GPMC.MSC from the **Start** menu, but in a different way than stated in our previous section about the **Start** menu. You see, the trick to using the **Start** menu in an efficient manner is not to use the **Start** menu at all. Instead, the way to make the **Start** menu an efficient tool that saves you time at the end of the day is to use only its **Search** function. You don't even have to use the mouse! Simply press the *Windows* key on your keyboard, and type the name of the application that you want to launch. In the following screenshot, you can see that I pressed my Windows, then typed gpmc.msc. After that, simply pressing the **Enter** key opens the console right up:

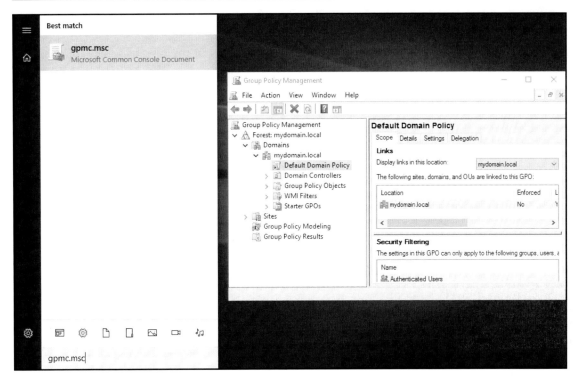

Figure 2.9

Accessing Group Policy remotely

It may not always be the case that you have access to launch the GPMC locally from a
DC server, so it is important to cover the bases on other ways that you can tap into these
settings. In fact, as you will soon read, this section may change your entire outlook on how
you interact with Group Policy, or, indeed, perhaps your outlook on how you administer
your servers in general.

Installing the GPMC on another server

At first glance, this heading might not make any sense. If all of my Group Policy data is stored on the DCs, and the GPMC gets installed by default on my DCs, why would I need to worry about installing the GPMC somewhere else? Won't I just log into a DC and launch the GPMC? Easy peasy, right?

DCs are critically important servers, arguably the most important servers in any network. They contain information that would be considered "keys to the kingdom," and security teams are turning more and more time and effort into making sure that their directory servers (DCs) are locked down and accessed only on an as-needed basis. In the past, pretty much anyone who worked in IT had a domain admin account that allowed them to log into anything, and do anything on those systems. While I still see many organizations operating under this mentality (please stop!), everyone really should consider this to be a terrible security practice, and put much more effort into making sure that user accounts are locked out of the things that they don't need to access. This includes IT user accounts.

All that to say—you may not have access to log into a DC server, even if you are an Active Directory administrator within a company. If that turns out to be the case now or in the near future, you'll still need a way to perform your daily duties within Active Directory and Group Policy, and this is where we start discussing the launching of the GPMC on a device other than a DC server.

Fortunately, tapping into Group Policy from a non-domain controller is super easy. Do you remember back when we prepped the test lab? When we were specifying that we wanted to install the Active Directory Domain Services role, we double-checked on the next screen (the **Features** screen) that there was an automatic checkmark placed next to **Group Policy Management**. That feature is all that is required to install and use the Group Policy Management Console on any domain-joined Windows server within your network.

I just spun up a new server in my test lab. This one is called WEB1, because perhaps someday I will use it as a web server. For now, I am simply going to use it as a management box to tap into Group Policy settings. After installing the operating system on WEB1, I gave it an IP address (making sure to specify DC1's IP as the Preferred DNS server, just as I did on my LAPTOP1), and then I joined it to the mydomain.local domain.

Now inside **Add Roles and Features**, I proceed on to the **Select features** screen, and check the box next to **Group Policy Management**. This is the only piece needed to manage Group Policy settings from this WEB1 server:

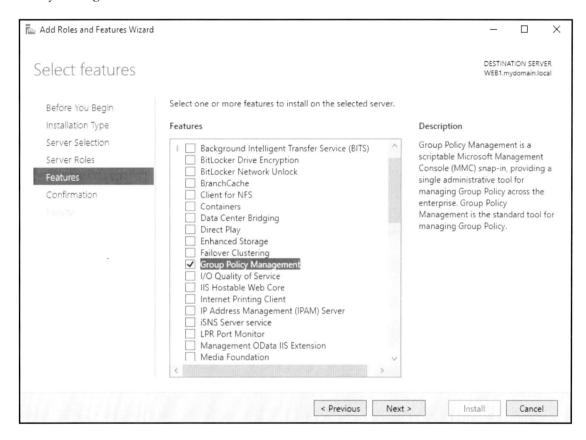

Figure 2.10

Once the feature finishes installing, the Group Policy Management Console is now fully capable on WEB1 and I can launch it in any of the standard ways, via **Start** menu, **Server Manager**, snapping it into the MMC or even running GPMC.MSC. Since I joined WEB1 to the domain, when we launch the GPMC, it automatically communicates with the domain, and knows that it needs to pull information from DC1:

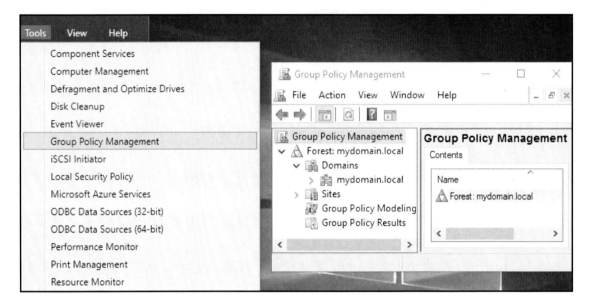

Figure 2.11

 An alternative to running through the **Add Roles and Features wizard** would be opening up a PowerShell prompt on this server and issuing the following command in order to quickly install the GPMC: **Add-WindowsFeature GPMC**

In an environment where you are running multiple DCs, it is sometimes necessary to connect the GPMC to a particular DC, or at least to a particular site to check the information that exists in that site. Active Directory (and therefore Group Policy) information gets automatically replicated between DCs, including across geographical sites, but sometimes this replication process takes a number of minutes or even hours, depending on the site construction of your network. There may be cases where you want to launch the GPMC and connect it directly to a particular DC, for example, if you are inputting some settings for a branch office and you want computers in that office to start receiving those settings immediately. Inputting the new settings on a DC in your primary site will eventually make their way over to the branch office, but if there is a DC in the branch office that you can connect directly to that DC, make the changes, and they will replicate out from there instead. This puts those changes "closer to home" right off the bat, so the client computers in the branch office can start receiving those settings sooner.

To force the GPMC to connect to a particular DC, open it up and then expand out the tree until you can see the `Domains` folder, with the name of your domain listed underneath. Simply right-click on the name of your domain, and choose the option for **Change Domain Controller...**:

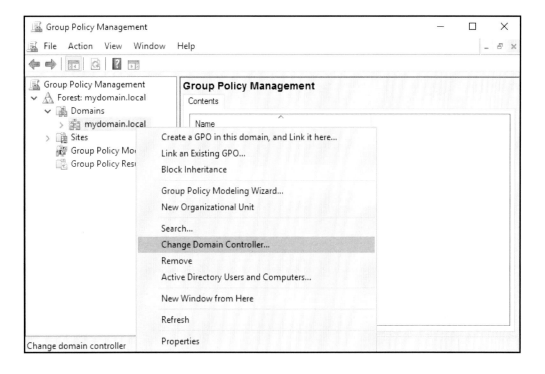

Inside the **Change Domain Controller** screen, you have a number of options for connecting to other DCs within your domain network. The easiest way to select a particular server is seen at the bottom of the following screenshot, under the **This domain controller** section. As you can see, I still only have one DC in my test lab, but if there were any additional DCs in my environment, they would be listed here automatically:

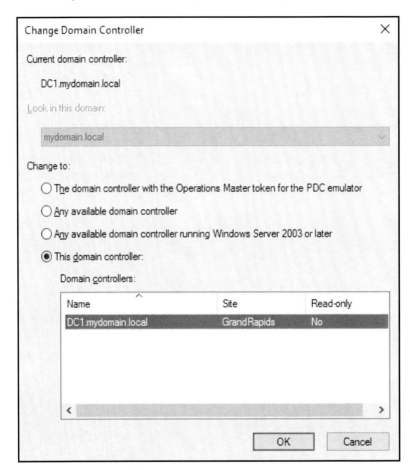

RSAT on Windows 10

While installing the GPMC onto a Windows Server operating system is quick and easy because the files for installation are already pre-built into each instance, launching the GPMC this way still means that you are having to log into a server of some kind anytime that you want to administer Group Policy. For some of us, that isn't a problem at all. I normally have RDP connections open to at least a half-dozen servers at any given time during my workday. But the larger the organization, the more segmented job roles are going to be, and wouldn't it be nice if we could configure Group Policy right from our Windows 10 desktop computer, without ever having to log into a server of any kind?

Yes it would. And that is exactly the purpose of the **Remote Server Administration Tools** (**RSAT**) from Microsoft. The RSAT toolset is much more comprehensive than just Group Policy tools, and installing RSAT onto a Windows 10 client is basically the same as having full Server Manager on your desktop. You will have many administration and management tools available natively on your workstation that will negate the need to log into a number of different kinds of servers in the future.

I already have a Windows 10 workstation running inside my test lab network, called LAPTOP1. I am going to download, install, and launch RSAT on LAPTOP1 to show you how easy it is to start using these features today. Every server administrator should give this a shot; I bet it'll save you time at the end of the day!

The current download for RSAT on Windows 10 is here: https://www.microsoft.com/en-us/download/details.aspx?id=45520

However, should this link ever change in the future, simply open https://www.bing.com/ (I know you'll actually use Google, but we're all Microsoft guys here, so you really should be using Bing!) and type download Remote Server Administration Tools for Windows 10 (or whatever the current client-side operating system is at the time of this reading).

Use the **Download** button on that page to download the installation file that is most appropriate for your Windows 10 workstation. I am running Windows 10 Version 1803, and so I am going to choose the **WindowsTH-RSAT_WS_1803-x64.msu** file, and run it once downloaded to install RSAT:

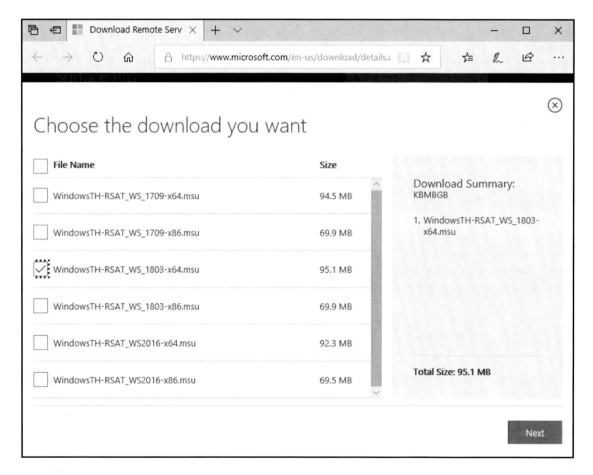

After installation is complete, click on your **Start** menu and you will see a new application installed called **Server Manager**, right here on your Windows 10 machine! Launching **Server Manager** brings you to a very familiar looking interface, from which you can utilize the same **Tools** menu in order to launch **Group Policy Management**, among many other things:

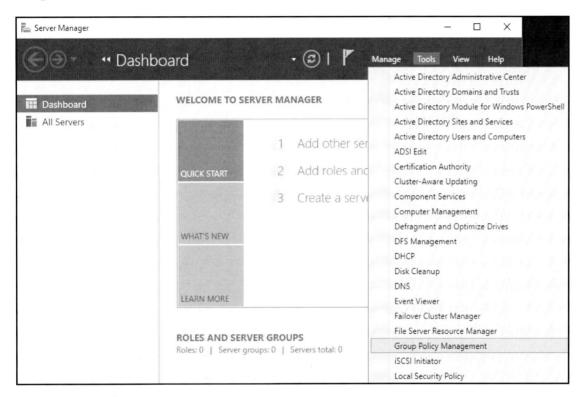

> Alternatively, just like on a Windows Server operating system, now that you have RSAT installed, you could also launch the GPMC via either the **Start** | search function, or by running GPMC.MSC on your Windows 10 workstation.

Keep in mind that getting the GPMC to connect successfully to the DC in order to pull Active Directory information means that you would need to be installing RSAT onto a workstation that is joined to your domain, and the user account that you are using to log into that computer should also be a domain account. This is typically the case with all workstations inside an enterprise organization, but it's worth mentioning for anyone who is trying to install RSAT on a standalone workstation that might not be joined to the domain, and is therefore receiving errors when trying to launch the administrative consoles.

It is very rare that I find server administrators who are making use of RSAT, but I strongly recommend anyone reading this to give it a try. This set of tools can definitively increase productivity, while at the same time increasing the security posture of your servers. Who knows – once you verify that you can handle your daily chores via RSAT, you may be able to do some major restrictions of access to your servers, and maybe even do things like block RDP access since, at that point, you wouldn't have much point logging into them anymore.

Exploring the GPMC

You now have the knowledge to be able to open the GPMC in about a hundred different ways, and from all kinds of different places. If you've been following along with your own server or test lab, I am sure you have already spent some time poking around inside the console to take a look at what screens and options are available, but we are going to take a look together as well. Throughout the rest of this book, we will be making continual use of the GPMC, so the majority of learning about this console will be through direct experience. Even so, we can't wrap up a chapter about the GPMC without actually looking inside the GPMC, so let's do that together now.

The GPMC is made up of two primary window panes. The left side is an organizational tree where you will find the different layers of Active Directory administration—Forests, Domains, Sites, and **Organizational Units** (**OUs**). Expanding any of these sections shows you additional information listed underneath. For example, a forest can have multiple domains within it. Furthermore, currently expanding the Group Policy Objects folder won't show you a lot of information, but eventually you will have many GPOs listed here. You can even see and explore your Active Directory sites right from this window. Expanding the domain further shows you the Active Directory-based OU structure. You will be able to see and click on every one of the OUs that you have created inside AD users and computers. All of this information becomes very important for our next chapters, `Chapter 3`, *Daily Tasks in Group Policy* and `Chapter 4`, *Advanced Filtering of Group Policy Objects*, when we start to discuss linking and filtering our GPO settings, which is the process of telling those GPOs where they need to apply.

In larger environments, it is easy to get lost while navigating through all of the various OUs and their corresponding GPOs. As you can see in the following screenshot, we can see multiple instances of what seems to be the same thing. The **Default Domain Policy** shows up twice, which can be confusing, but what is really happening here is that we are looking at both the actual GPO that is called **Default Domain Policy**, and also an active link to the Default Domain Policy GPO. When you expand the **Group Policy Objects** section, you are looking at the master list of Group Policy Objects that are stored inside Active Directory. So this is a common place to visit when you are looking for a particular GPO, perhaps to make a change to it. But up above where you see Default Domain Policy listed underneath **mydomain.local**, this is *just a link* to that GPO. In other words, links are *associating* the GPOs with different locations within Active Directory. You can see the difference in the icon next to the text. The link has a little arrow on the icon. This is your visual indicator that the **Default Domain Policy** is linked on to the root of the domain:

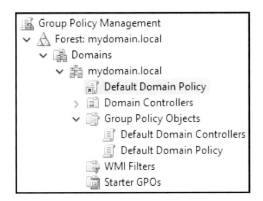

Then the pane on the right-hand side shows additional information about whatever you have selected on the left. Sometimes, there is nothing listed on the right, but other times there are multiple settings and tabs on the right where you will need to be spending some time. One of the primary places you will find yourself revisiting time and time again inside the GPMC is the information that is presented whenever you have a particular Group Policy Object selected.

The following screenshot of the GPMC shows both the left and right sides, and you'll notice that I have clicked on a GPO—the **Default Domain Policy**—and on the right there are multiple options and tabs-worth of information that I can use that are related to this single GPO:

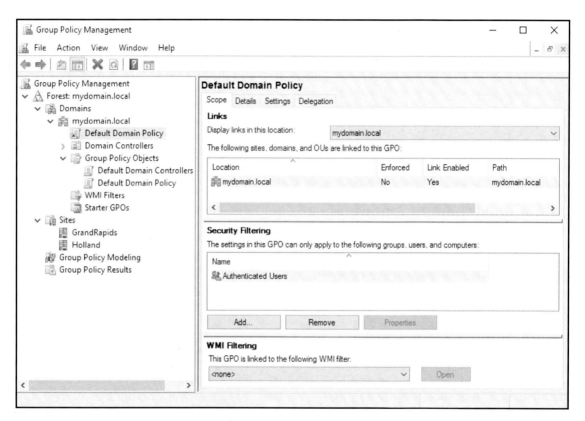

Whether you have clicked on the actual GPO listed under `Group Policy Objects` or if you have clicked on one of the links associated with the GPO, the right pane of the GPMC will display almost exactly the same tabs and information associated with that GPO. The only exception is that clicking on the GPO itself will display one extra tab called **Status**, which is not very commonly used. When needing to make changes to GPOs or GPO filtering, you can accomplish the same tasks whether you have chosen the GPO itself, or one of the links to that GPO.

We start out on the **Scope** tab, which is one of the most common places to visit inside the GPMC. Scope shows you information about where and to whom this GPO is applying. The links section shows you all of the locations that this GPO has been linked to. In the screenshot, you can see that the **Default Domain Policy** is linked to the domain. If we had selected a GPO here that was linked to five different OUs, you would see all five of those listed on this screen. Below the links we see the security filtering section. We will be doing some work here later on, but this is showing you that within those Links, this GPO is being filtered to only these users and/or devices. In this case, the **Default Domain Policy** is applying to **Authenticated Users**, which essentially means everyone.

Moving on to the **Details** tab gives you a little bit of information about the GPO itself. You can see some ownership settings, and important dates about when the GPO was created and last modified. Version numbering can become important when troubleshooting GPOs. Each time that you make changes to a GPO, versioning numbers increment, so this screen can be a nice resource when comparing GPOs between different DCs to make sure replication is happening properly, or to be able to help track changes:

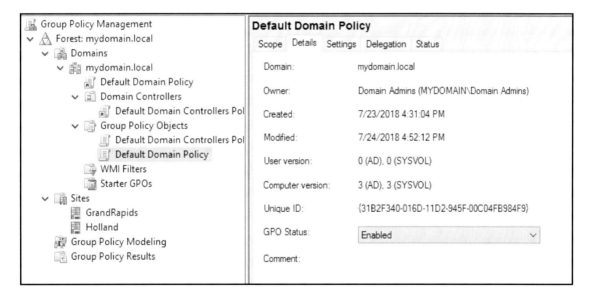

The **Settings** tab is next, and this one is hugely important. The **Settings** tab will display for you all of the settings contained within a **Group Policy Object**. This is extremely useful for tracking down settings, and from which policies they are applying. I certainly expect that you will be visiting the **Scope** and **Settings** tabs much more frequently than any other location within the right pane of the GPMC. Here's a quick example that shows some of the settings that exist within the **Default Domain Policy**:

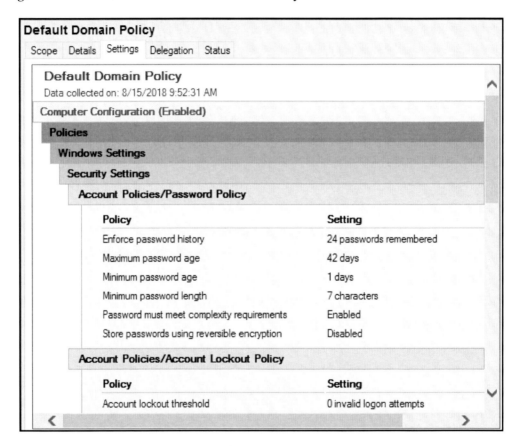

The **Delegation** tab gives us insight into the permissions associated with this GPO. Here, you can view the information that already exists about who has access to read or manipulate the GPO and its settings, and this is also the screen where you make modifications to these permissions. The **Delegation** tab can be important to your overall Group Policy security strategy:

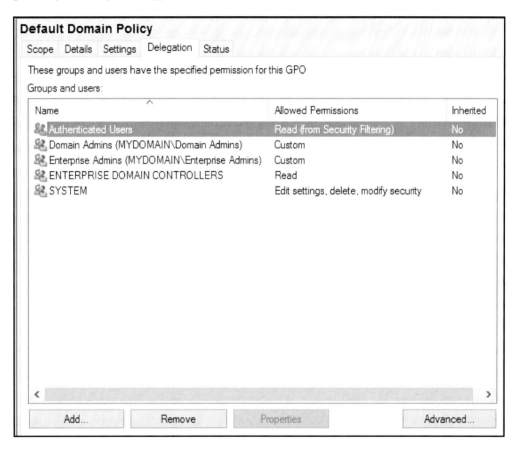

The final tab (if you have selected the GPO itself and not just the link) is called **Status**. We don't need to take up any more space looking firsthand at this one because it's pretty self-explanatory, and won't show us very much information because my lab environment has only a single DC. In a larger environment with multiple DCs, this screen can be helpful, because it will poll and display some health information related to the DCs and their replication status.

I also want to point out that right-click menus are just as important inside the GPMC. As with most Microsoft management screens, right-clicking on different things gives you different options. It will be a very common occurrence for you to utilize the right-click menus to create GPOs, link GPOs, and edit the settings within those GPOs. Just as a quick example, here is the menu when right-clicking on the root of your domain:

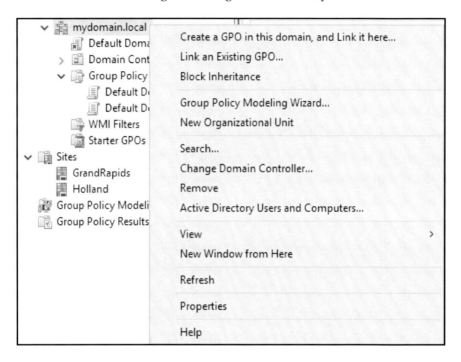

As one final example of the right-side window pane inside the GPMC, go ahead and click on the name of your domain. This changes the right side of your screen to display information that is no longer about a specific GPO, but rather information that is higher level, things associated with the domain as a whole. Go ahead and click on the **Linked Group Policy Objects** tab. As you can see, there is currently only one GPO linked at this level of the domain. This screen can become very useful, however, if you have multiple GPOs being linked at the same level (whether that level is here at the domain, or at one of the different levels, such as an OU). This screen can be helpful when troubleshooting GPO settings that seem to be contradicting each other, as you will be able to view the **Link Order** on this screen, and help determine which GPO is supposed to be processing last, aka winning the fight, between GPOs that contain conflicting settings:

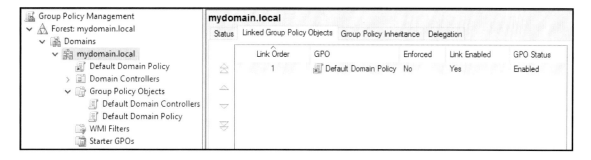

Summary

The GPMC is absolutely the primary tool that Active Directory administrators use to work with Group Policy settings. This console is critically important to your role as a Windows Server administrator. In addition to giving you a glance into the console where we will be spending so much time over the course of this book, I hope this chapter prompts you to start thinking outside the box about other server management duties in the future. Using the RSAT package on a regular workstation can completely change your server security stance.

Join me as we dive next into the meat and potatoes of Group Policy—the common tasks that you will be required to handle on a daily basis.

3
Daily Tasks in Group Policy

In this chapter, we will get more hands-on with Group Policy. There are certain functions within the **Group Policy Management Console** (**GPMC**) that will be so common that you may literally be performing them every single day in your role as a directory administrator. Let's cover those topics now, and keep them lumped together in a single chapter so that this can also serve as a quick reference guide for any reminders that may be needed in the future.

The following topics will be covered in this chapter:

- Default policies and permissions
- Modify an existing **Group Policy Object** (**GPO**)
- Creating a new GPO
- More on GPO links
- Everyday command-line tools

Default policies and permissions

After installing **Active Directory Domain Services** (**AD DS**) and therefore Group Policy, there are a few settings that start taking immediate effect within your network. Not many, but some, and so it is important to know where these are and understand what they are doing. These settings do have the potential to conflict with other GPO settings that you might intentionally put into place, and could cause confusion if there are policy settings on your workstations that you weren't expecting. Fortunately, these items are pretty visible, and we will take a minute to take a look at them here.

Furthermore, there are some default permissions settings associated with Group Policy that you, as an administrator, should be aware of. We will discuss those as well.

Default Domain Policy

As you have probably noticed while following along with our lab build so far, there is this thing hanging out inside GPMC called the **Default Domain Policy**. This is a GPO that always exists by default in a fresh domain implementation. In fact, I have never seen an environment where this policy did not exist, so it is not a common practice for anyone to remove or delete it.

The Default Domain Policy contains a handful of security-related settings. The most important part to understand about this default policy is that it applies to everyone: a users on all domain-joined systems. Any settings you plug into the Default Domain Policy will roll out on a very large scale, which could cause you a lot of grief if not done properly. So it is recommended to basically leave this GPO alone unless you are absolutely sure about the settings that you are going to use within it.

Oftentimes, what I see in smaller environments is that the IT staff (sometimes just one person) has made a little bit of use of the Default Domain Policy, perhaps modifying the password policy as we will be doing in just a few pages. This probably happens because there are plenty of blog posts and how-tos out there that guide an IT administrator through modifying the corporate password policy to make it stronger, and the easiest way to show this procedure is through a simple edit of the default policy. Often this GPO is the extent of how Group Policy as a whole is used in these smaller businesses, which is unfortunate because of how immensely powerful Group Policy can be when used more extensively. As you can see in the following screenshot, there are not many settings inside the Default Domain Policy, and most of them are related to user passwords. If you have ever wondered why or how complex passwords are required right off the bat, even in a brand-spanking-new installation of Active Directory, this GPO is your answer:

Default Domain Policy
Data collected on: 8/15/2018 9:52:31 AM

Computer Configuration (Enabled)

Policies

Windows Settings

Security Settings

Account Policies/Password Policy

Policy	Setting
Enforce password history	24 passwords remembered
Maximum password age	42 days
Minimum password age	1 days
Minimum password length	7 characters
Password must meet complexity requirements	Enabled
Store passwords using reversible encryption	Disabled

Account Policies/Account Lockout Policy

Policy	Setting
Account lockout threshold	0 invalid logon attempts

Account Policies/Kerberos Policy

Policy	Setting
Enforce user logon restrictions	Enabled
Maximum lifetime for service ticket	600 minutes
Maximum lifetime for user ticket	10 hours
Maximum lifetime for user ticket renewal	7 days
Maximum tolerance for computer clock synchronization	5 minutes

Since we are talking about a policy that applies to everyone, let's explore the reason why the Default Domain Policy applies to everyone.

Authenticated users

Settings inside the Default Domain Policy apply to everyone and everything inside the domain for two reasons. The first is that this GPO is linked to the root of the domain automatically. Based on our Group Policy hierarchical understanding we have already established, you know that this means the GPO will attempt to apply itself to everything listed under that domain tier.

The second is that the Default Domain Policy has **Authenticated Users** specified inside the **Security Filtering** section of the GPO settings. If you open GPMC, click on **Default Domain Policy,** and navigate to the **Scope** tab, you will see **Authenticated Users** listed near the bottom of the screen. We haven't discussed **Security Filtering** yet, because we have Chapter 4, *Advanced Filtering of Group Policy Objects*, coming up shortly. But for now, you simply need to understand that this specification means that the settings inside the Default Domain Policy GPO are going to attempt to apply to every domain user on every device:

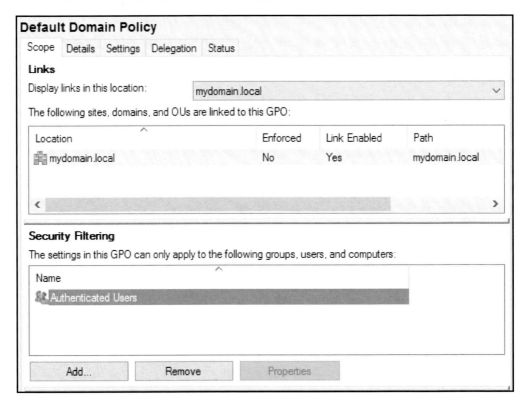

 Authenticated Users even includes administrators! This is important to note because you as the IT admin are not automatically immune from Group Policy settings, and so it is very possible to lock yourself out of functionality that you need in order to do your work. Tread carefully with the Default Domain Policy or any other GPO that filters to **Authenticated Users**.

Default Domain Controllers Policy

The second GPO that exists by default in even a fresh installation of Group Policy is the **Default Domain Controllers** (**DCs**) Policy. As the name implies, this policy is for your DC servers, and taking a look at the policy itself shows us that it is linked to only one location inside Active Directory, an OU called Domain Controllers. Only your DC servers end up inside the DCs OU, so settings in the Default Domain Controllers Policy only ever apply to DCs, but it is once again important to take into account that there are settings inside this policy and so they are applying to all of your DCs immediately upon creating the new domain.

The settings inside this GPO are fairly self-explanatory; it is a policy dedicated to keeping a baseline of security on the DC servers themselves. Settings here include things such as restrictions on who is allowed to log in to DCs, who is allowed to shut down DCs, and who is allowed to do other seemingly innocent tasks such as changing the system time. All of these functions are locked down by default to only certain users and groups of users being able to access them, namely those user accounts who are inside administrative containers and are therefore declared to be administrators:

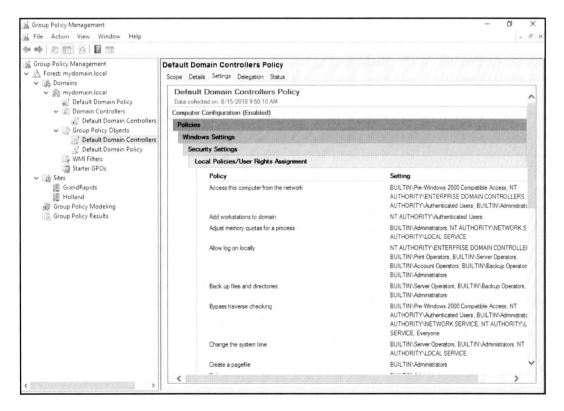

Unless you have some experience here, it may seem silly that the ability to change the clock on a DC is locked down. However, all machines in the domain receive their time automatically from DCs, and if the computers in your domain fall out of time synchronization with each other, it can create an extremely broken environment. Time management is actually a really big deal within a domain!

Permissions

If you are following along with a lab of your own, you are currently having no trouble or limitations because you are probably logging in to your servers or management workstations from an account that is part of the domain administrators group. In fact, you may even be logging in as the domain administrator account.

Sidenote: Do not use the domain administrator account to log in to servers! In a test lab, that's fine. But in a production network, you should absolutely be getting away from ever touching that account. It should be locked down and locked out, and your IT staff should not know what the password is so they can't use it even if they forget that they shouldn't use it. Using the domain administrator account can turn into a major security hole so fast it'll make your head spin. I see far too many server admins using it for everyday tasks that could easily be done with their own accounts.

Now, moving off my soapbox, domain administrators and enterprise administrators have access to do whatever they want inside Group Policy. Anybody else, however, is limited. This is important to understand as you move into Group Policy administration. In the wild, by far the most common way to grant an admin access to manipulate Group Policy is to add their domain user account to the Domain Admins group, which is fine but not ideal. There are more fine-grained ways of giving permissions inside GPMC that don't require quite this level of access.

Later in the book, we will explore delegation of privileges within Group Policy, essentially showing you an alternative way to give a user the rights they need in order to administer only parts and pieces of Group Policy, but for now we just need to understand that you won't get very far in GPMC without being a member of either Domain Admins or Enterprise Admins.

A quick aside regarding sites. Even though we will be able to delegate some permissions later to non-admin type users, this is not the case with site administration. To be honest, flagging GPOs to be applied at the site level is not a common practice. It's very rare that I find people doing that, because it's a rare use case that would deem it practical. However, should you discover the need to modify Active Directory sites or link GPOs at the site level, you will need to use an account that is a Domain or Enterprise Admin. Again, since most server administrators are already either Domain Admins (though this is becoming less common as security levels increase), or have access to a Domain Admin account on an as-needed basis, that is most often the level of permissions you will have when working within Group Policy, which will allow you to do whatever you need.

Modifying an existing GPO

Group Policy is pretty pointless without plugging settings into GPOs. (That's a lot of words that begin with the letter P!) So one critical skillset needed for Group Policy administration is familiarity with modifying GPO settings. So far, we are still working with the items that are pre-built into our fresh installation of Group Policy, but that will soon change. As a general practice, you don't usually touch or change the Default Domain Policy, but something that is commonly put into place here is generalized password settings that you want applied to all users within your domain. We will update those settings to meet our current password needs.

Using the newest GPMC

Our test lab is running brand-new instances of the latest Windows 10 and Server 2016, so we have no concerns about old technology or outdated consoles. However, in production environments, there are almost always old pieces of equipment still being used. This seems to be particularly true with DCs. Many administrators make their Group Policy changes by using GPMC on their DCs, because that is where GPOs live and it makes some common sense to use DCs as centralized points of administration. We already covered the reasons why this isn't a best practice, but alas it is simply the way things are in many organizations.

The rub comes in because, for numerous reasons, it seems like DCs are always the last servers to get updated to the newest operating systems. Or at least your PDC Emulator. I have witnessed domains consisting of literally hundreds of DCs all track back to a PDC that is still running Server 2008 R2. I have also seen networks where brand-new Server 2016 DCs were still happily running right alongside Server 2003 DCs.

I cover all of this to simply say that Group Policy administration should always be done from the newest platform that you have available to you. If you don't have any Windows Server 2016 servers, it should at least be easy enough for you to gain access to a Windows 10 computer where you can then install the RSAT tools (see `Chapter 2`, *Group Policy Management Console (GPMC)*). The reason you want to be running a newer operating system is that GPMC has included updates as the years have progressed and new features have been released. Within the same domain, opening GPMC on a Server 2008 R2 and opening it side by side on a Server 2016 will result in there being different options and functionality between the two. *Most* of what you will find is still exactly the same, but functionality introduced in the newer platforms will only be visible from the Server 2016 console.

There is also the chance that opening GPMC from an older platform will have "invisible" settings inside. If a colleague with Windows 10 adds a setting to a GPO that is related to a brand-new feature, and then you open GPMC from a Server 2008 and navigate to that same GPO, you simply will not see the setting that is contained inside that GPO. The setting is there, but the older GPMC is unable to display it to you, and you have no idea that it exists.

Long story short—always run GPMC on the newest operating system that exists in your environment.

Editing settings inside a GPO

Changing or introducing settings into a GPO is quite simple. As with everything related to Group Policy, you start inside GPMC. Once opened, expand the trees on the left-hand side until you find the GPO that you want to modify. It is generally easiest to find a particular GPO by expanding the `Group Policy Objects` folder, as they will all be listed there.

Now right-click on the GPO that you want to modify, and choose **Edit...**:

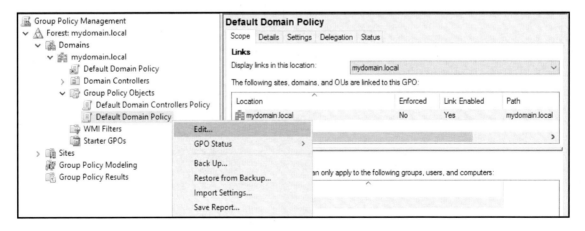

This launches a familiar-looking console, the **Group Policy Management Editor**. This should remind you of the console presented when we first launched `gpedit.msc` in order to see the underlying settings structure that can exist within the local policy settings. We are now viewing the "guts" of the Default Domain Policy, and any changes that we make inside this screen will take immediate effect within the domain. This is the same process you would take to edit any setting within any GPO; simply right-click on the GPO and choose **Edit...** in order to see Group Policy Management Editor with the GPO's settings snapped into it:

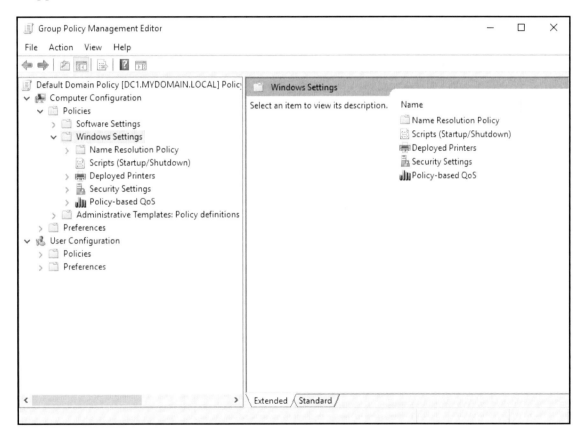

Quickly finding your settings

For the purposes of modifying an existing setting within a GPO, it would make all kinds of sense if there was a way to edit the GPO and force the Group Policy Management Editor to take you directly to that particular policy setting, so that you could simply make the change. Unfortunately, this common sense does not translate into functionality within GPMC; rather, what you will soon discover is that any time you edit any GPO, the **Management Editor** will bring you to the root of all policy settings. You are left on your own to find the settings that you want to manipulate. When you are building out new settings that don't already exist in the GPO, this usually means you are hitting your favorite internet search engine in order to find the exact location. However, there is a shortcut available to use if you are only interested in changing an existing setting. You are already familiar with the **Settings** tab inside GPMC, where it shows you a quick layout of all settings within a GPO. By opening the **Settings** tab side by side with the **Group Policy Management Editor**, you can use the information shown on the **Settings** screen to quickly navigate to the proper location inside of your **Group Policy Object**.

For example, at the end of this section, we are going to update a password setting in the Default Domain Policy. You can see in the following screenshot that I have opened the **Settings** tab of that policy inside GPMC, and I am using the information displayed to find the location inside the editor that I need to navigate to, in order to make my changes:

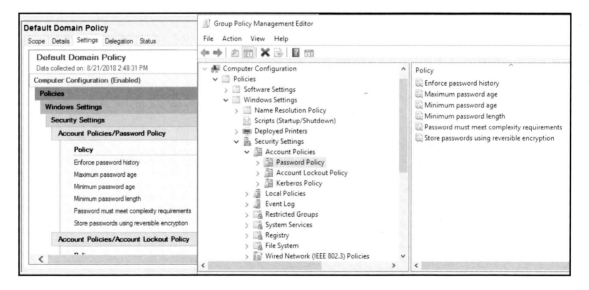

An annoying Internet Explorer popup

If you have been working in GPMC from RSAT on your Windows 10 workstation, then this section is not for you. You won't be having this problem! However, I suspect many of you continue to work with GPMC on a Windows Server operating system, which is entirely fine, but you have probably realized by now that every time you open up the **Settings** tab within a GPO, you get an annoying Internet Explorer pop-up screen:

This happens because the **Settings** tab inside GPMC utilizes pieces of Internet Explorer in order to display its information. Internet Explorer is locked down by default on any Windows Server operating system with something called Internet Explorer Enhanced Security Configuration. By simply clicking **Close**, you can proceed past this message and see the Settings information, but that gets old in a hurry. An alternative is to completely disable IE Enhanced Security Configuration on the server, but that is a very bad habit to get into from a general security perspective. The better solution is to click on that **Add...** button, and then click **Add** again on the next screen in order to add `about:security_mmc.exe` into IE's **Trusted sites** list. This ensures that IE trusts the process that GPMC is calling for, and allows this information to be displayed in the future without a warning message:

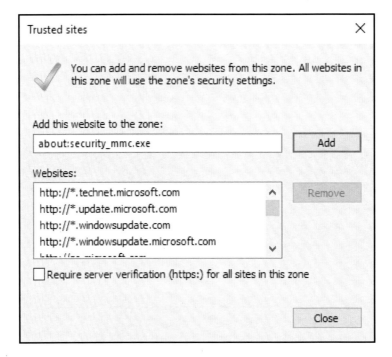

Updating the default password policy

Flowing on right from our previous screenshot, we already have the Default Domain Policy opened for editing, so let's go ahead and make a change to verify that this whole Group Policy thing works! Some of the primary settings inside this policy are rules and restrictions surrounding password requirements for user accounts within the domain. If you navigate to **Computer Configuration** | **Policies** | **Windows Settings** | **Security Settings** | **Account Policies** | **Password Policy**, you will see the currently configured password requirements:

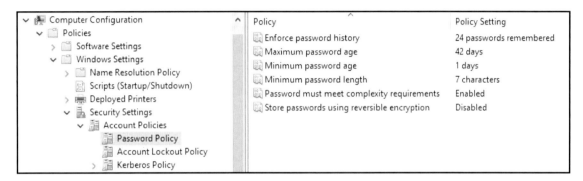

To make a change, all you need to do is double-click one of the entries on the right-hand side of the screen, and update the information. In order to prove that this change really works, I want to make an adjustment that will have immediate impact on my existing user accounts. Currently, the password for my login is only eight characters long. I am going to update the **Minimum password length** to 12 characters:

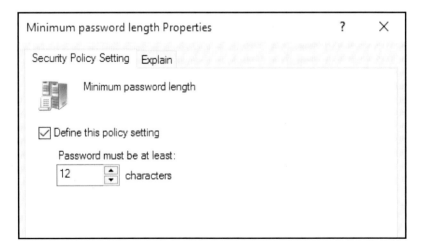

After clicking **OK** in order to accept the change, this updated setting is immediately saved into the GPO and replication starts pushing it out to the rest of my network. In order to really test this setting, I am going to also force my user account to require a password change during my next login. This is accomplished from inside my user account properties inside **Active Directory Users and Computers**. Once I have checked the box labelled **User must change password at next logon**, I then walk over to my Windows 10 workstation and try to log in as myself. I am presented with a password change notification screen, and if I try to set a new password that is less than 12 characters in length, it fails:

Not configured versus enabled versus disabled

When we double-clicked on the **Minimum password length** setting in order to make a change, the screen that presented itself was pretty short and sweet. You selected the checkbox for whether or not you wanted to enforce this policy setting, and then you set a number of characters. No real questions there, but if you wanted a more in-depth explanation on what this setting was all about, you could have clicked on the **Explain** tab in order to get some additional information. This is important to remember when working within Group Policies, as sometimes the settings are not so clear-cut. GPO settings always have a tab with some details explaining what the setting is for and how to use it.

Oftentimes, you will find policy settings with three choices: **Not Configured**, **Enabled**, or **Disabled**. Depending on which option you select, that opens the door to additional settings or configurations within that particular policy setting:

- **Not Configured**: This one basically means to ignore this setting. If a policy setting is configured as not configured, Group Policy will not take any active steps to change the settings on the device where the policy is applying. If the user has manually adjusted that setting on their own workstation or some other management tool has made a change to it, the GPO will ignore it and leave whatever settings are already in place.
- **Enabled**: This forces Group Policy to take action on this particular setting. Choosing Enabled often enables a drop-down box or fields for additional configuration that is needed, depending on what the setting is all about. We will see this in the following example.
- **Disabled**: Sometimes, setting a policy setting to Disabled can mean an active squashing of that setting, forcing it to be disabled. Other times, setting to Disabled can be more akin to an ignore-type situation. When changing a setting to Disabled, it is usually helpful to read over the explanation settings to make sure your selection is going to really do what you want it to do.

Example – configuring Teredo

Let's look at an example of a setting that has these three options. Teredo is an IPv6 transition tunneling protocol, and oftentimes I have to touch Teredo via Group Policy when working with a customer to get their client-side tunneling behaviors to line up with best practices. We create a new GPO, link and filter it to the appropriate places so that this GPO applies to the client workstations, and then configure Teredo in one of a couple of different ways. Usually, we are setting it either to a specific status that we want to enforce, or we are setting it to Disabled because we want to make sure the Teredo adapter on those workstations is always disabled.

No need to walk through this one in your own lab, because I doubt you have a pressing need to change your Teredo behavior at present. But follow along with the following screenshots for a helpful example on not configured versus enabled versus disabled.

Navigate to the following location to view the Group Policy settings associated with Teredo: **Computer Configuration** | **Policies** | **Administrative Templates** | **Network** | **TCPIP Settings** | **IPv6 Transition Technologies**. You can see here that there are a number of different settings related to Teredo, as well as settings regarding other IPv6 transition tunneling adapters:

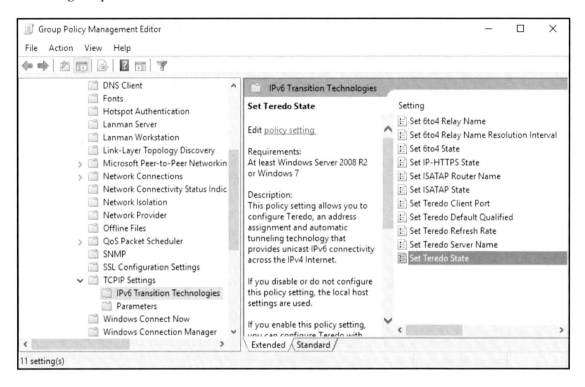

We want to manipulate the Teredo State, so we double-click on **Set Teredo State**. When changing a policy setting, you always want to think about this setting as if you were coming from the recipient's point of view: "On my desktop computer, I want to Set Teredo State to (insert your setting here)". Inside **Set Teredo State**, you can see we have radio buttons for **Not Configured**, **Enabled**, and **Disabled**. You can also see that there is a **Help** field that explains these settings and how each one will affect the behavior of Teredo upon the devices on which the setting is applied.

In the following screenshot, I have chosen **Enabled**, and that has presented me with a new drop-down menu of choices to choose from. You can see those selections as well as the **Help** pane previously mentioned:

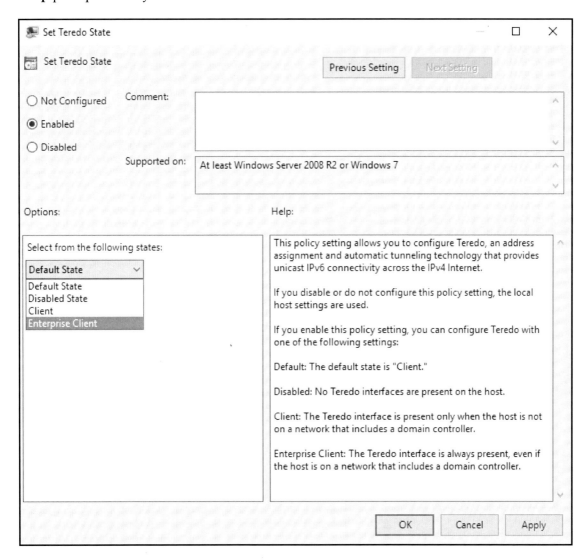

If you are intending to make use of Teredo, it is often a best practice to set this to **Enterprise Client**. You can select that choice, click **OK**, and be done. However, the real reason I chose this particular setting for our example is that it also portrays one of those strange ways for doing a disable. In the case of Teredo, you can see in the **Help** pane that it says if you set the policy setting to either **Not Configured** or **Disabled** radio buttons, that this policy would do nothing and that the localhost settings would be used. That's not what we want at all; that would mean that Teredo would remain enabled it if were already enabled, which it is by default in Windows. Instead, if we wanted to actively set Teredo to the Disabled state, we would have to select the **Enabled** radio button, and choose **Disabled State** from the drop-down list. Many times, Group Policy is used to disable functionality that is not needed on corporate workstations in order to heighten security on those devices, so the likelihood that you will have to take this same procedure with your own settings is actually quite high.

Creating a new GPO

Creating a new GPO is not rocket science, but walking through some examples will give us the opportunity to discuss some practices surrounding GPO creation that will be good to keep in mind. We have already modified an existing policy, but there is rarely a good reason for modifying the Default Domain Policy; much more commonly you will be creating brand-new GPOs for settings that you decide need to be rolled out to your workforce. Creating GPOs yourself will give you much more control over settings and filtering within your environment.

For this section, we are focusing on creating the object at GPMC level. Under the hood, a GPO is not really a single object but rather a combination of an AD object and some files that sit on the DCs. We will further discuss the "what and where" in Chapter 8, *Group Policy Maintenance*.

Naming your GPOs

You can name your GPOs however you want, but the mindset you take when deciding on those names could benefit or harm your Group Policy environment down the road. In the beginning stages of a fresh Active Directory installation, it is quite easy to find anything inside Group Policy, and you will generally remember offhand where you placed all of your policies. The larger you grow, the more difficult it will become to distinguish between them and track back to changes you made months or even years ago.

There are two typical mindsets that I often see in the wild. They are quite different. The first is to name GPOs according to the places where they will be applying. In this instance, you will see GPO names such as "HR Department Settings" and "Accounting Computer Lockdown Policy". While these aren't terrible names, going this direction generally means that each of your GPOs is a culmination of all kinds of different settings. They may all work together in order to define security for your devices, but these GPOs will generally be quite large and have many settings, which means they will be more difficult and dangerous to make changes to in the future.

The second mindset, which I am in much larger agreement with, is to keep minimal settings inside each GPO, and simply have many more GPOs. In this case, you will see GPO names more like "Disable IPv6", "Set the idle lockout policy to 2 minutes", and "Set Teredo to EnterpriseClient status". As you can see, each of these names is quite specific, and that may mean that you only have one policy setting inside each of the GPOs. This certainly means that you will be creating many GPOs where in the alternative mindset you may get away with putting all of these settings into a single GPO, but having them separated like this makes GPOs very easy to identify, and means that you can be extremely flexible with the placement of these policies. For example, if you need to set the idle lockout policy on both HR and Accounting computers, you simply link that one GPO to both OUs for those groups, whereas if you had a single GPO for each department, you would now have to modify both of those production GPOs in order to include this setting, which doesn't give you much room for error. If you mess something up, it messes it up for all of those computers.

Configuring many GPOs that all have a very limited number of settings also gives you more flexibility should the day ever come that you need to disable or delete GPOs. You can much more easily remove individual settings without the potential to wreak havoc on your workstations.

Creating the GPO

Go ahead and open up GPMC, and let's walk through the steps of creating a fresh GPO. Navigate to your primary `Group Policy Objects` folder, right-click on that folder, and choose **New**:

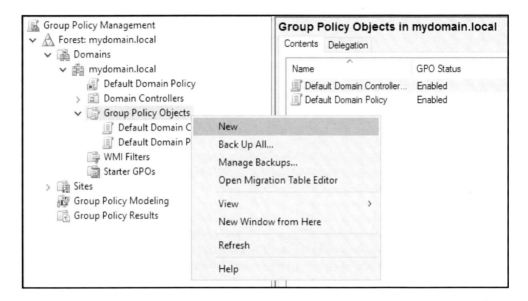

The only thing you need to do here is specify a name for this new GPO. Remembering the previous advice to specify a GPO name based on the settings I am going to put inside, I will call my GPO **Set Desktop Wallpaper to Blue 1**. This name will make sense soon.

That's all it takes to create a GPO! You will see your new GPO sitting waiting for you underneath the `Group Policy Objects` folder. This GPO does not yet contain any settings, which we will resolve right now.

Configuring the policy to apply a desktop wallpaper

I named my new GPO based on the setting I plan to put inside; I would like to utilize this policy in order to set a specific desktop wallpaper onto my accounting workstations. Again, sticking with a name that indicates only the setting inside allows me future flexibility to be able to assign this GPO to many different departments if I ever have the need to do so.

Right-click on the new GPO and choose **Edit...** in order to launch the Group Policy Management Editor. Now we need to navigate to the setting we want to use. Setting wallpaper settings can be done from **User Configuration** | **Policies** | **Administrative Templates** | **Desktop** | **Desktop**. Inside this location, you will see a few policy settings available to us; the one we are going to modify is called **Desktop Wallpaper**:

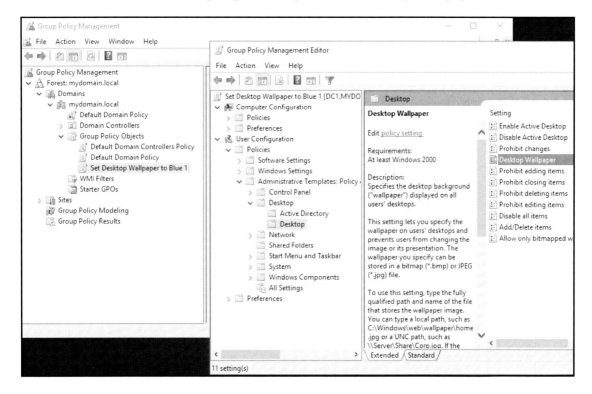

Double-clicking on **Desktop Wallpaper** brings us to the screen where we get to manipulate the policy setting and tell the GPO which wallpaper we would like to apply to the machines where this policy gets pushed. Set this policy setting to **Enabled**, and then specify the necessary information. I have specified the location of my Blue1 wallpaper inside the GPO, and I also used the drop-down menu in order to tell the wallpaper to **Fill** the screen. As you can see in the screenshot, the options available here in this drop-down menu are the same options you would have if you were to be changing the desktop wallpaper manually on a Windows computer:

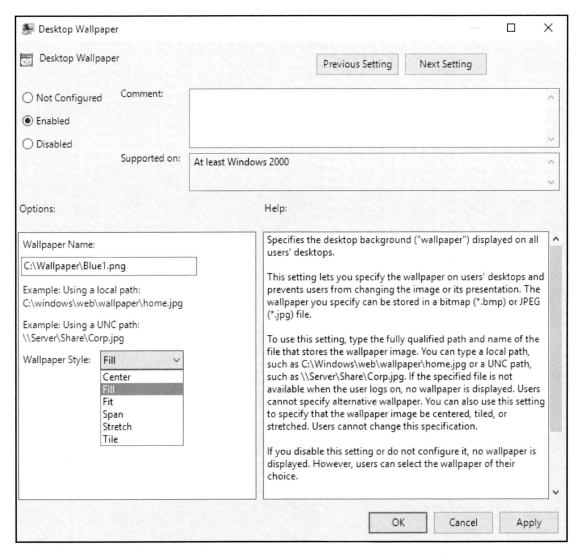

Take note that I am specifying a PNG file that sits inside a folder called `C:\Wallpaper`. Your Windows computers will not have this same directory and file, of course, because I created these images. If you are copying these steps precisely then you will need to ensure that whatever images you want to use for wallpaper do reside on the user's hard drives. On the computers in my test lab, I actually have two PNG files sitting on the hard drive of my `LAPTOP1` workstation that we are going to use to play around with as we build these GPOs.

I would say "let's go ahead and try this out!", except that, even though we now have our GPO configured with a desktop wallpaper setting, we have to remember that this GPO is not linked anywhere at present. The GPO exists, but is currently just sitting in the main `Group Policy Objects` containing folder, which doesn't necessarily mean it is doing anything. A GPO is only as powerful as its links, and since we have not yet established links to any locations inside our domain, this new GPO is currently not going to be assigned to anybody. We will link and then finally test this new GPO in the very next section of this chapter.

More on GPO links

There are a few more items to understand when it comes to GPO links. You already know about the Group Policy processing order and how GPOs filter down to client computers in the order of sites, then domains, then OUs, and then nested OUs. This is important to remember any time that you are working within Group Policy. The question still remaining is: how or where do you determine when a GPO needs to apply at one of those tiers? How do you take a GPO and apply it somewhere? To a particular site, domain, or OU? The answer to this question is GPO links. You use links to associate GPOs with places inside Active Directory. Sometimes, this means that each GPO is linked to only a single location, like a very specific OU because that GPO is for a very specific purpose. Other times, you may find GPOs that need to be linked to many different places. Perhaps you have a GPO setting that you want to roll out to many of your workstations, but it's not quite appropriate to link it all the way at the top of your domain because you don't want or need everything in the domain to receive that setting. In this case, your GPO might be linked to dozens of different OUs that contain the computer accounts where you do want the GPO to apply. Linking GPOs to many different places is a very normal practice.

The difference between GPOs and GPO links

We have already inferred this information based on other items that we have talked about, but it is critically important to understand the difference between GPOs and GPO links. GPOs are the objects stored inside Active Directory that contain all of the settings that you want to apply. By themselves, GPOs do nothing at all. They are simply objects sitting around inside the `Group Policy Objects` folder inside GPMC. You could spend years creating 1,000 different GPOs and still never have a single one of them applying to anything in your environment.

GPO links are where the rubber meets the road. You link GPOs to places inside Active Directory. Sometimes GPOs get linked to a site, and that GPO setting is then applied to everything inside that site. More commonly, GPOs might be linked to a domain, in which case it filters down from that level, again creating a pretty wide path as it spreads that setting around. Most often, GPOs are linked to individual OUs. This provides very minute and focused attention of the GPO settings only to those machines and users to which you desire them to be applied. One GPO can be linked to numerous places, and a single OU could also have many different GPOs linked to it. Each link is unique and treated individually when Group Policy processes.

The GPO link warning message

Following on the heels of our clarification of GPOs versus GPO links, let's discuss that GPO link warning message that you have undoubtedly seen 100 times already as you have started clicking around inside GPMC. By default, unless you have already turned it off, every single time that you click on a GPO link, you will see the following warning displayed:

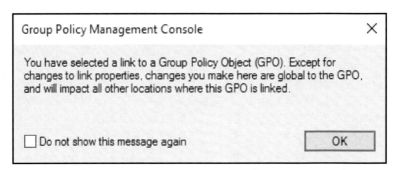

This is super annoying, and thankfully it is easily disabled by checking the little box that says **Do not show this message again**. However, it is very important to read this message at least once, and to take it to heart. This warning is telling you, in case you didn't know, that while you have clicked on a mere piddly link to a GPO and not selected upon the GPO itself, changes that you make here will change the GPO itself! Remember, a GPO is only stored in one centralized location. There may be numerous links to that same GPO, which sometimes makes it appear as if they are separate GPOs. If you were to click on a link to a GPO that is listed under an Accounting OU and make a change, and that same GPO is linked to human resources, any settings that you change will affect human resources as well.

If you have disabled this message and want to re-enable it for the sake of a new administrator or simply to start giving yourself that reminder once again, it is easily done by opening GPMC and visiting the **View** menu. Open **View** | **Options** | **General** and re-select the box for **Show confirmation dialog to distinguish between GPOs and GPO links**:

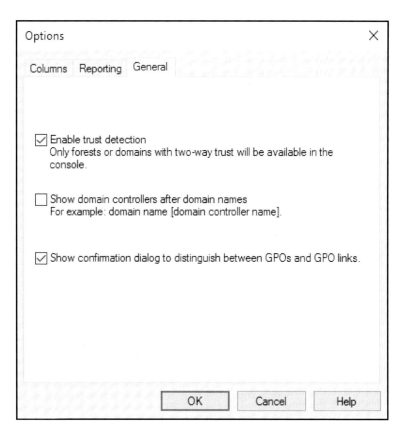

Linking our new GPO

Our test lab has Active Directory, Group Policy, a few OUs created, and now we even have a new GPO with a setting inside that should set the desktop wallpaper of whatever computers the policy applies to. We are finally ready to test this GPO to make sure it really works; our final remaining step is to link the GPO to a location so that it starts applying. We could link the GPO at the root of the domain and (without additional filtering) it would then filter down to all of the machines that are joined to my domain, but I don't want to be quite that extensive. I just want to test my new GPO out on a single workstation for now, which is a very common task when creating any new GPO or adding a new setting into a GPO. Always test before rolling out to production.

I have created an OU called **Accounting**. My LAPTOP1 workstation is currently sitting inside this OU. All I need to do in order to link my policy is to open GPMC, find the Accounting OU, and right-click on it. From the menu, choose **Link an Existing GPO...**:

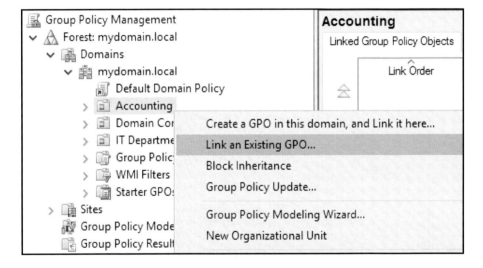

You will now see a screen called **Select GPO**. This displays for you all of the GPOs that exist inside your domain. Simply select the new GPO we created called **Set Desktop Wallpaper to Blue 1** and click **OK**:

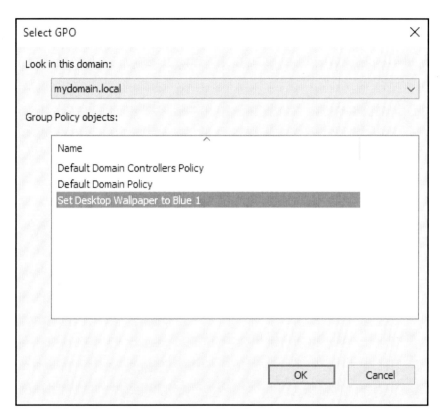

That's all you have to do! Back inside GPMC, you can now see that the **Set Desktop Wallpaper to Blue 1** GPO is linked underneath the **Accounting** OU. This change is immediate; the policy is now associated with that OU and the next time that any computers inside Accounting do a Group Policy refresh, they will see and apply this new setting.

For Group Policy testing scenarios, there is a command-line tool that is very commonly used to force policies to apply manually, but usually when making changes at a production level, you simply make the change inside GPMC, and then let it "sit and bake". The changes will roll around to all of your workstations over the next few hours; there is no need to manually touch each computer. That would be a nightmare! In our case, I'm not quite ready to cover the command yet because we will talk about it later in this chapter, and I also don't want to sit around and wait for the policy to apply naturally, so I am going to simply reboot LAPTOP1. Group Policy processes during boot/user login so we will take that approach. To be honest, I'm not sure that I have rebooted LAPTOP1 anyway since moving it into the Accounting OU, and so I really should do so to make sure that change is also recognized by the workstation. After rebooting LAPTOP1, I log in to it and, sure enough, my desktop is displaying a blue number one!

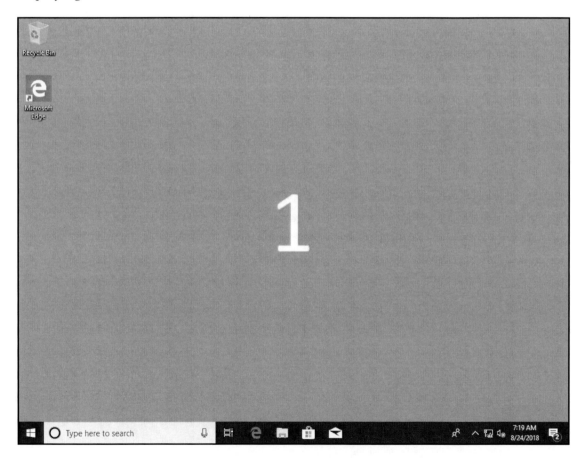

An aside regarding OU moves and reboots. Moving workstations from one OU to another inside Active Directory is a fairly normal process, but not everyone realizes that a reboot of the computer is necessary before the computer will recognize that location change. The computer will continue to think it is inside the old OU until you restart, upon which the new location is recognized.

Creating and linking new GPOs at the same time

We just finished working through a two-step process to make my desktop wallpaper "pretty". We created the GPO, and then we later linked the GPO. For those worried about wearing out the mouse clicker and wanting to save a step, there is an alternate method where you can perform both of those steps at the same time.

Inside GPMC, navigate to a location where you might want to build a new GPO. In my example, let's look at an OU called **IT Department**. When right-clicking on **IT Department**, the top option in the context menu is **Create a GPO in this domain, and Link it here...** (you can also see this option in the first screenshot in the *Linking our new GPO* section, where we right-clicked on **Accounting** in order to link our desktop wallpaper policy).

Create a GPO in this domain, and Link it here... is a very long title for a tiny little menu, which makes me laugh a little bit. Granted, it is very descriptive and this option does just what the name implies. Clicking upon this will ask you to specify a name for your new GPO, and that's all you have to do. It will create that new GPO and automatically link the new GPO to the IT Department OU (or wherever it is that you have right-clicked upon). You can see in the following screenshot that I have a new GPO linked under the IT Department OU. All I have done to create and link this GPO is choose **Create a GPO in this domain, and Link it here...** and then type in a GPO name. This new GPO is now ready for editing, and as soon as a setting exists in this GPO, that setting will immediately start rolling around to my IT Department machines:

Create a GPO in this domain, and Link it here... only works at two of our processing tiers. You can use this option to create and link a GPO at the root level of the domain, or at a specific OU level. This option is not available at the site level.

Linking at the site level

When creating and linking new GPOs, it is almost always at either the Domain level, or an OU-level tier. As you know, there is also the ability to link GPOs to a particular Active Directory site, and so we should cover that in case you ever have the need. This is a little bit trickier than linking GPOs to an OU, because your sites are not visible by default inside GPMC.

Open up GPMC, and attempt to expand the Sites folder. You will notice that nothing is listed there by default. We must manually add the sites that we want to display inside GPMC. Right-click on **Sites**, and then choose **Show Sites.**

Now select the sites that you want to display inside GPMC, and click **OK**:

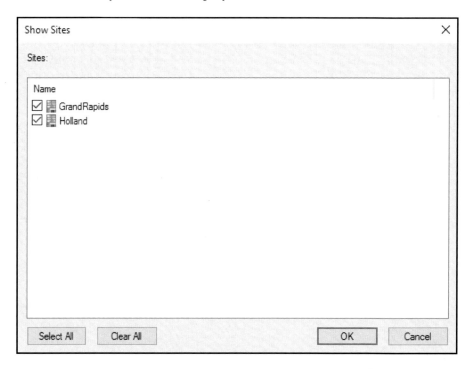

Now, back at the primary GPMC console screen, you can successfully expand the `Sites` folder and see all of your sites listed here. You now also have the ability to right-click on a particular site, and choose the **Link an Existing GPO...** option in order to link a policy to the entire site:

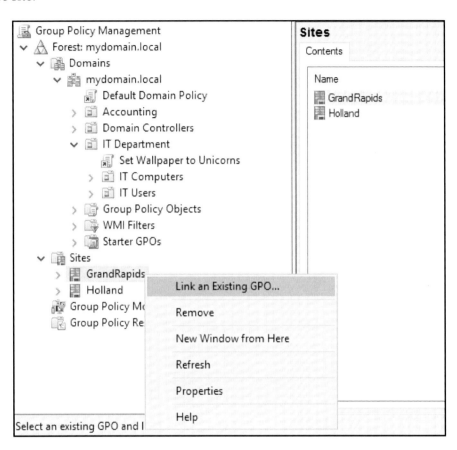

Deleting a GPO link versus deleting a GPO

If all of the information we have discussed regarding the differences between GPOs and GPO links makes sense to you, then this topic is probably already sorted in your brain. The topic of deleting these items is still worth discussing, though, because a deletion of these objects can have serious implications in your network.

Deleting a GPO link

Deleting links to GPOs is the more common task that you will be accomplishing. It is quite common that there are many more links inside an Active Directory domain than there are GPOs, because one GPO can be linked to many different places. The process for rolling out that GPO setting along with its links was probably an extended affair, starting with the creation of the GPO itself, moving on to testing those GPO settings by linking to test OUs, finalized by creating links to production OUs inside your environment in order to start pushing the settings to production computers. The reverse is generally the smart way to go when removing settings. It is most common to delete the links to the GPOs before you delete the GPOs themselves. This retains the GPO and all settings inside the GPO, so that you can reverse ship if needed and re-link those GPOs in the event that the link deletions start to cause problems.

Deleting GPO links is very simple: you right-click on the link and choose **Delete**. However, it is super important to make sure that you are deleting the *link*, and not the GPO itself. In the following screenshot, you can see the GPO called **Set Wallpaper to Unicorns** listed under **Group Policy Objects**, and you can also see the link to that same GPO listed under the **IT Department** OU. You could easily delete either thing inside GPMC, but you only want to delete the link. The icon for links always has the little arrow on top of the scroll. There aren't any links that show up underneath the Group Policy Objects folder, so make sure you are not deleting something down there. Instead, we are right-clicking on the link that is hooked to the IT Department OU, and choosing that **Delete** function:

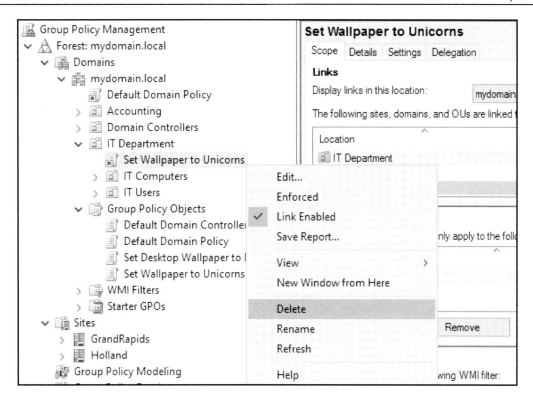

Deleting a GPO

Alternatively, you could delete the GPO itself. This is a far less common scenario, but sometimes you just need to do a little bit of AD cleanup. The process for deleting a GPO is the same: simply right-click on it and choose **Delete**, but the location where you are making that deletion is different. When deleting GPOs, you drop down the `Group Policy Objects` folder, and accomplish the deletion from there. This ensures you are deleting the GPO itself and not just a link to it.

 It is really smart to double-check the GPO's **Scope** tab before deleting any GPO! Here you can see any links that might still be active. This helps to ensure that you aren't deleting a GPO that is being used by another administrator in your company. Note that deleting your cubicle neighbor's important GPO could result in you having to take said co-worker out for a beer after work.

Disabling GPO links

Instead of deleting GPO links, the option also exists to disable those GPO links. In most cases, this is a smarter approach. Perhaps you run into a case where an existing GPO is pushing some settings into place, and you now have a need to adjust those settings. You could delete all of the GPO links to make sure it is no longer applying to your computers, then modify and test the GPO, and then re-link it to all of the locations. But what if you forget where they are linked? I hope you documented them all.

Instead, we can simply right-click on a GPO link and uncheck the option for **Link Enabled**. As expected, this sets the link into a Disabled state, so the GPO will no longer apply to that linked location. Later, when you have made your changes and are ready for the newly improved GPO to make its appearance, you simply find your existing links, right-click on them again, and re-select the **Link Enabled** option to put them back into action.

When you disable a link, it is a little bit difficult to identify the fact that it is disabled. The image for the link does turn a bit of a grey color, but you can hardly tell the difference on most monitors. So, instead, to get a quick feel for whether a GPO link is enabled or disabled, you could right-click on it and reverse-engineer whether or not the **Link Enabled** checkbox is present, or you could left-click on the GPO link itself and take a look inside the **Scope** tab. You will see a field called **Link Enabled** and it will display **Yes** or **No**:

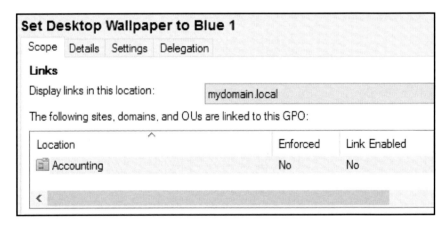

Everyday command-line tools

When working with Group Policy, it is very common to find yourself inside a Command Prompt or PowerShell window, throwing some simple commands at servers and workstations in order to test out settings, push settings into place, or verify that Group Policy settings have been applied successfully. We will save the PowerShell-specific cmdlets for later in the book, and here discuss a few commands that can be run from either command-line interface.

GPUpdate

One command-line tool that is baked into every version of Microsoft Windows is **GPUpdate**. Based on the name, you can probably guess that this command has something to do with updating Group Policy settings. Think of GPUpdate as a client-side tool that allows you to initiate a new "pull" of Group Policy settings. When you create a new GPO or make changes to an existing GPO, those changes will roll around naturally without any manual user input, but that rollout happens on a schedule which could leave you waiting 90 minutes or more in order to test your new settings. GPUpdate is the tool that speeds up that process.

There are a number of switches that can be used alongside the `gpupdate` command, each serving different purposes. Before we discuss the different switches and their uses, it will be important to understand the two different ways that Group Policy processing happens on a machine.

Background refresh

This is the processing that you are typically trying to speed along when testing out new settings. Group Policy background refresh happens naturally in the background on a periodic basis. The default timer for new updates is 90 minutes. Every hour and a half, workstations will check in with Active Directory and ask whether or not anything in Group Policy has been updated. If not, it won't do anything. If there have been changes, then those policies changed will be re-processed on the client machine, thereby putting the new settings into place.

Foreground refresh

Group Policy foreground refresh is a little bit different in that it is only triggered by specific events. These events include boot or shutdown of the computer, as well as user logons or logoffs. Foreground refresh sequences are the only times that something like a logon or logoff script would be able to be processed.

Knowing the differences between refresh cycle types is necessary because some of the switches that can be used with GPUpdate initiate different tiers of the refresh cycle. Here is a list of those switches.

GPUpdate.exe switches

- gpupdate: The gpupdate command can be used on its own. This will initiate a regular background refresh cycle, meaning that it will only process GPOs that have been changed or updated within Group Policy. In my experience, running the command on its own doesn't usually do much.

- gpupdate /Force: By far the command that I issue most frequently, the /Force switch causes Group Policy to re-process and re-apply all of the policy settings. If you ever have a policy that doesn't seem to be applying, make sure to run this command at least once before doing any in-depth troubleshooting. This often clears it up. /Force causes a refresh at both the background and foreground levels.

- gpupdate /Sync: The /Sync switch doesn't actually initiate an immediate refresh of Group Policy like the other switches do. Instead, it flags the next foreground refresh to happen "synchronously". During a normal, everyday Windows login process, Group Policy processing is happening asynchronously, which means the login process will proceed and bring the user to a desktop even while Group Policy is still finishing its business in the background. Unfortunately, there are some processes that don't work super well with this asynchronous mentality, namely some ways of mapping drives or doing folder redirection. If you want to force the Windows login process to happen synchronously with Group Policy, thereby making sure that your policies are processing in order and properly during the next Windows login, for example, you could issue the gpupdate /Sync command and the next user login would follow that process.

- gpupdate /Boot: This causes the machine to restart after applying GPO settings, if one of the GPOs asks for a restart. Some policies are only able to apply during the computer boot process, such as software installation. Using /Boot is the switch to force that behavior.

- `gpupdate /Logoff`: Similar to `/Boot`, the `/Logoff` switch causes the user to be logged out of the computer after Group Policy has finished updating. This sounds useful because some policy settings can only be applied during the user login process, but this switch is a little silly because simply logging off the computer and logging back in will also cause that policy refresh cycle to happen, so I have never actually seen anybody use this switch.
- `gpupdate /Wait <30>`: Feel free to replace `30` with your own number of seconds. This switch causes Command Prompt to wait a certain number of seconds for GPO processing to finish, before returning to the cursor. This switch is generally only useful for scripted operations.
- `gpupdate /Target:<User or Computer>`: The `Target` switch can be used to refresh only one side of the GPO, or the other. If you want to test a change that you know is on the User side of policy, you can specify `gpupdate /Target:User` and update only that part of the policy. The same is true for Computer. The advantage to using this switch is purely for efficiency of that refresh. If you only need to pull a setting from one side, it shortens the amount of time that the Group Policy refresh takes to finish.

In order to test the `gpupdate` command, simply log in to the workstation where you want to test Group Policy refresh, open up Command Prompt, and enter `gpupdate /Force`. Group Policy will process, and any errors within that process cycle will be displayed. If everything has gone swimmingly, you will see the following, which indicates a successful run:

GPResult

If `gpupdate` is used to update Group Policy settings, then `gpresult` must be used to show us some kind of results from Group Policy updates, right? Absolutely. GPResult is another client-side command-line tool that can be used to show you some details about which GPOs have been applied or not applied to a particular workstation.

 When I talk about workstations, what I really mean here is any device within your domain that can receive Group Policy settings. This includes both Windows 7/8/10/and so on workstations, as well as Windows Server operating systems. `gpupdate` and `gpresult` are just as useful on both client and server operating systems.

Switches also exist for GPResult, which are quite common to use because oftentimes when you are reviewing GPResult data, you are trying to home in on some particular GPO or piece of information, and the switches can be most helpful for narrowing down the scope of displayed info:

- `gpresult /R`: The R is short for **Resultant Set of Policy (RSoP)**. This switch will show you the results of the policy settings that have applied to this machine. Without using the `/R` switch, the `gpresult` command doesn't tell you much of anything other than how to learn how to run the `gpresult` command. You almost always use `/R` when working with `gpresult`.
- `gpresult /Scope <User or Computer>`: This helps to narrow down the results to display for you either information from the User side of Group Policy, or results only from the Computer settings. When trying to narrow down a search to ensure a particular GPO is being successfully applied to a workstation, it is quite common to use this switch so that you have less data to sift through.
- `gpresult /X or /H`: Both of these switches perform similar tasks, but with different results. Using `/X` will save your `gpresult` report to an XML file, whereas `/H` will save as an HTML document.
- `gpresult /S`: Use `/S` to specify a remote computer name. This allows you to check Group Policy results remotely, without having to log in to that computer.
- `gpresult /U`: Specifies a user context for running the `gpresult` command. If you are logged in as a standard user and have a non-privileged Command Prompt open, you will probably have to specify an administrative user account with your command in order to get any useful data.
- `gpresult /P`: Use this switch to specify the password that goes along with the user account that you specified in `/U`.

There are other switches that can be used with `gpresult` but are less common. For a full report, type in `gpresult /?` to review the whole set. Also keep in mind that many of these switches can be used in combination to further modify your results. We will see an example of this below. I am going to use `gpresult /R /Scope:Computer` in order to show the RSoP (the list of policies that have been applied) for only the computer-based policy settings. This report does not, therefore, list any policies that apply at the user level:

```
Administrator: Command Prompt

C:\>gpresult /r /scope:computer

Microsoft (R) Windows (R) Operating System Group Policy Result tool v2.0
© 2018 Microsoft Corporation. All rights reserved.

Created on 8/ 29/ 2018 at 4:46:47 PM


RSOP data for  on LAPTOP1 : Logging Mode
------------------------------------------

OS Configuration:          Member Workstation
OS Version:                10.0.17134
Site Name:                 GrandRapids
Roaming Profile:
Local Profile:
Connected over a slow link?: No


COMPUTER SETTINGS
-----------------
    CN=LAPTOP1,OU=Accounting Computers,OU=Accounting,DC=mydomain,DC=local
    Last time Group Policy was applied: 8/29/2018 at 4:13:28 PM
    Group Policy was applied from:     DC1.mydomain.local
    Group Policy slow link threshold:  500 kbps
    Domain Name:                       MYDOMAIN
    Domain Type:                       Windows 2008 or later

    Applied Group Policy Objects
    ----------------------------
        Default Domain Policy

    The following GPOs were not applied because they were filtered out
    ---------------------------------------------------------------------
```

One of the particularly cool things about this result is that it shows you not only the GPOs that have been applied successfully to your machine, but also points out the GPOs that have been specifically filtered out, and are therefore not applying. This will become very helpful in later, advanced troubleshooting scenarios where you are tracking down whether or not a GPO is working.

Sending the output to a file

As stated previously, the /X and /H switches can both be used in order to export the gpresult data to a file. This can be helpful for submitting reports, for logging data during a troubleshooting session, or simply to be able to view the Group Policy data in a more user-friendly format. I prefer exporting to and viewing RSoP data inside an HTML file. If you open up Command Prompt, browse to the C:\Temp directory and issue the following command, the Group Policy summary will be exported to the C:\Temp folder on your machine:

```
GPResult /H GPOs.html
```

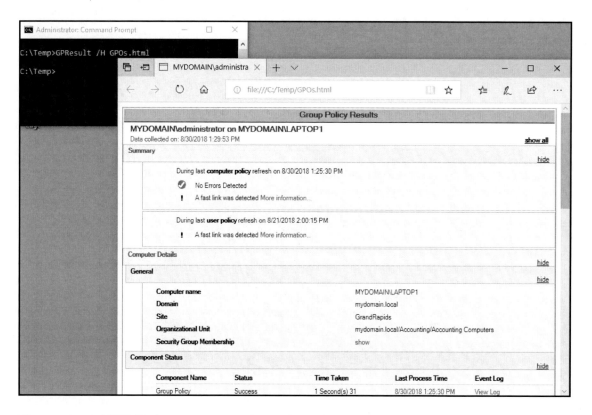

The generated HTML document is easily read inside a web browser, and displays all of the data about which GPOs were applied or not applied. This is much nicer and easier to read than skimming this information from inside a Command Prompt window.

Checking GPResult data from a remote machine

In keeping with our centralized administration mindset, let's cover an example of looking up this information remotely. Today, I am logged in to my DC1 server, but I am going to utilize GPResult with a few switches in order to query the Group Policy data that is sitting on my LAPTOP1 workstation. I also want it to display GPO information for my primary user account on that system, which is called Jordan. Here is a command that will tell GPResult to reach out to LAPTOP1 and pull not only its computer information, but also the information related to the user Jordan:

```
GPResult /s LAPTOP1 /user JORDAN /r > JordanLaptop1.txt
```

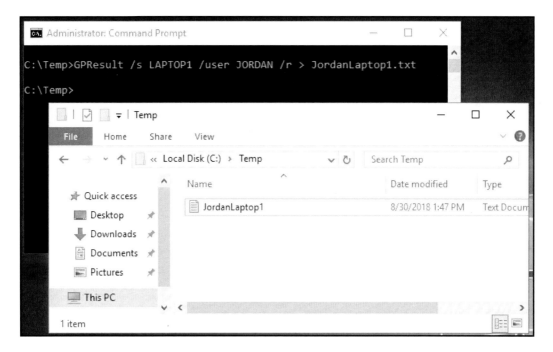

As you can see, I appended yet one more way to send the resultant data out to a file, this time a text document. This is no different than reading the data inside Command Prompt, but it is now saved so that I can store it and reference it later.

If you open up that text document, you will see the output of the GPResult command. It shows me information about both computer policies as well as user policies applied to the Jordan account. Scrolling down to the user information, we can see confirmation that my Set Desktop Wallpaper to Blue 1 GPO is still being applied to this user account:

Resultant Set of Policy

Throughout the previous few pages, we have already been viewing RSoP data. RSoP is the "end result" of which settings are sitting on a machine after all tiers of Group Policy processing have finished. The GPResult command is useful for displaying this kind of information for us, but there is another tool called RSOP.MSC that can also be used to take a look at the data in a slightly different way.

Log in to one of your machines, open Command Prompt, and simply type RSOP. Then press *Enter*. A new window will open that allows you to browse through all of the policy settings currently applied to your machine. The layout is the same as Group Policy Editor, so this can be another useful way of tracking down the location of a particular setting if you have a need to edit the GPO and change it.

In the following screenshot, I have run RSOP.MSC on my workstation. Drilling down into the menus, I have easily discovered the policy setting that is applying my blue desktop wallpaper to this machine:

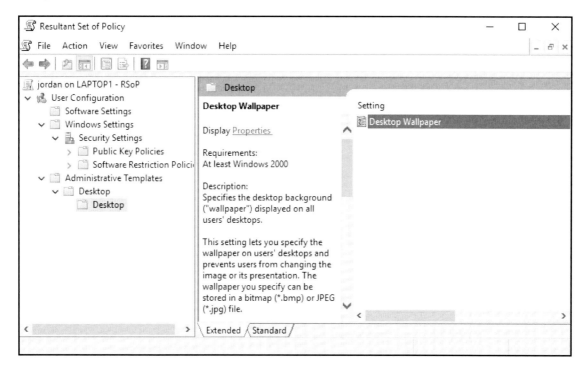

Summary

In this chapter, we covered many of the daily duties and tasks that you will find yourself enthralled with as an Active Directory/Group Policy administrator. Being comfortable with these items will enable you to immediately start doing real work within a Group Policy infrastructure, and can probably pass muster for 80% of the necessary functionality for most companies. We covered GPO creation and linking information, editing GPO settings, deleting and disabling said settings, and the everyday command-line tools that can be used to interact with Group Policy.

In Chapter 4, *Advanced Filtering of Group Policy Objects*, we will focus on pinpointing your GPO settings to ensure they are only applying to the workstations and/or users to which you want them to apply. You currently have a basic understanding of how to divide up that access, but there are some additional tools and features that can be used to further enhance your GPO filtering prowess.

4
Advanced Filtering of Group Policy Objects

We have been discussing GPO links in every chapter of the book so far, diving a little bit deeper each time that links are mentioned. If you couldn't tell, having the ability to manipulate GPOs by their links is essential to successful Group Policy administration. In this chapter, we take it a little bit further still, and look at some of the more advanced filtering scenarios for your GPOs. Sometimes GPOs can be filtered simply by strategically placed links, true, but there are many cases where you need to filter the application of GPOs even more specifically than what a simple link allows for. This chapter is all about those advanced filtering capabilities.

The following topics will be covered in this chapter:

- Link order precedence
- Blocking GPO inheritance
- Enforcing GPOs
- User settings versus computer settings
- Exercises with **Organizational Units** (**OUs**) and links
- Filtering GPOs with security filters
- Filtering GPOs with WMI filters

Link order precedence

We have already learned "on paper" that there is a hierarchical system to the way that Group Policy processes through GPO links. As a quick refresher, those tiers are (from first to last):

1. Site level
2. Domain level
3. OU level
4. Nested OU level

Since processing starts at the top of that list and finishes at the bottom, this means that for any conflicting settings that exist across the different tiers, the ones closer to the bottom will win. Domain policies beat site policies, OU-linked policies trump domain-linked policies, and so on. Within that hierarchy, I would like to briefly both prove this out so that you can see it with your own eyes, and also shed light on some of the more advanced options within these tiers so that you can prepare to handle conflicts in the future.

OUs trump domains

A GPO that is linked to a specific OU should process after a GPO that is linked at the root of the domain, and those settings in the OU-linked GPO should win out in the end, correct? This is the scenario we are proving out today. You probably remember the GPO I created previously that set my desktop wallpaper to the color blue with a large number 1 in the center. This policy is linked at the root of my domain, as you can see in the following screenshot, and as you can also see, it is successfully applying to the LAPTOP1 workstation where I am currently logged in:

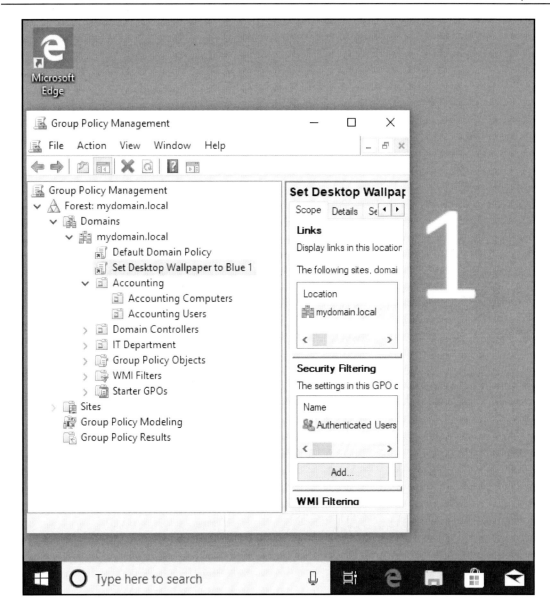

Now I am going to create a second GPO that sets the desktop wallpaper to the color orange, with a number 2 in the center of the screen. This wallpaper setting is in direct conflict with the wallpaper setting in my old GPO, and so if both GPOs apply to a workstation, only one of them is going to win at the end of the Group Policy processing cycle.

Remember that simply creating this new GPO will do nothing until we link it to a location. I have created my new **Set Desktop Wallpaper to Orange 2** GPO and, as seen in the following screenshot, I have linked this new GPO to the **Accounting** OU. This OU happens to be the place where my LAPTOP1 workstation resides:

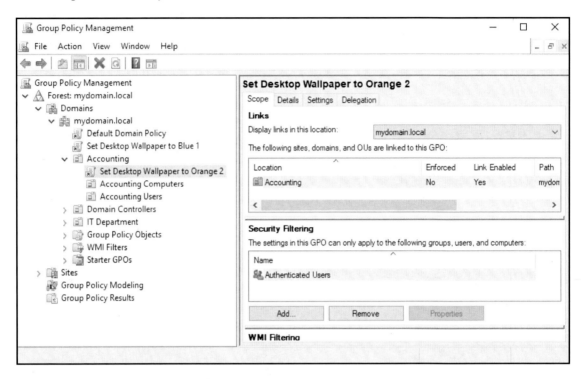

When I reboot LAPTOP1 and log in, Group Policy processes both settings. It first applies the **Set Desktop Wallpaper to Blue 1** GPO because that GPO is linked to the root of the domain. It then proceeds to apply the settings from the **Set Desktop Wallpaper to Orange 2** GPO that is linked to the Accounting OU, and when the login process is finished, you can see that the wallpaper configured on my client is orange with the number 2:

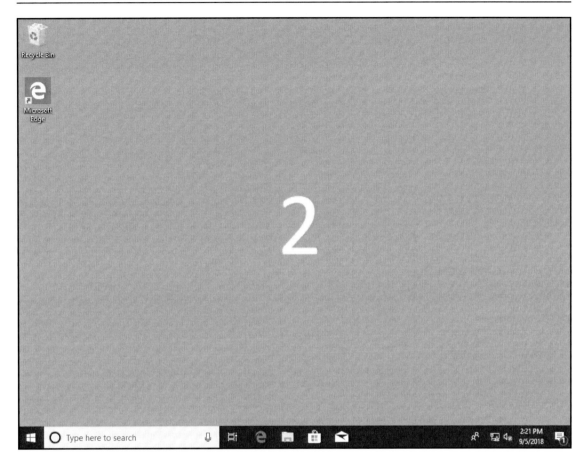

This example is nothing earth-shattering, but is definitive proof that I'm not making this stuff up, and that conflicting settings will overwrite each other depending on the GPO processing hierarchy.

Multiple GPOs linked at the same level

Taking this link precedence discussion one step further, what do you suppose happens when there are multiple GPOs linked to the same tier, but that contain conflicting settings? One of them must win, but how do we determine which settings are going to end up on our devices? GPMC can once again come to the rescue and clue us in as to what is happening under the hood. Let's say that I were to link both of my desktop wallpaper GPOs to the same place. I will link both of them to the Accounting OU. Now I have two GPOs that are both trying to modify the same setting on my workstation, and they are both linked at the same level. Which one has priority?

Inside GPMC, I am going to click on the **Accounting** OU. Then, over on the right-hand side of the screen, we are looking inside the **Linked Group Policy Objects** tab. This tab displays the list of GPOs that are linked to this OU, whether or not they are enabled, and, most importantly, something called **Link Order**.

As you can see in the following screenshot, my Accounting OU has both of our desktop wallpaper GPOs linked to it. They are both visible inside **Linked Group Policy Objects**, but they have different **Link Order** numbers. These numbers can be a little bit confusing; it is most helpful to think of this Link Order number as if the GPOs are competitors running a race that has just finished. Most races end with a first place winner, second place, third, and so on. That thought process is the same for the GPO **Link Order**. Whichever GPO has **Link Order** number 1, that GPO is our *winner*. In our case, my desktop wallpaper is going to end up as Orange 2, because that GPO has **Link Order** number 1:

The reverse way of thinking about it is that the GPOs will process in reverse order of their **Link Order** number. In our example, the Blue 1 GPO is link number 2, which means it processes first. Then the Orange 2 GPO is link number 1, which means that it processes last. And remember, last always wins in Group Policy. I find this to be the more confusing way to remember how the processing order works, so maybe stick with the first, second, and third place race winners!

Changing the order of link precedence

If you ever find yourself in a position where multiple GPOs are linked to the same place and they are fighting each other for settings, it will probably be in your best long-term interests to revisit those GPO settings and edit them so that you can create harmony between all of the GPOs that are linked to a particular location. However, sometimes this is simply not possible, and so you may have to throw those GPOs into the boxing ring and let them duke it out.

Thankfully, changing the priority of GPOs is very easy. We do this from the same location we have been working in previously, inside GPMC's **Linked Group Policy Objects** tab. When multiple GPOs are listed here and you want to change the **Link Order** so that higher-numbered policies start taking precedence over lower-numbered policies, you simply choose the GPO that you want to re-prioritize and click on the up or down arrow buttons that are displayed along the left-hand side of the window.

In previous screenshots, you have seen that my Set Desktop Wallpaper to Orange 2 GPO is **Link Order** number 1, and is therefore the GPO setting that is being pushed into place on the client workstations that reside inside my Accounting OU. I now have the desire to make sure that my Set Desktop Wallpaper to Blue 1 GPO is the one who wins, and so I have clicked on that GPO and then simply clicked the up arrow button shown here:

Link Order	GPO	Enforced	Link Enabled
1	Set Desktop Wallpaper to Blue 1	No	Yes
2	Set Desktop Wallpaper to Orange 2	No	Yes

Accounting

Linked Group Policy Objects | Group Policy Inheritance | Delegation

You can see that the Blue 1 GPO now has **Link Order** number 1 priority, which means that this GPO is the one that is going to apply last on my workstations, and therefore be in place when I log in to LAPTOP1. Let's test it out. As with most changes inside GPMC, these link order adjustments take immediate effect, and so all I have to do is restart LAPTOP1, log in to it, and see that my wallpaper has changed:

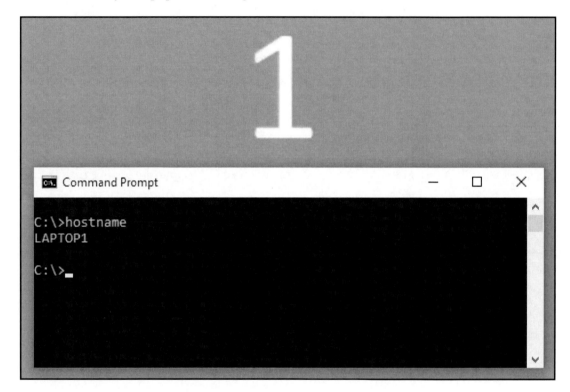

Seeing the big picture

One honorable mention while we are inside this part of GPMC: if you navigate one tab further to the right, you will find some more helpful information on this link precedence topic. I am talking about the **Group Policy Inheritance** tab, as shown in the following screenshot:

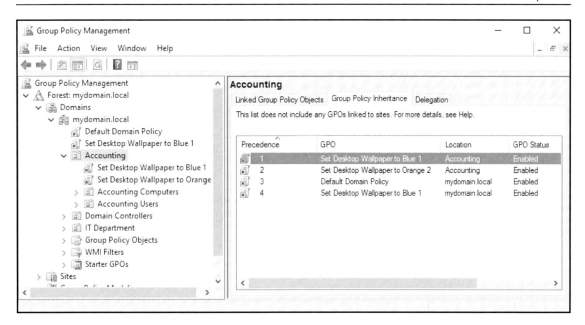

This helpful screen shows us not only the precedence of GPOs that are linked directly to this OU, but encompasses those GPOs that are linked at higher tiers and are therefore also applying to this OU via inheritance. Specifically, you can see in the preceding that my Blue 1 and Orange 2 wallpaper settings are linked to the OU itself, and you can see that those GPOs are precedence numbers 1 and 2. Even more specifically, you can see that Blue 1 is first in the list, because we just changed the link order in order to make this GPO be the last one that gets applied.

Then, further down in the list, we also have two additional GPOs on this screen. These GPOs are both linked at higher processing tiers, namely, they are both linked at the root of my domain. One is the Default Domain Policy, which makes sense because that policy is linked by default to the root of the domain and I have never changed that in my test lab environment. The last GPO in this list may be a bit of a surprise though: it seems to be another instance of my **Set Desktop Wallpaper to Blue 1** GPO. Why does this show up here? It is because when I linked that GPO to my Accounting OU, I forgot to delete the link that already existed at the root of my domain. Actually, I didn't forget at all, I left it on purpose for the sake of this example.

When Group Policy processes on computers in this Accounting OU, they will actually put the blue wallpaper into place (precedence number 4), then switch it to orange (precedence number 2), and then switch it back to blue (precedence number 1).

Each link is individual. Creating a new link to a GPO never automatically deletes previous links to that same GPO. This is very important to remember as you start doing Group Policy administration.

The **Group Policy Inheritance** tab inside GPMC can be an invaluable tool for quick reporting on all of the GPO settings that are applying to a particular OU, no matter which tier those GPOs happened to be linked to. Similar to the **Linked Group Policy Objects** tab, the precedence numbers displayed here are best thought of as first place, second place, third place, and so on. Number 1 is always the winner, but he wins because he crosses the finish line last. Clear as mud, eh?

Blocking GPO inheritance

As your Active Directory and Group Policy environments grow and expand, you will inevitably have multiple GPOs applying across the various tiers in order to make sure your workstations, servers, and users have all of the settings they need in order to stay safe and secure. Occasionally, you will have a need for a particular device or group of devices to step back from all of these rules and regulations, and be untouched by Group Policy settings. During my day job, I live on the Windows Server side of the IT house, and it is a very common occurrence that we are spinning up a new server for a particular role, and we want to make sure that this new server is not going to be immediately affected by a dozen GPOs as soon as we join it to the domain. Usually, when joining new client workstations to the domain, that is exactly what you want to happen—you rely on Group Policy to put all of the appropriate settings and configurations into place on those machines, but oftentimes new servers are being introduced for new technologies coming into your network, and there will be testing phases that accompany those rollouts. During the testing phases, to ensure everything is working on those new servers before they are "muddied up" with policy settings, it would be helpful to have a quick and easy way of excluding those servers from being manipulated by GPOs.

Thankfully, there is exactly such a functionality. I often refer to it as inherency blocking, though technically the term is *blocking inheritance*. As the name implies, this function inside GPMC allows you to block the inheritance of GPO settings for a particular location. Namely, you can right-click on any OU and choose the **Block Inheritance** option. You can see this option in the following screenshot, as well as the fact that I have already blocked inheritance for my OU called IT Department. This fact is recognized by that little blue icon next to the OU name:

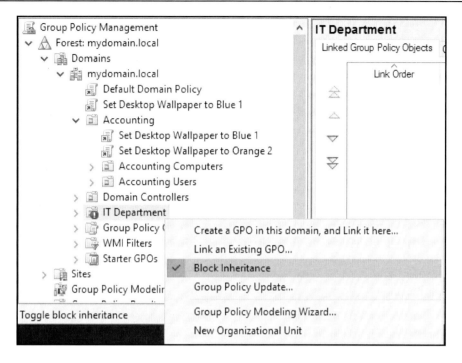

Once you have blocked inheritance for an OU, any device or user that you place into that OU will be unaffected by Group Policy settings that would be inherited down the chain to that OU. For example, any GPOs that are linked at the Site level or the Domain level would not apply to anything that was inside the IT Department OU, or any nested OUs listed under IT Department.

 Links directly to the OU will still apply! Keep in mind that even if an OU is flagged for **Block Inheritance**, any GPO that you have linked directly to the OU will still be in effect.

Let's cover a quick example to pull it all together. I often work with a Microsoft remote access technology called **DirectAccess** (**DA**). A successful DA deployment is heavily dependent on solid networking practices on the DA server. In many networks, it is common to find GPOs that do things such as disabling the Windows Firewall or configuring the IPv4/IPv6 stack in a way that certain functions within networking are squashed by default. While this is considered a good security practice for some of the machines inside a domain, it can be detrimental to a DA server. If you were to bring a new DA server online, plug it into your network, join it to your domain, and automatically get such policies, your DA server would be broken before you ever start configuring DA.

Because of this, I now consider it standard practice to put DA servers into an OU that is blocked from GPO inheritance. This ensures that any policies that might be automatically filtering down to that OU will not be processed, and will not break my new server. Then the flip side of that coin is that many of the settings DA uses are actually rolled out to the DA server via a new GPO that we create. Once we get to the end of the DA configuration process, a new GPO is created and filled with settings, and those settings need to make their way down to the DA server or servers. Since those servers are sitting inside an OU with **Block Inheritance** enabled, by default they will not receive the settings that they need. In this case, we right-click on the OU and manually link the new GPO directly to that OU. This link then works and pushes only those settings to the DA servers, while continuing to block inheritance from other GPOs that may be filtering down from higher levels in the processing tier.

It is important to remember that **Block Inheritance** is not a full-on kill switch for GPOs. Any policies linked directly to the OU will still be processed on the machines inside that OU.

Enforcing GPOs

On the heels of a discussion about inherency blocking, why don't we spin things around and discuss an option that overrides that blocking. Boy, this almost sounds like we are working in an environment where the administrators are fighting for control.

While blocked inheritance is associated with an OU-level mentality, blocking the ability for GPOs to filter down into or beyond particular OUs, the option for enforcing GPOs is flagged to the GPO link itself. It is a fairly simple setting; if you have a GPO that you want to enforce to be processed, even blowing through the borders of inherency blocking, this is the ticket.

To enforce a GPO link, all you need to do is right-click on the link and choose **Enforced**, as seen in the following screenshot. Here, I am enforcing my **Set Desktop Wallpaper to Blue 1** that is linked to the root of the domain. This means that this policy will apply to all machines in the domain, even those machines that reside inside the IT Department OU, which has inherency blocking enabled.

You can see there is also a visual indicator inside GPMC for an enforced GPO. A little lock icon shows up on top of the GPO link graphic:

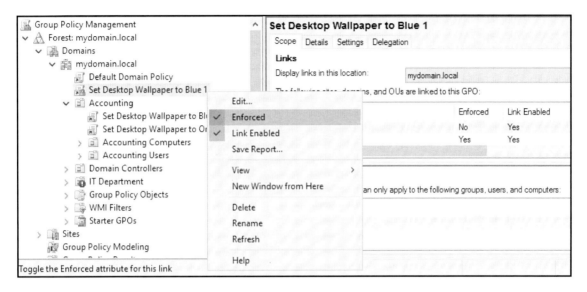

Remember, setting a GPO to be enforced does not mean that it will be applied *everywhere* in your environment, unless your link is way up high in the domain structure. Even with enforcement enabled, the GPO still regulates itself to only applying to the places where it is linked and filtered. The key difference between an enforced GPO and a non-enforced GPO is that enforced GPOs will blow through the **Blocked Inheritance** setting and apply themselves to that OU anyway.

Will enforcing GPOs affect GPO precedence?

You bet it will! You'll remember my two GPOs that contain conflicting settings; one is setting the desktop wallpaper to a blue number 1, and the other to an orange number 2. Prior to enforcing anything, my Blue 1 GPO was linked at the root of the domain, and my Orange 2 GPO was linked at the Accounting OU. Since OU links process after domain links, my Accounting computers were all receiving the Orange 2 wallpaper setting.

However, now that I have right-clicked on my domain-level Blue 1 policy and chosen to enforce it, my Accounting computers will all change over to the Blue 1 desktop wallpaper. We see an explanation as to why this happens if we click on the **Accounting** OU and then navigate to the **Group Policy Inheritance** tab. Here you can see that **Set Desktop Wallpaper to Blue 1** (note how it is the one linked at the domain tier) has jumped to the top of the priority list because it is being **Enforced**:

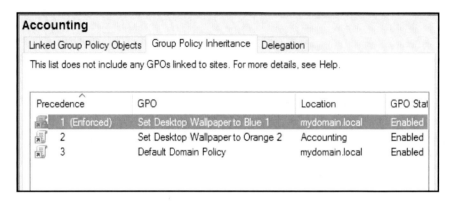

User settings versus computer settings

Now that you have some experience with editing GPOs, you may have noticed that inside each GPO are two separate groups of settings. There are **Computer Configuration** settings, and there are **User Configuration** settings, as seen in the following screenshot:

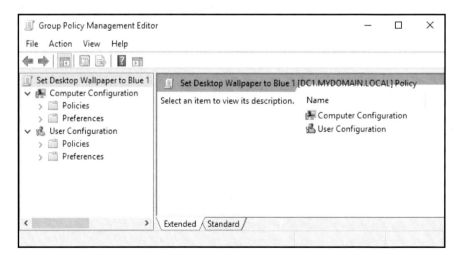

At first glance, it almost looks like Group Policy is set up so that the same policy settings are available for either computer accounts or user accounts, but that is actually not the case at all. If you expand some of the folders and settings listed inside Group Policy Management Editor, you will shortly discover that most settings do not overlap; they are unique between the two sides.

It is most common to find organizations who only make use of either **Computer Configuration** or **User Configuration** for each individual GPO. This is a good practice, especially considering our previously mentioned best practice of having GPOs be configured for very individual tasks. So, most often, you will find GPOs with computer settings being linked to OUs that contain computer accounts, and GPOs with user settings being linked to OUs that contain user accounts. There is certainly the potential to cross over settings, but organizing these settings and troubleshooting them later will be much more straightforward if you stick to the plan.

Computer Configuration settings get applied to computers, regardless of which users log in to those computers. When creating a GPO with computer settings, try to think outside the scope of users logged in to the machine and focus on security and settings of the physical machine itself. Then **User Configuration** settings are applied to users, no matter which computers they are logging in to. In an AD environment, user settings will follow the user to any domain-joined computer that they log in to. In the event that you have a GPO with both user and computer settings and they conflict, then in general the computer policies will win and take final effect.

Occasionally, you may have the need to issue user settings to anybody who logs in to a particular computer or group of computers. This capability is handled by something called **Loopback Policy Processing**, which we will discuss further in `Chapter 5`, *Deploying Policy Settings*.

Disabling half of a GPO

One controversial option that exists for every Group Policy Object is the ability to disable half of its settings. Namely, you can easily select to disable the entire set of computer settings (allowing only the user settings to work), or you can disable all user settings (which allows only computer settings within the GPO to function). The purpose of this capability is to speed up Group Policy processing when a machine boots or a user logs in. Oftentimes, we create GPOs with specific purposes in mind. Usually, the settings that we plug into a GPO are only ever going to be on one side of the house or the other. It is quite rare that you would create a GPO that contains both user and computer settings; typically, you would want to scope user and computer settings separately and so you would create separate GPOs to contain those settings. When Group Policy processes its settings, it runs through all of the settings in each GPO. This happens very fast, but what about in an environment with 400 GPOs? If you were able to disable the unused half of each GPO, that literally cuts in half the amount of time and processing power that Group Policy needs when running a refresh on a machine, which can become substantial.

Why is this option controversial? Because it is easy to forget that you have flagged a GPO to be halfway disabled. Imagine the troubleshooting hours that you may have to put into a setting that you have added to a GPO but simply isn't working no matter what you try. After banging your head against the wall for hours looking into links, scopes, and filtering options, you may only then stumble on the screen where it allows you to disable large parts of a GPO and discover that the setting you are putting into place is being ignored because someone set the GPO to be half disabled.

All in all, I believe that if you are aware of this option and how to check its status, then it is safe to use and can speed up logon times in your environment. Most of the time, when I build GPOs, I am only putting computer settings into that GPO, and usually I am creating GPOs that I don't want anyone to manipulate down the road, so I frequently disable the **User Configuration** settings part of my GPOs. Let's take a look at this option together, so that you know exactly where to configure it, and where to check to find out whether or not this option is configured for any GPO in your environment.

Inside GPMC, expand your `Group Policy Objects` folder and click on any GPO that exists in your environment. Then, on the right-hand side of the screen, click on the **Details** tab. Here, you can see some statistical information about the GPO itself, and at the bottom is an option labeled **GPO Status** that contains a drop-down list of options:

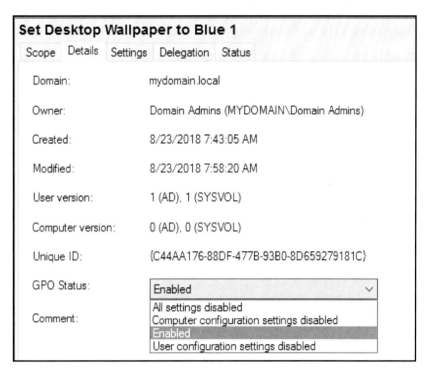

The options are as follows:

- **Enabled**: This is the default status for any GPO. This means that the GPO will process both user and computer settings when it applies to an object.
- **Computer configuration settings disabled**: Select this option to immediately disable all processing of the computer settings within this GPO. Only user-side items will function.
- **User configuration settings disabled**: Select this option to immediately disable all processing of the user settings within this GPO. Only computer-side items will function.
- **All settings disabled**: This option will cause all settings within a GPO to stop functioning, effectively disabling the GPO. This option is rarely used, but could be useful if you ever had the need to immediately stop some settings from getting pushed into place. Disabling or unlinking GPOs could also work, but that generally means you are disabling multiple links, which takes more time, and then you have to do all of that work again when it comes time to turn the GPO back on. By disabling it at this level, you have one single click to immediately and effectively disable the entire GPO. **All settings disabled** can also be useful when building out a new GPO. Maybe you need to input a whole list of settings into a GPO, but you already have it linked out to some OUs and you don't want these settings to start rolling out to the client computers before you finish populating the GPO with all of the remaining settings. By temporarily disabling the GPO inside the **Details** screen, you will stop that GPO from putting any settings out in the wild until you have confirmed it is 100% ready to roll.

You don't have to find and click on the actual GPO in order to make this GPO status change. If you were to instead click on any link associated with that GPO, you would also be able to manipulate this drop-down box. Remember that this change affects the entire GPO and will also change the settings for any other links that are hooked to this GPO!

Exercises with OUs and links

Enough theory, let's get our hands dirty for a little while. You are now familiar with many of the tasks inside GPMC that are required to be a Group Policy administrator. However, there are other functions associated with these tasks that so far we have been taking for granted. We talk an awful lot about OUs and how your users and computers are going to be magically organized inside of these OUs. You now know how to manipulate GPOs so that they are linked to particular OUs or nested OUs, but who created all of those OUs and how did all of your user and computer objects get sorted into those OUs in the first place? The answer may surprise you: it's the lesser-known tale of the OU Fairy, distant cousin of the better-known Tooth Fairy. Don't take my word for it: if you pull out a magnifying glass and take a look at your own business card, listed in very small letters under your job description should be the words "OU Fairy". If it's not there, you should set up a meeting with your HR department immediately.

Let's take a few minutes to cover some of the need-to-know items that are necessary for working with OUs, because you'll need to be able to do this in order to make your way through this book and your life as an IT professional.

Creating or deleting OUs

This first step is pretty important; it's difficult to link GPOs to OUs if the OUs don't exist in the first place! It is possible to create or delete OUs from within the **Group Policy Management Console** (**GPMC**), but these functions are more commonly performed from inside **Active Directory Users and Computers** (**ADUC**). Let's take a quick look at how to do it inside either console.

OUs inside ADUC

You can launch ADUC in the same ways that you launch GPMC, through the **Start** menu or via Server Manager's **Tools** menu. ADUC is also included in the RSAT tools, so if you have taken the steps to install those on your workstation, this console already exists there as well. Most commonly, I find myself launching these management consoles via Command Prompt, because I tend to always have one up and running on my machine. You are familiar with GPMC.MSC in order to launch the GPMC, but is there a similar command-line shortcut for ADUC? Yes, though you may have to type it in a few times before it gets committed to memory because it's not the most intuitively named MSC:

DSA.MSC—this is the MMC shortcut command that you can launch from Command Prompt, from PowerShell, or from **Start | Run**. DSA.MSC will open up **Active Directory Users and Computers**:

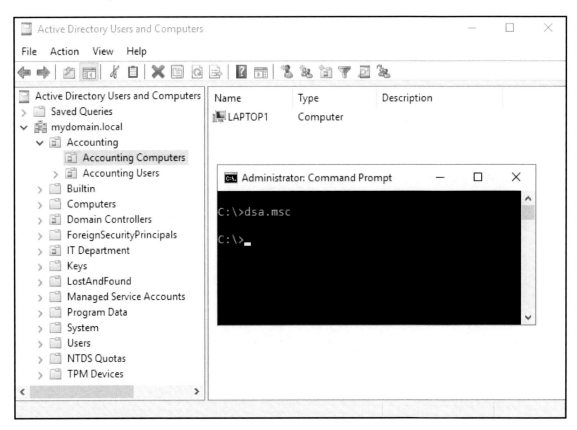

We are now looking inside Active Directory. You can see many containers that exist by default here, and some that I have added. OUs, our purpose for visiting this console today, are distinguished by the little icon on top of the folder. While I'm not exactly sure what that little icon is supposed to be, you can see in the previous screenshot that there are many folders/containers displayed, but only Accounting, Accounting Computers, Accounting Users, Domain Controllers, and IT Department have the little extra icon sitting on top of their manila folder. Only these five are OUs.

Creating new OUs or deleting old OUs is extremely simple. Right-clicking on an existing location inside ADUC will present for you a menu from which you can choose **Delete** to remove an OU, or you can expand the **New** menu to see all kinds of options. As you can see, there are many more things that can be done here beyond the scope of generating new OUs, but for our purposes you would select **New** | **Organizational Unit**:

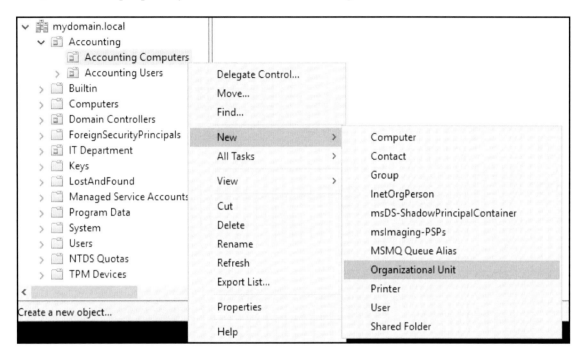

You can create new OUs directly under your domain, so they reside within this top tier of the domain, or you can create **nested OUs** by right-clicking on an existing OU (as I have done in my screenshot) and then choosing to create a new OU. In the example provided, when I click on **New** | **Organizational Unit**, I would be creating a new nested OU that resides under my Accounting Computers OU.

OUs inside GPMC

You are already familiar with opening and working within GPMC, but one thing we have not covered is the ability to create or delete OUs from inside this console. Similar to ADUC, when you open GPMC, you can see all of the OUs that are present inside your domain, and creating or deleting new OUs is as simple as right-clicking and choosing the appropriate action. You can see in the following screenshot that I have mirrored what I did earlier inside ADUC, right-clicked on my `Accounting Computers` OU and now see the options to either **Delete**, or to create a **New Organizational Unit**:

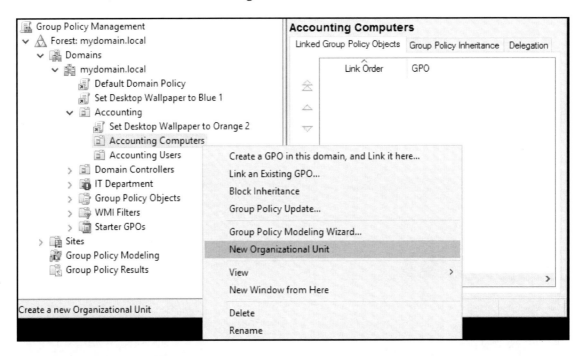

Is there a right or a wrong answer as to which console is the better place to perform these functions? Generally, you always want to be manipulating your OUs by using ADUC. While all of your Group Policy-related functions are requiring you to be logged in to GPMC, it is worth the few extra clicks to get ADUC open, because working with OUs inside the GPMC has some limitations. Most importantly, when inside GPMC, you cannot see inside of the OUs! There is no way to tell what user or computer accounts exist inside the OU that you are working with, so if you decided to do something such as deleting an OU, you could potentially also be deleting items that you couldn't even see!

Let's show a quick example. We will pretend that I want to do some cleanup and delete my `Accounting Computers` OU. Inside that OU, however, there are still four computer objects that I will lose if I delete this OU. When I click on `Accounting Computers` from inside ADUC, I can see these computer objects. When I click on `Accounting Computers` from inside GPMC, I have no idea that there are items inside this OU, and I could easily delete something accidentally:

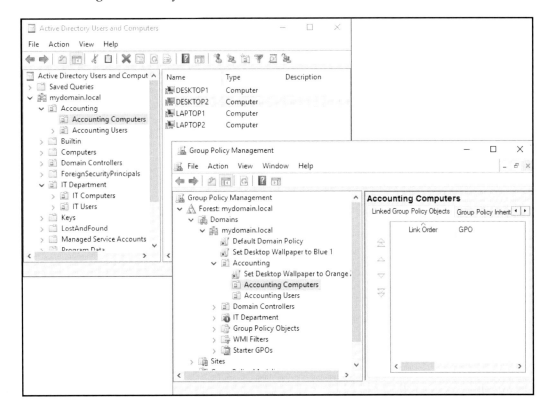

If you do find yourself in the position of making some changes inside ADUC and others inside GPMC, remember to refresh the consoles occasionally! When you create a new OU or delete an existing OU inside one of the consoles, the other is *not* automatically refreshed. You will need to right-click on your domain name inside the consoles and choose the **Refresh** option to re-populate the newest information. This also applies when multiple people are administering Active Directory and Group Policy in your organization, because changes they make will not be reflected in your console until you refresh.

Default containers that are not OUs

Remember when you learned how to identify the OUs inside ADUC by that little extra icon graphic that sits on top of the manila folder? It is important to distinguish between OUs and non-OUs when working with your GPOs, because you are going to be linking GPOs to your OUs, but you will find that you are unable to link GPOs to those non-OU containers. Inside GPMC, you won't even see them.

This point is worth talking about primarily because there are two default, generic containers that exist in any installation of Active Directory called `Users` and `Computers`. The `Users` and `Computers` containers are not OUs! This is very important to realize because it would make common sense to create new user objects inside that `Users` folder, and by default, whenever you join a new computer to the domain, guess where the new computer object gets placed inside Active Directory? You guessed it—inside that `Computers` container. This is a problem because you are not going to have good control over what policies these computers and users can get as long as they reside in these default containers.

All in all, it is common good practice to make sure that you are not using these built-in `Users` and `Computers` containers other than as a very temporary resting place for new accounts. As soon as you are able, make sure to move all new user or computer objects out to real OUs for their final locations.

Moving machines from one OU to another

Now that we have created some new OUs, what about placing objects inside of these OUs? Every domain user account that you have, as well as every device that is joined to your domain, has an object inside Active Directory that has a home somewhere. In well-organized directories, that home is probably in an appropriately named OU. If you run IT for a company and this is the first time you are learning about OUs, then at this point in time it is likely that all of your computer objects are sitting inside the default `Computers` container, which as we just learned is not an OU at all.

Moving objects from one location to another inside Active Directory is quite simple, and is best accomplished from inside ADUC. As you can see in the following, my `LAPTOP1` computer object currently resides inside the `Accounting` OU. I have recently created more specific nested OUs called `Accounting Users` and `Accounting Computers`, and I am now interested in moving `LAPTOP1` into the more specific OU that is called `Accounting Computers`. Right-click on the `LAPTOP1` object itself, click **Move...**, and then simply choose the new OU where you would like `LAPTOP1` to reside:

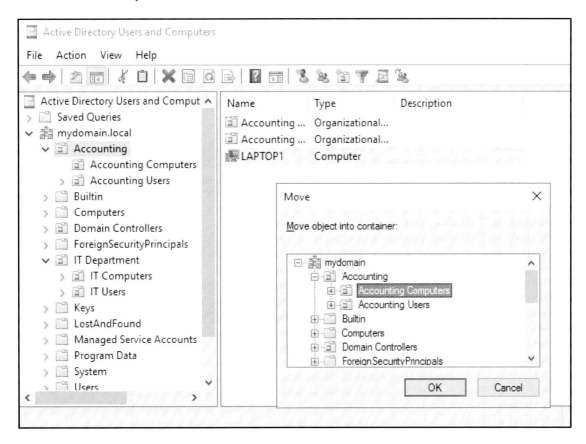

What is extremely important to note here is that this move from `Accounting` to `Accounting Computers` will result in some changes on my `LAPTOP1` workstation. While we have no indication of these changes inside ADUC, we are actually changing which GPOs are going to be applied to `LAPTOP1` when we make this transition. By heading back into GPMC, you can see that my **Set Desktop Wallpaper to Orange 2** GPO is linked at the `Accounting` OU, and so that GPO was applying to `LAPTOP1` previously. Now that we have moved `LAPTOP1` into the `Accounting Computers` OU, you can see that the **Set Desktop Wallpaper to Blue 1** GPO is going to start applying to my workstation, because it is linked specifically to the `Accounting Computers` OU where `LAPTOP1` now resides:

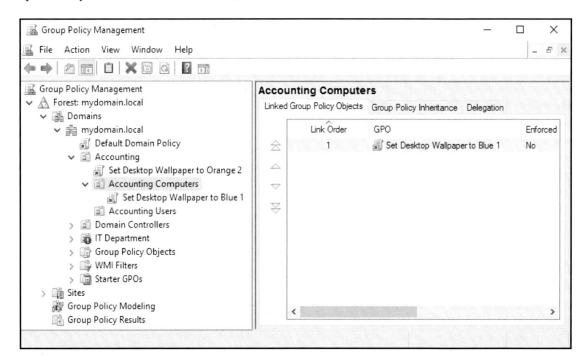

You can see how administering Group Policy and administering Active Directory are inseparable functions. While we sometimes need to utilize a combination of both the GPMC and ADUC consoles, it is critically important to always be comparing changes side by side in both consoles so that you can fully understand the implications of the changes you are making. One simple move of a computer object from one OU to another could completely alter the policy settings that it is receiving.

After moving a computer object from one OU to another, it is important to reboot that computer before you can expect the move to be recognized and the new policy settings to be applied.

OUs protected from accidental deletion

If you went ahead and created some of your own OUs as part of the previous exercise, then you probably noticed the little checkbox that appears and is automatically checked whenever you create a new OU. This checkbox is called **Protect container from accidental deletion**. Sounds like a good thing, right? But what does this checkbox really do?

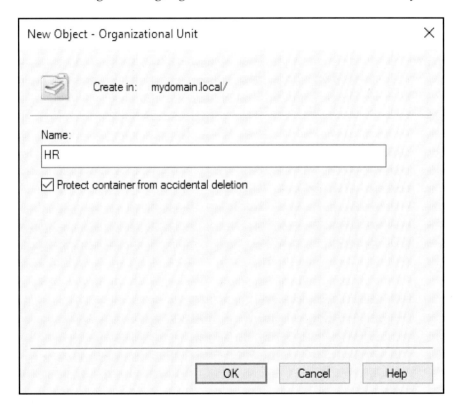

Leaving this option selected when creating a new OU means that you won't be able to delete the OU without some extra effort. This applies even to domain administrators. As an example, I have just created a new OU called HR, but now I want to delete this new OU. It should be a simple matter of right-clicking and selecting **Delete**, right? But when I do that, I get the following error message:

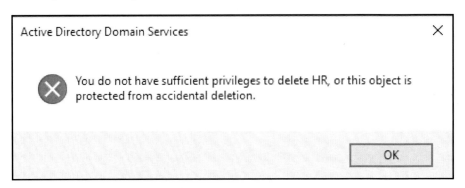

Whoops, that's a problem. This is something you will often encounter when trying to delete OUs that have been created by other administrators, because usually everyone leaves that accidental deletion checkbox enabled whenever they create new OUs.

If you are really sure that you want to delete this OU, here are the extra steps you will need to take in order to accomplish that deletion. We essentially just have to clear out the permission setting on the OU that is currently blocking our ability to delete it, but where do I find the permission settings for an OU? Inside ADUC, these permissions are hidden by default. Open up ADUC and click on the **View** menu, then choose the option for **Advanced Features**. This option enables some additional screens and information inside ADUC. Regarding our OU deletion process, what it enables is additional tabs inside each OU's **Properties** page.

Now that **Advanced Features** are enabled, I can right-click on my HR OU, and go into **Properties**, and I now have access to a tab called **Security** (this tab did not exist prior to enabling **Advanced Features**):

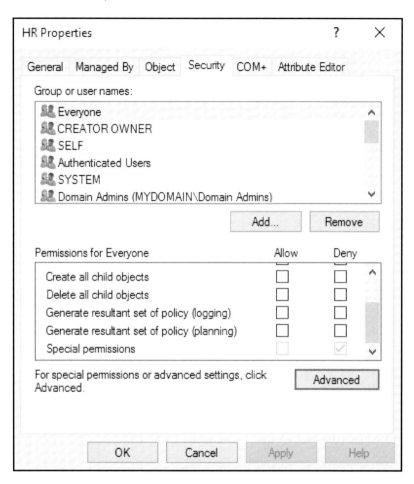

You can see that the top listing inside this OU is a specification for **Everyone** to have **Special permissions**. Go ahead and click on the **Advanced** button, and you can see that the special permission it is talking about is a big fat **Deny** rule that applies to **Everyone**. This setting is the thing that is currently blocking us from being able to delete the HR OU:

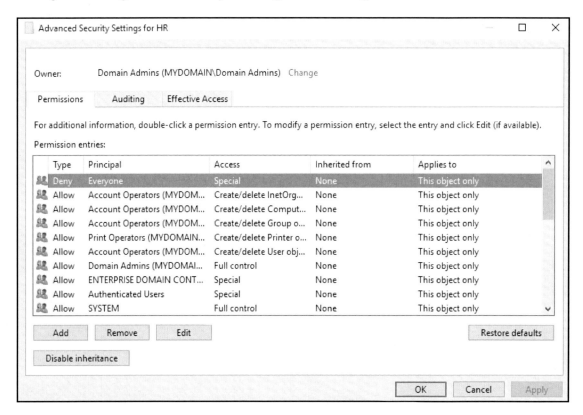

Simply select that **Deny** rule (if not already selected), and click the **Remove** button. By removing this special permission from the HR OU, you will find that you can now successfully delete the HR OU with no problems whatsoever.

A warning on cross-domain policy linking

In our test lab, we have no plans to grow into a large enough environment where there would be multiple domains being hosted, but this is certainly a scenario that you could stumble into when doing IT work for a business. When multiple domains exist inside Active Directory, there is the opportunity to link GPOs from one domain to OUs in a different domain.

Don't do it!

This is called cross-domain policy linking and is generally a bad practice. It is very easy to lose track of these links, or for an administrator in one domain to mistakenly interfere with settings that another administrator in another domain put into place. Furthermore, you may have admin access to your own domain but not in other domains, and so your options will be limited at best. Cross-domain links are always at a higher risk of being broken or deleted unknowingly. If you happen to be relying on that policy when it gets deleted or broken, that leaves you in a big bind and catches you completely unaware.

What is the better method for dealing with a multi-domain scenario? Duplicate your GPOs across each domain. It is more work up front to recreate all of your GPOs and settings inside each domain, but will be much better in the long run.

Filtering GPOs with security filters

A newly created GPO does not apply its settings to anybody or anything until you link that GPO to a particular location, such as an OU. Once linked, that GPO then typically starts applying to everything listed underneath that OU. In the case of a domain-level link, this is even more widespread as GPOs linked at the root of the domain will, by default, attempt to apply themselves to everything within the domain (other than OUs where inherency blocking is enabled, as we already discussed). All of this sounds good if your intentions are for these GPO settings to roll around to that many people and workstations, but there are instances when you create GPOs that only need to apply to particular groups of computers or users, and those groups do not always line up exactly with the way that you have structured and organized OUs within Active Directory. Indeed, if OUs were the perfect organization platform, then we wouldn't even have a need for **Active Directory Security Groups** (**AD Security Groups**), would we? But alas, AD Security Groups do exist and are used by every company in the world, so clearly we sometimes have the need to lump machines or users together in these special groups in addition to their existing organization and placement within OUs.

Where am I going with all this? Wouldn't it be great if we could link a GPO to a high-level tier (such as at the domain level), but then require additional filtering on that GPO so that it only applies to something more specific, such as a particular AD Security Group? That is exactly the option we are here to discuss. Even though you cannot create a link directly to a security group, you will find yourself quite often utilizing security groups in order to filter your GPO settings.

A security group usually contains a set of users that you want to keep together for one purpose or another, or it contains a group of computers that you want to lump together to meet a specific need. It is very rare that you would ever create a group that contained a mix of both user and computer accounts. This lines up well with our mentality of trying to keep GPO settings organized for one purpose or the other. A GPO created with only computer configuration settings is well prepared to be applied to a group of computer objects. And on the other hand, a GPO containing just user configuration settings could be applied to a group of users that you put together. Just one more example of how it makes sense in the big picture and through all facets of administering Group Policy to keep the two sides of the house split, and retain some separation between user and computer settings.

How to filter a GPO to a particular Active Directory group

AD Security Groups are created from inside the ADUC toolset, and on their own accord security groups don't necessarily have anything to do with Group Policy. So the creation of these groups is outside the scope of our instructions here, but we will assume you have some groups already created that we can play around with. I have created two new groups called "Users needing Blue 1 Desktop Wallpaper" and "Users needing Orange 2 Desktop Wallpaper". Recall that we already have GPOs that are assigning these graphics to people's desktops, and we have done some creative linking in order to get those GPO settings to apply to certain users as they log in to their workstations.

Within the `Accounting` OU, I have a need for some users to receive the Blue desktop wallpaper, and other users must receive the Orange wallpaper settings. Organizing these GPO links is starting to become cumbersome, as what I really want to do is to have all of my Accounting users inside one single OU. Linking both of those GPOs to this OU is going to result in either one or the other GPO having priority, and so all of my Accounting users would receive the same wallpaper setting. I could split up the wallpaper access by creating an additional OU and then moving half of my users over to that other OU, and linking the GPOs separately to the two different OUs, but that makes the OU structure more confusing. Instead, I am going to leave all user accounts inside the `Accounting Users` OU, link both of my desktop wallpaper GPOs right to the "parent" `Accounting` OU, and then utilize the **Security Filtering** section of those GPOs to specify particular security groups to which they should apply.

Utilizing security filtering is a way of filtering GPO settings to apply to certain users or devices; there is not accommodation inside the **Security Filtering** section to block these settings for only certain users or devices. While we will discuss a capability to block or deny access for certain people a little later in this chapter, it is important to remember that when you are using the **Security Filtering** section for manipulating this access, your groups need to contain the list of users or computers that you would like the GPO to successfully apply to. In other words, any users or computers that are *not* part of this group will *not* receive the GPO settings.

You can see in the following screenshot that I have now adjusted my GPO links so that both policies concerning desktop wallpaper are linked to the `Accounting` OU. All of my Accounting computers are in the corresponding nested OU, and the same is true for my Accounting users. As of now, those two GPO settings are going to conflict when a user logs in to a computer, and all users will receive the same wallpaper based on the link order priority inside Group Policy; basically, whichever GPO processes last will win:

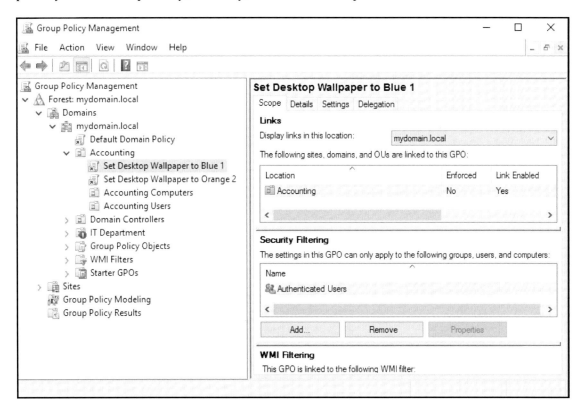

Also seen in the preceding screenshot is that we are looking inside the **Scope** tab of the **Set Desktop Wallpaper to Blue 1** GPO, and you can see here the section called **Security Filtering**. Currently, the only thing in that list is **Authenticated Users**, which means that this GPO will apply to any user that resides under this link.

 Actually, **Authenticated Users** refers to *any user or any computer*. This explains why computers receive policies as soon as GPO links are created. **Authenticated Users** even includes administrators! Keep in mind that you are not automatically immune from receiving GPO settings just because you are an admin.

To adjust the scope of this security filter, the first thing we want to do is remove **Authenticated Users** from the list. To do this, simply choose **Authenticated Users** and click the **Remove** button, and it will disappear. Now that the **Security Filtering** list is empty, this GPO will no longer apply to anyone or anything, even though it is still linked, until we input something new into the **Security Filtering** section.

 Remember that you are modifying **Security Filtering** for the entire GPO, not just the link! Any additional links to this GPO will also receive the same **Security Filtering** settings.

Now click the **Add...** button, and search for the AD Security Group to which you would like this GPO to be filtered. As you can see in the following screenshot, I have selected my new group of users that I would like to have the Blue 1 desktop wallpaper:

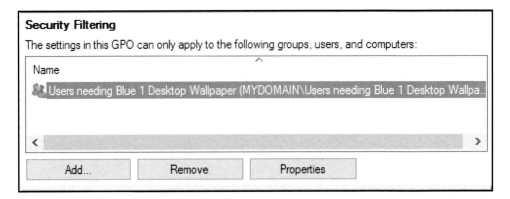

I will also adjust the security filtering on my Orange 2 GPO so that only my other new security group, the one that contains users who need the Orange desktop wallpaper, will receive the appropriate settings. I have now successfully filtered both of these GPOs so that they are only applying to users who are listed inside those AD Security Groups. Now if I have new users that need the settings, or users who no longer need those settings, giving or taking away their wallpaper configurations is as simple as adding or removing them from the AD group membership.

In fact, you can modify that AD group membership right from this same screen of the GPMC. At the bottom of the **Security Filtering** section, next to the **Add...** and **Remove** buttons, is a third button called **Properties**. Select a group from the list, click on **Properties**, and you will see the list of users or computers that are included inside this list. You also have the ability to add or remove objects from here. Alternatively, you could of course perform this function from inside ADUC:

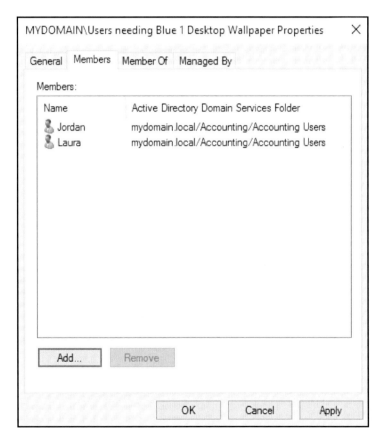

While our example focused on user accounts because the desktop wallpaper settings are a user configuration inside Group Policy, what I find myself doing more often in day-to-day Group Policy administration is filtering GPOs to computer accounts. The process for security filtering a GPO to a group or groups of computers is exactly the same. Simply create your AD group, add a bunch of computer objects to it, and then set that group as your filter inside GPMC. I often help companies roll out certificates to all of their workstations as part of remote access projects. We roll out those certificates through a process known as **autoenrollment**, which can be configured via Group Policy. As you can see in the following screenshot, I have created a new GPO for **Autoenrollment** settings, linked it to my domain, and then security filtered it to two specific groups of computers. Since this GPO is linked way at the top of the domain, if I had left **Authenticated Users** in that list, I would be sending out certificates to every computer in the domain. However, I was careful to set my **Security Filtering** settings prior to putting the actual **Autoenrollment** settings inside my GPO, and as such, only those computers that I manually add into these AD groups will be receiving my **Certificate Autoenrollment** settings:

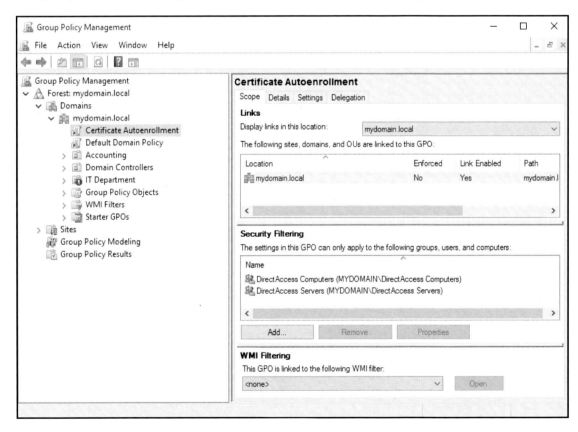

Filtering to specific users or computers

Not only can you add AD Security Groups into the **Security Filtering** section, you can add individual user or computer objects as well! For my **Set Desktop Wallpaper to Orange 2** GPO, I would like to test this GPO out on just a couple of users prior to rolling it out to the entire AD group. As can be seen in the following, I have security filtered this GPO to only two specific user accounts, so that those employees can test this setting and make sure it is working properly. *Only* these two user accounts will receive these GPO settings at the moment. This capability can also be very useful for testing out new security settings that you want to roll out to computers, or to servers. You need to be very careful before allowing any GPO to roll out to a server, lest you hose that server. Filtering a GPO to an individual machine for testing before making that filtering more widespread can save your bacon!

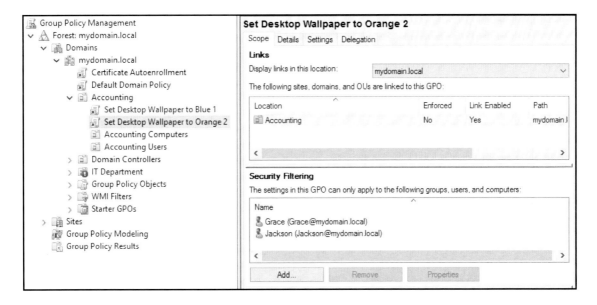

Security filtering – permission changes

When configuring **Security Filtering** settings on a GPO, what you are really doing is changing security permissions on the GPO itself. You see, for a computer or user to be able to apply any given Group Policy Object, that computer or user needs to have two different "rights" to the GPO. It needs to be able to "read" the GPO, and it needs to be able to "apply group policy".

You can view the permissions for any GPO by clicking on the GPO (or any one of its links), then visiting the **Delegation** tab. Here, you can see a general overview of the permissions on the GPO, but you won't see the full story until you then click on the **Advanced...** button. Clicking **Advanced...** shows you the full picture of permissions on this GPO, as seen in the following screenshot:

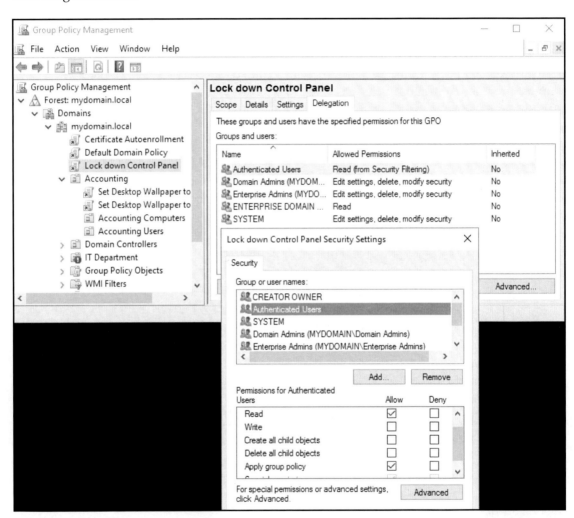

The preceding screenshot shows permissions on my brand-new GPO called **Lock down Control Panel**, which is currently still being filtered to the default **Authenticated Users** group. Inside the permission settings, you can see that **Authenticated Users** has two **Allow** settings—**Read** and **Apply group policy**. The combination of these two allowances is what tells the GPO to successfully process on anyone who is an Authenticated User.

Any users, computers, or groups of users or computers that you have listed inside **Security Filtering** will show up inside this list of permissions, and will have both of these rights assigned to them. This is the "under-the-hood" view of what really defines who gets the policy applied, and who does not.

How to block a GPO from a particular Active Directory group

So far, we have learned that the **Security Filtering** section is all about granting access to GPOs, but what if you want to flip things around? What if you have a GPO that is linked to a particular location, and you want everyone in that location to receive the GPO settings, *except* for just a handful of people? The **Security Filtering** section does not have any accommodation for such a request (to deny specific users, computers, or groups), but there is a way to do it. We will make use of the advanced **Delegation** properties that we viewed in the previous section of this chapter.

The newly created GPO for **Lock down Control Panel** is a good example. This policy is linked at the domain level and is currently security filtered to **Authenticated Users**, so at this point in time as soon as I add settings to this GPO, it will start applying to every computer and user in the entire domain. That is almost what I want to do, except that I certainly don't want to lock myself out of using the Control Panel, so I want to create an exclusion to this policy to prevent my own user account from receiving these settings.

We will leave the **Security Filtering** section alone so that the majority of everyone continues to receive these settings, by continuing to have **Authenticated Users** listed there. Then, inside the **Delegation** tab of the GPO, I will click on the **Advanced...** button. Now we are viewing the permissions associated with this GPO, and I am going to use the **Add...** button to add in a new group that I just created called **IT Gurus**. Once added, **IT Gurus** will automatically have **Read** access to the GPO, and that is fine—no need to modify that setting. What we do want to modify is the **Apply group policy** permission setting, by checking the box called **Deny**:

Deny permissions trump **Allow** permissions, so in this configuration everyone will receive these Control Panel lockdown settings, except for any users who are added to the **IT Gurus** group. This GPO will pass over those user accounts, and they will continue to be able to use the Control Panel on the machines they are logging in to.

While this is a very powerful way of manipulating GPO permissions, it is also a dangerous one. The fact that you create **Deny** permissions here does not show up anywhere else inside GPMC. Namely, the **Security Filtering** section does not in any way express these changes; it will continue to show you that **Authenticated Users** should be receiving this policy, and you would have no idea when looking at the **Scope** tab that there were any further permissions in place. So this is a choice you will have to make whenever setting **Deny** permissions—is it worth the potential trouble in the future? What if you forget about these **Deny** capabilities? Are you going to check the **Delegation** | **Advanced** settings every single time that you work with a GPO? What if you transition to another role in the company and some other administrator needs to fill your shoes? How likely is it that they will know how to utilize **Deny** permissions to create exclusions for GPO application? These are all good questions to consider before making this a regular practice in your environment.

Filtering GPOs with WMI filters

Using security filtering to apply GPOs only to particular groups of users or computers is an extremely powerful capability, and I find that it is typically the lowest level of filtering that the average Group Policy administrator takes in most domains. I would completely understand if you stopped here and did not read this last section of the chapter. However, at some point, you may discover a need to filter the scope of a GPO even further, or perhaps all of this group creation just for the purposes of filtering a GPO sounds like unnecessary work (after all, you do then have to administer those groups and group membership on an ongoing basis).

WMI filters are a way to narrow the focus of your GPO filtering even further. This is a way to look at the WMI information that exists on Windows computers, query on that information, and then filter GPO settings based on the results of that WMI query. Using WMI filters is essentially a way to tell Group Policy to only apply the associated GPO settings if the computer meets particular criteria, and those criteria are determined through WMI.

Now, WMI is an enormous topic and we certainly can't cover it all here. We can get our feet wet with an example, and instruct you on exactly how to put WMI filters into place so that you know how to use them within Group Policy, but piecing together the WMI queries themselves will take some legwork. Thankfully, they just invented the internet and these things called search engines, and you will be able to easily find sample queries of all shapes and sizes.

The list of specific criteria that you can search for inside WMI is huge, and is potentially different depending on your computer manufacturers and model numbers. Just to give a very basic overview of some of the things you can pull out of WMI: operating system version numbers, operating system names, the kind of CPU the machine has, how much RAM it has, the amount of available disk space, whether or not particular KB/hotfixes are installed, whether or not certain third-party software is installed; the list goes on and on and on. You can query against hardware, software, and sometimes even firmware (BIOS) on your machines. Then, once WMI has sucked in those results, you utilize those results to determine whether or not a particular GPO should apply to that device.

Thinking this through, WMI filters enable you not only to do things such as "only install this huge piece of software if there is at least 5 GB of available disk space" but can even be used for a decision such as "only implement these firewall settings on machines that are running a Windows Server operating system".

One real-world example that I encounter often is a WMI filter that flags remote access settings only to "mobile hardware". The Microsoft Remote Access Management Console is a tool used to configure VPN and DA settings on a Windows Server, and when it rolls around DA settings, you have the option to enforce a WMI filter that only allows those GPO settings to apply to any hardware that comes back at the WMI level as a laptop or tablet. Any systems that WMI identifies as traditional desktop or server hardware will not receive those GPO settings, because you only need remote access settings on your mobile hardware.

When WMI queries against a machine, it comes back with basically a "true" or "false" response, based on whether or not the WMI criteria have been met. If a machine tests "true", that GPO will apply to the machine. If a machine tests "false", that GPO will not apply to the machine, or in some cases will actively remove those GPO settings if they already exist on the machine. It is important to note that you cannot flag only some settings inside a GPO to be used by this WMI filter. Just like with security filtering based upon AD groups, a computer will either receive or not receive the entire GPO based on whether or not it passes the WMI filter test.

WMI filters could cause a performance hit

As you already know, Group Policy processes settings during computer startup and shutdown, and user logon/logoff. It also does a background refresh cycle every 90 minutes as the users are working on their computers throughout the day. The goal for Group Policy processing is to be as fast as possible, hopefully measured in milliseconds, so that your employees are not wasting time sitting around and waiting for these settings to finish processing.

To this end, in a normal GPO background refresh cycle, the computer evaluates whether or not GPOs have been modified. If they have since the last cycle, then of course the computer needs to spend time and energy processing through those modified GPOs. But if the GPO is completely unchanged from the last refresh, it can skip that GPO to make the process more efficient.

When you apply a WMI filter to a GPO, by nature of the way the filters work, you then cause that GPO to be reprocessed every time that Group Policy refreshes. This happens because the filter needs to re-evaluate the machine criteria every time that the GPO attempts to apply. This will have some form of performance impact, though hopefully very small. Some WMI filters evaluate within milliseconds, which probably won't be noticeable, but some can take full seconds to complete. It is important to always seclude and test GPOs with WMI filters applied before rolling them out to production, to ensure processing performance is within acceptable standards.

Try to keep WMI filters only applied to GPOs that are pretty selective to begin with. Appending a WMI filter on a GPO that only applies to a single nested OU is going to cause a very minuscule change in GPO processing, but setting a WMI filter on a GPO that is linked at the domain level instantly increases processing time on every machine in your network. Yikes!

Applying a WMI filter to our GPO

Let's work together to apply WMI filters to some of our existing GPOs. I have the need to treat the Windows Firewall rules differently based upon whether a machine is a laptop, or is not a laptop. Effectively, I want my laptops to have some specific firewall settings and rules that I have defined inside a GPO called **Set Firewall Rules for Laptops**. On the flip side, any machine in my network that is not a laptop doesn't need the Windows Firewall running at all, so I have a second GPO named **Disable Windows Firewall**.

I could accomplish this scenario by using an AD Security Group and the GPO **Security Filtering** section, but that means I need to create the group and then add all of my laptop computers into that group. Sounds like a pain. I could also do some really creative things with WMI to make it self-identify the hardware and probably determine what is or is not a laptop purely from the WMI side of the house, but that is too complicated for a simple example like this, and since I have numerous different kinds of laptop hardware, I'm not sure that WMI query would be perfect anyway.

Instead of any of that, I have smartly named all of the domain-joined devices in my network with hostnames that indicate what kind of a system they are. Most importantly, all laptops in my domain have names that begin with the word "LAPTOP". This is something that I can easily query with a WMI filter, the hostname of the device. Using this information, we will cause the **Set Firewall Rules for Laptops** GPO to apply to all laptop computers, and **Disable Windows Firewall** on all non-laptops.

First, we must create the WMI filter itself. Open up GPMC and find the folder called WMI Filters. It is listed just below the Group Policy Objects folder. Right-click on **WMI Filters**, and select **New.**

Now populate **Name** and **Description**, and **Add** in the WMI query or queries that you want to be included with this filter, as I have done in the following screenshot. The following query will filter to computers whose hostnames include the word LAPTOP:

```
Select * From Win32_OperatingSystem Where (CSName like '%LAPTOP%')
```

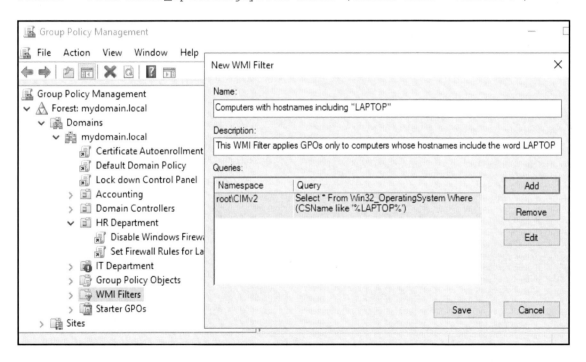

Click **Save**, and you can see our new WMI filter inside GPMC. In fact, while I am here, I am going to create a second WMI filter that does the opposite. The following query will identify computers whose hostnames do *not* include the word LAPTOP:

```
Select * From Win32_OperatingSystem Where Not (CSName like '%LAPTOP%')
```

Now, both of my WMI filters are visible inside GPMC:

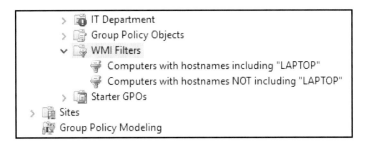

Just like with GPOs, these new WMI filters are created but they don't actually do anything until you associate them. In order to do that, we simply select the GPO to which we want a filter to apply, and visit the **Scope** tab. Underneath our **Security Filtering** section, you will see another section entitled **WMI Filtering**. Inside this screen is a simple drop-down menu where you can select one of our existing WMI filters. Once selected, that WMI filter is now applying to the GPO. In our screenshot, I am choosing to require the **Computers with hostnames including "LAPTOP"** WMI filter for the **Set Firewall Rules for Laptops** GPO. Then I have also selected the **Disable Windows Firewall** GPO and chosen the **Computers with hostnames NOT including "LAPTOP"** WMI filter to be applied there. You can see that both of my new GPOs are linked to the HR Department OU, but now when these GPOs process, the firewall settings will land on all of my laptop computers, and the firewall will be disabled on all non-laptop computers:

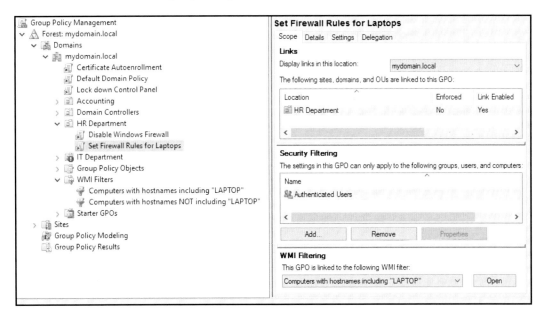

Summary

This chapter was all about applying and filtering your GPOs. We explained link order precedence and showcased the areas of GPMC where link priority can be viewed and manipulated. We also discussed some need-to-know features such as blocking inheritance, and enforcement of GPO settings. Following discussion of the differences between user and computer settings inside the Group Policy Management Editor, we ran through some exercises of normal tasks associated with links and filtering. We wrapped things up with details on two very important options that exist for any GPO: security filtering and WMI filtering. After reading this chapter, you should be able to take any GPO in your environment and apply it with precision to only the computers or users to which it needs to apply.

Turn the page to continue exploring Group Policy functionality. In the next chapter, we will take a closer look at the Group Policy Management Editor, and the settings contained within, as we start to take this idea of centralized management via Group Policy and turn it into reality by creating some real policy settings and pushing them out to our computers.

Deploying Policy Settings **5**

In this chapter, we will be discussing Policies. We are finally ready to talk about and look at actual policy settings within actual **Group Policy Objects**. As you have seen, much discussion and learning needs to have taken place to understand the management of policies and the options that exist for issuing and filtering those policies. It's kind of like learning how to lasso a wild horse before stepping into the arena next to one. We can't go all willy-nilly creating GPOs and filling them with policy settings until we have learned to control those policies, which is what we have been doing thus far. With great power comes great responsibility, right?

Of course, we have been working within a test lab environment during this reading, so let's blow things up! Of course, we're not really going to do that but we don't need to be nearly as careful as you would when making changes to your production environment. In this chapter, we will talk just a little bit about some topics related directly to the policies themselves, and then we will get our hands dirty by doing a step-by-step implementation of some sample policy settings that you can use to improve life for your workforce.

The following topics will be covered in this chapter:

- Managed versus unmanaged policies
- Administrative Templates
- Computer Configuration Policies
- User Configuration Policies
- Group Policy Loopback Processing

Managed versus unmanaged policies

There is an important distinction that every Group Policy administrator needs to understand about policies. There are two different types of policies, and they behave very differently. You can think of the two types as managed versus unmanaged, and also as policy versus preference. The word preference in this case is not necessarily the same distinction between the lumping of policy settings being separated from Group Policy Preference settings inside the **Group Policy Management Editor**. Those preferences we will be discussing in Chapter 6, *Group Policy Preferences*. In this sense, I am talking only about settings that exist in the traditional Policy locations inside GPME, namely inside the Administrative Templates section, but they are settings that behave more as if they are preferences in the user's eyes. On the flip side, policies are more stringent and generally more powerful.

Managed policies behave like true gentlemen. These are the settings that you put into place and expect results, but when you request these policy settings to back away from the places they are applied, they happily comply. What do I mean by that? When you plug some policy settings into a GPO and then filter that GPO to a location, you expect those settings to be put into place on the machines or users to which you have filtered the GPO. And that happens just fine with all policy settings inside the Group Policy Management Editor. But what about when that GPO no longer applies to a machine? What if you change the Security Filtering of the GPO, or if you move a workstation from one OU to another and it no longer receives the same GPO? Do those settings that were previously applied continue to be applied? Or are they removed from the machine now that the GPO is no longer filtering to it? The answer to that question differs based on what Group Policy settings we are talking about. True managed policy settings will behave in the way you would expect—when you retract a GPO, the settings disappear as well. They are reversed and removed from the workstation. Then there are other settings that really behave like preferences. These are settings that get applied to the computer via Group Policy, but when that GPO later falls out of scope and no longer applies to the computer, these preference settings do not retract automatically and are left hanging around on the machine. Most of the time, when dealing with these different kinds of settings, we are working within the Administrative Templates section of the GPME. So let's segue into a talk about Administrative Templates themselves.

Administrative Templates

The policy settings that are available to choose from out of the box in Group Policy are lumped together into folders visible inside the **Group Policy Management Editor (GPME)**. If you expand either **Computer Configuration | Policies** or **User Configuration | Policies**, you will see three folders called `Software Settings`, `Windows Settings`, and `Administrative Templates`. Actually, that last one is officially called **Administrative Templates: Policy definitions (ADMX files) retrieved from the local computer**. That's a bit of a mouthful, but the name of that folder reflects the reason why we treat the settings inside Administrative Templates a little bit differently than the other policy settings.

ADMX/ADML files

Administrative Templates showcase the flexibility of Group Policy. Rather than being a static bundle of settings that can be changed inside the operating systems, all of the settings that are available inside GPME under the Admin Templates heading are settings that are being pulled from template files. The template files are .ADMX files that reside on your Domain Controller servers.

These ADMX files contain the information that the GPMC needs to display the available configuration settings in a friendly manner. There are primarily three important pieces of information inside ADMX files: the name of the settings, the registry key(s) that the setting is going to modify do its job, and a description for how it should look and work inside the Editor. Things such as what options it needs to have, drop-down boxes needed, what the description fields should say, and so on.

ADMX files are language-agnostic, so each ADMX file has an accompanying ADML file that defines the language for those settings.

Now, before we get too far I will point out that for Windows XP and earlier, these file types did not exist. The settings inside Administrative Templates were based on ADM files instead. But, as we have already stated, this book really pertains only to Windows 7 or newer, since in our organizations we should only ever be dealing with operating systems that are still currently supported by Microsoft. Heck, Win7 is going to fall out of support before we know it! ADMX and ADML files combine to create setting configuration options for the Group Policy Editor. These templates are the secret sauce that causes the settings to magically appear inside GPME.

We will look much further into the practical application of ADMX and ADML files in Chapter 8, *Group Policy Maintenance*. This is an area of Group Policy that you could be dealing with often, and adding new templates is technically digging under the hood of Group Policy a little. So, we will save the details for later. For now, a quick screenshot will show you that sitting on the hard drive of my Domain Controller is a folder containing all of my ADMX files. These files contain all of the information that is telling GPME how and what to display inside the Administrative Template settings groups:

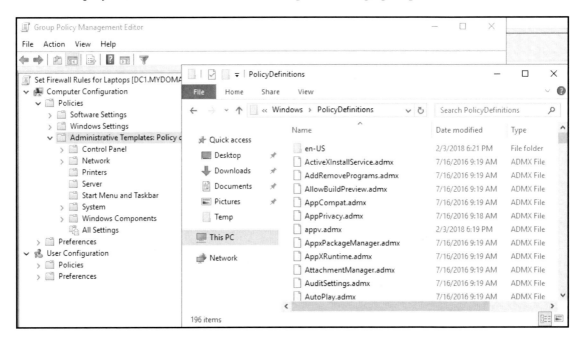

Self-regulating policies

Most policy settings that exist inside Administrative Templates by default (the ones baked into Windows when you build a Domain) have the ability to self-regulate, or to self-remove when the policy is no longer applied to a machine. When you tweak a setting inside Administrative Templates, and that GPO then filters down and applies to a workstation, what you are really doing on that client machine is modifying a registry key that lives in a special section of the registry that is unavailable to the users, so they can't edit these settings. That makes sense and lines up with everything we have learned so far, as soon as a GPO has settings and the client computer does a background refresh, those settings are put into place.

Furthermore, when you stop a GPO from applying to a machine by causing it to fall out of scope (for example, if you deleted the link to the GPO so that the GPO is no longer applied to your workstation), those settings will be reversed. That may seem like no big deal, of course it's supposed to work that way, right? Actually, this is an incredible capability that is going on under the hood. You see, those registry keys that were put into place don't know how to remove themselves, but Group Policy processing does treat these areas of the registry as special, and when the GPO no longer applies, Group Policy will know that it needs to reverse those settings. This is the under the hood procedure that allows you to force settings via GPO, and have those settings removed again by simply unlinking the GPO, or moving the computer account to a new OU, or whatever method you use that causes a GPO to no longer apply to your client machine.

Special registry keys

So, again, whenever GPO settings make tweaks to special sections of the registry on a client machine, those settings will self-regulate, that is, reverse themselves—when the GPO no longer applies to that computer. When Group Policy processes, it double-checks four special sections of the registry. When new settings inside these keys appear, the machine knows they need to be put into place immediately. When settings inside these keys disappear (GPO removal), the settings are reversed. Here is a listing of those four registry keys that are being watched by Group Policy:

- `HKLM\Software\Policies`
- `HKLM\Software\Microsoft\Windows\CurrentVersion\Policies`
- `HKCU\Software\Policies`
- `HKCU\Software\Microsoft\Windows\CurrentVersion\Policies`

Sticky preferences

If you haven't played around with implementing a lot of settings inside Group Policy before, you might be scratching your head a little at this point. The idea of self-regulating policies that remove their settings when the GPO no longer applies—that makes perfect sense, right? Isn't that simply the way that all GPO settings work?

Nope! There is another class of settings inside Group Policy that is not self-regulating, and does not have the ability to remove itself when its issuing GPO falls out of scope on a workstation. These settings get left behind, and continue to be present inside the registry of the machine long after the GPO has fallen away and is no longer applying to the computer.

Almost all of the GPO Policy settings that exist out of the box inside Group Policy will be self-regulating, so if you only ever use pre-built settings, you will rarely need to worry about this. At least not for Policies, so most of these stock settings are what I consider to be **managed policies**. What is perfectly critical to understand though, is that in any given deployment of Active Directory and Group Policy, the potential exists for there to be settings mixed into Administrative Templates, which are unmanaged. In other words, settings that apply to the workstation, and are then stuck in place. Even if you de-scope the GPO so that it no longer applies to that machine, these unmanaged settings will hang around in the registry and continue to be in effect on that computer.

The unmanaged settings are left behind on the workstation simply because they are settings that exist outside of those four special registry keys. Only settings inside those keys are re-evaluated every time that Group Policy processes. But the registry is enormous, right? So any settings that utilize keys or values inside the registry that sit outside of those four keys are not re-evaluated every time Group Policy runs, which means that those settings get left in place even when the GPO is no longer in scope and no longer being actively applied to a client computer.

Unmanaged Policies versus Group Policy Preferences

A good word for these unmanaged policies would be "preferences", though that could get confusing because the preferences we are talking about here are different than the actual Group Policy Preferences, which we are going to discuss in Chapter 6, *Group Policy Preferences*. But they do work similarly. There are two key differences between a managed policy and a preference.

Preferences can usually be overwritten by a user

Keep in mind that whenever issuing an Administrative Template setting that is unmanaged, or when deploying a GP Preference, your settings could be overwritten by the user's own hands. Policies are traditionally set firmly into place so that the user cannot manipulate them, that is kind of the point of Group Policy. Preferences, on the other hand, are just that—configuring preferred settings to make a user's life easier or more efficient. Many things inside **Windows Settings** or the **Control Panel** are good examples. You may use preferences to manipulate all of your machines to behave one way when they are deployed, but perhaps your users want to tweak those settings to their own liking. Maybe items such as screen settings, mouse settings, or speaker settings—things of that nature. So Group Policy sets it to your administratively-defined default setting, and then allows the user to overtake that setting and change it according to their own preferences.

Preferences stick around after the GPO is removed

And, once again, always remember that both unmanaged policies and true preferences within Group Policy are not self-regulating, but rather "sticky" inside the registry. If a GPO applies settings to a machine and an administrator then tweaks settings inside GPMC so that the GPO no longer applies to that same machine, anything that is a true managed policy setting will be automatically removed from the workstation, but anything that is a sticky preference will hang around until changed by the user, or until flipped back via a new GPO.

Both of these data points apply whether we are talking about Group Policy Policies that are unmanaged, or if we are talking about actual Group Policy Preferences. The big difference between unmanaged policies and Group Policy Preferences is which section of the GPME they reside in. Unmanaged policies are under the Policy section, inside Administrative Templates. Actual GP Preferences, on the other hand, have their own folder inside the Editor and are lumped together there. Why the separation? Because while you can't really modify or add to the real preferences folder, that is exactly the point of Administrative Templates. I don't believe I have mentioned it yet, but you have the ability to create your own policy settings.

Creating or importing new templates

That's right; you can create your own Group Policy settings. As you probably suspect, this is done by creating your own ADMX/ADML files. Again, we will get more hands-on with these template files later in the book. However, there are some important topics to discuss beforehand because it is very possible you will never actually create your own ADMX file, but you very well might utilize an Administrative Template setting that has been built upon an ADMX file created by someone else (such as Microsoft), and you need to remember that those settings could be managed, or they could be unmanaged. One purpose for creating your own template files would be to manipulate settings for a particular software application that you are running on your machines. Maybe you need to tweak some of the application's settings for all of your users, and don't want to walk around and perform those changes by hand on all of the computers. Almost all software applications utilize the registry in Windows, so it makes sense that you could use an Administrative Template in order to tweak some of those registry settings. Yes, this is true and can be very helpful, but it is most likely that an application's registry settings do not exist within our four special sections of the registry that are managed. Therefore, remember that if you are going to be creating new template settings, it is most likely that they will not be managed, and that your settings will continue to exist inside the registry of your workstations even after the GPO no longer applies to the machine, perhaps even after the piece of software is uninstalled from that computer.

Your custom Administrative Template settings that fall into the unmanaged category also have the potential to be usurped by users. You may set something via this policy, only to find that a user has used their own keyboard and mouse to counteract your setting and configure it differently.

If the registry keys you are manipulating with your own Admin Template are actually contained within one of those four special sections of the registry, you're in luck! Your homegrown, customized settings would be managed policy settings, and behave just like those settings built into Group Policy by default.

Sometimes Microsoft puts time and effort into creating ADMX/ADML templates that you can then import into Group Policy to plug new settings into the Group Policy Editor. This may be the case for a particular piece of Microsoft technology that can utilize Group Policy settings, but is perhaps a technology that not everyone will deploy in their environments, and so those settings are not part of the out of the box Admin Templates inside Active Directory. We will walk through an example of importing such a template in Chapter 8, *Group Policy Maintenance*.

How can you tell the difference?

When looking at settings inside the Group Policy Management Editor, you can quickly tell the difference between a real policy setting that will self-regulate itself off the machine when the GPO stops applying, and those other preference settings that stick around on the machine even after the GPO disappears. Inside GPME, the managed policy settings are designated by little icons that look like pieces of paper, like a little checklist. The weaker preference settings are instead designated by icons that are the same little pieces of paper, with a prominent down arrow sitting on top of the paper. This can be a quick reference for you to determine which settings will behave in each way. The following is a screenshot with a list of Administrative Template policy settings that shows a mix of managed and unmanaged settings:

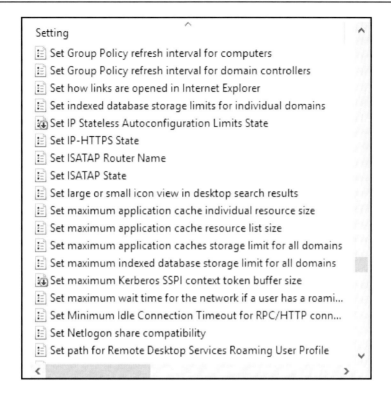

Computer configuration policies

This *Deploying Policy Settings* chapter is all about, well, deploying policies. There are more than 5,000 unique policy settings available to choose from within any GPO, so this chapter will obviously not be a comprehensive covering of all available policy settings. What we are going to do is implement a handful of helpful and common policy settings, some from the **Computer Configuration Policies**, and later some from the **User Configuration Policies**. By walking through these step-by-step instructions, you will be equipped to take the same procedures, combine them with a little search-engine browsing, and be able to configure anything you can dream up via Group Policy.

Idle-time lockout policy

Let's start with a policy setting that every company in the world should be putting into place for their users and computers. The purpose of having user accounts in the first place is to make sure that you can limit access to certain things based on who is logged in, and to be able to track which users are accomplishing which tasks. Therefore, it should be part of any company's employee handbook that users always lock their screens when they walk away from their desk. This is especially important with mobile computers, such as laptops. Imagine logging into your machine, connecting your company VPN, and then walking across the coffee shop to grab your drink. Just that quickly, someone sitting at the table behind you could open up your mapped drive and start deleting everything. Always lock your screens! But alas, not everybody will remember that they are supposed to do this. To counteract this potential malicious activity, we can utilize Group Policy to force an idle-time lockout policy that will automatically lock the screen after a certain amount of idle (inactive) time has passed on any domain-joined computer.

For this first example, I will walk through the steps for creating and linking our new GPO. I know we have already covered this topic, but it's a good and quick refresher for anyone new to Group Policy administration. For the remainder of the tasks outlined in our chapter, we will assume that you already have a firm handle on how to create your GPOs, link your GPOs, and filter your GPOs.

Open GPMC, and the first thing we need to do is create our new GPO. Right-click on the **Group Policy Objects** folder and choose **New**. I have named my new GPO **Idle-time lockout policy**, as you can see here:

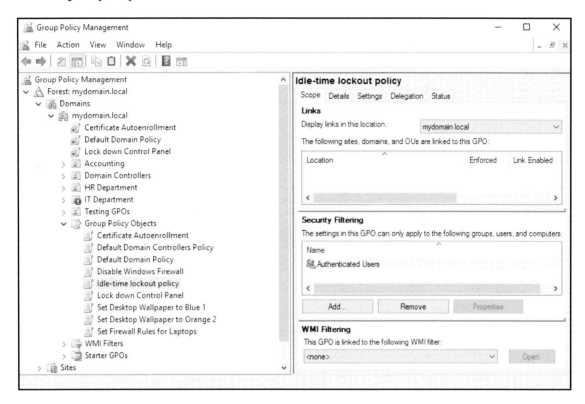

You will also notice in the **Scope** tab that this new GPO is not yet linked anywhere, so at the moment it is not applying to anybody. This is a good thing, as we want to do some thorough testing on this new GPO setting prior to rolling it around to our workstations. Next, we want to populate this GPO with the setting that it needs to be able to tell the client computers how to enforce an idle lockout timer. Right-click on the new **Idle-time lockout policy** GPO, and choose **Edit....** Then browse to the setting that we are going to manipulate, which is located at **Computer Configuration** | **Policies** | **Windows Settings** | **Security Settings** | **Local Policies** | **Security Options** | **Interactive logon: Machine inactivity limit**:

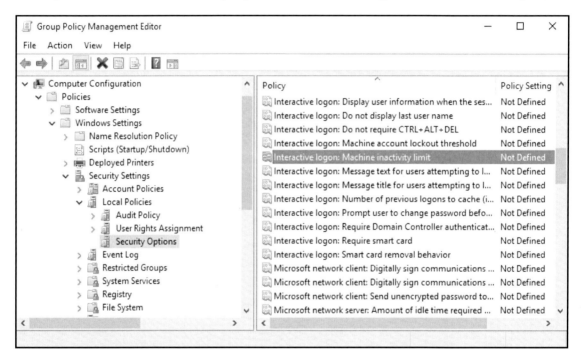

Double-click on the **Interactive logon: Machine inactivity limit** setting, and configure it accordingly for your environment. In order to easily test that this is working on my LAPTOP1 machine, I am going to set the idle timer very low, at one minute (60 seconds actually, as the setting needs to be specified in the number of seconds). That way, I can filter the GPO to my machine and know whether it is working in a very short amount of time:

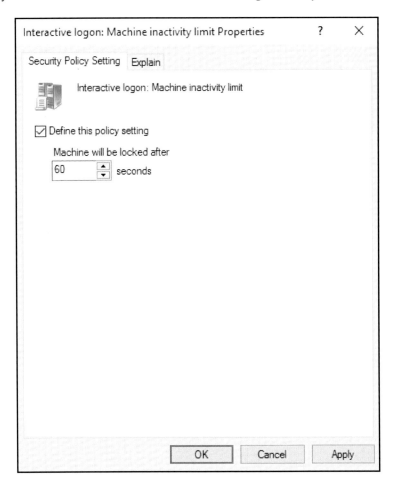

Before clicking on **OK**, take a peek over at the **Explain** tab. This tab is always incredibly useful for showcasing what exactly each setting is going to do, so that you can be sure it will accomplish the task that you are asking of it:

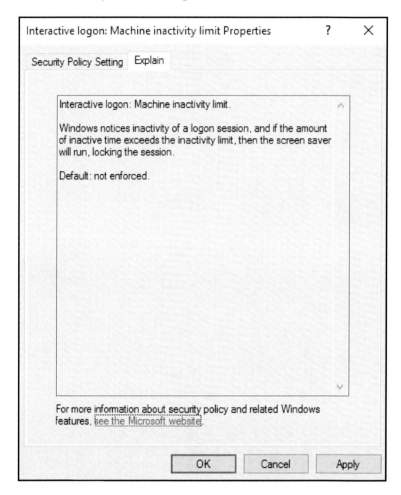

After clicking **OK**, this 60-second idle timer is now configured inside the new GPO. The final step to test this out is to apply the GPO to a client computer and see what it does. I have an OU that I use for testing all of my new GPO settings, appropriately called **Testing GPOs**. I will now right-click on that OU from inside GPMC, and choose the option to **Link an Existing GPO...**, after which I am presented with a list of all the GPOs in my environment:

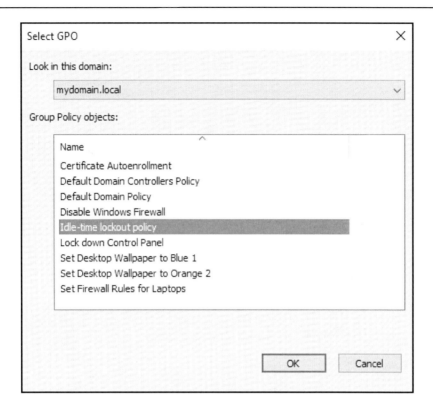

Selecting the new **Idle-time lockout policy** and clicking **OK**, my GPO is now successfully linked to the Testing GPO's OU. I then use Active Directory Users and Computers to move my LAPTOP1 computer object inside that Testing GPO's OU, and after restarting LAPTOP1, it is now receiving the new GPO setting. We can verify this by logging into LAPTOP1 and running the GPRESULT /R command:

After letting my LAPTOP1 workstation sit around without any mouse or keyboard input for a solid 60 seconds, we can see that, yes indeed, the screen has locked itself out and is now forcing me to re-enter my password to continue with my work:

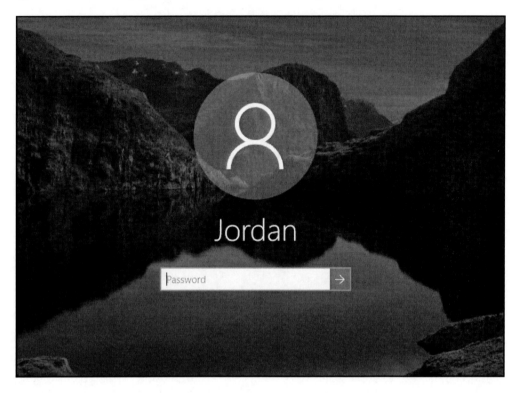

Now, remember, implementing security and maintaining user-friendliness is always a sliding scale. The more strict your security posture, the more annoyed your users are going to be. How many Christmas cards would you like to receive this year? Make sure to cross-check your policy settings with a little bit of common sense. Do you really want all machines to lock themselves out after only one minute of inactivity? Will that drive users crazy? Maybe there is a more realistic compromise, something such as 3-5 minutes.

What about Windows 7?

Those of you who are familiar with this idle timer policy setting are probably screaming at the page right now, because you know that this particular setting is actually new starting with Windows 8 clients, and that it will not work on Windows 7 machines. While most settings that you configure via Group Policy will be able to successfully apply no matter what the endpoint operating system, there are some new features introduced with each new OS rollout, and as such there are specific settings crafted into Group Policy that are also new as of each new iteration of Windows. That is true of this machine inactivity limit policy. I chose a tricky one like this on purpose, to showcase that you always want to test, test, and test again whenever you create new policies. Make sure the new settings do what you want them to do on each kind of client machine that you have.

This option was available to click on and configure inside GPMC because we are running GPMC on a Server 2016 platform, which of course has the newer settings introduced by Windows 8 and Windows 10 clients. If we were to run GPMC on an older box, such as a 2008 Server, this setting would be missing.

When you plug newer settings into a GPO, settings that will only do something on Windows 8 and newer, for example, and then push that policy to something older, such as a Windows 7 workstation, the Win7 client simply ignores that setting. Windows 7 doesn't know what to do with the Machine inactivity limit setting, and so it laughs at you and ignores it.

Thankfully, there is a way to configure an idle timer on Windows 7 as well; it's just a little bit more complicated. You have to utilize a combination of four different settings to make it happen, but those settings are all sitting right alongside one another, so it's not too terrible to implement. Even though this is the Computer Configuration section of our chapter, we are going to jump over to User Configuration just for a minute so that you have the ammunition you need in order to roll this idle timer out to all of your workstations.

Back inside the Group Policy Management Editor, navigate to the following section:

User Configuration | Policies | Administrative Templates | Control Panel | Personalization

There are numerous settings available inside **Personalization,** and we are going to employ four of them in order to configure our idle time lockout to work on Windows 7 computers. You will need to **Enable screen saver**, **Force specific screen saver** (in order to tell it which one to run), set a **Screen saver timeout** (60 seconds), and **Password protect the screen saver**:

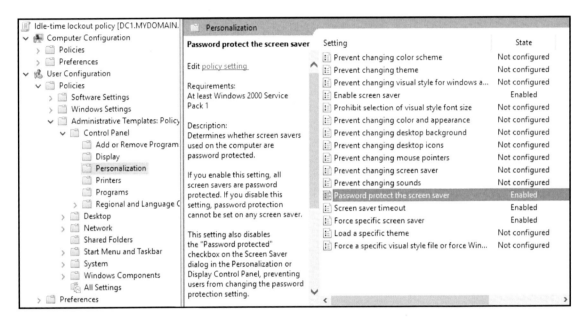

This combination of settings will force Windows 7 clients to flip on a screensaver after 60 seconds, or whatever you determine that idle interval to be, and to require the users to enter their password in order to come back to the desktop after the screensaver has been started. It is now obvious why Microsoft implemented the new policy setting for Windows 8 and newer clients; it's much easier to deploy!

Also note that you have the choice of implementing the Win8+ setting in one GPO and the Win7 settings in a different GPO, or you could put all of the settings together inside the same GPO and roll them out to all of your workstations. Either way would accomplish what you are looking for technically—the decision is yours as to what fits your GPO-filtering mentality better.

Launching an application upon login

Users have to log into their computers each morning. Once logged in, they open the applications that they will be utilizing throughout the day. A timesaver that could make their day more efficient would be a policy that was configured to automatically launch a certain set of applications whenever someone logs into a computer. This could be especially useful for a kiosk machine of some kind, where numerous different people might log into it, and you wanted an application to auto-launch in the event that any user logged into that computer. Again, we won't cover the creation, linking, or filtering of GPOs from this point forward; instead, we'll focus on the settings themselves, where they are located, and how to use them. To configure an application autolaunch policy, head to the following location inside your GPO:

Computer Configuration | Policies | Administrative Templates | System | Logon

The setting that we are going to configure is called **Run these programs at user logon**. Set this to **Enabled**, and then click on the **Show...** button to define the applications that you want to launch when any user logs into this computer. This is not limited to a single application, as you can see here, I have created a policy that will launch both Notepad as well as Calculator:

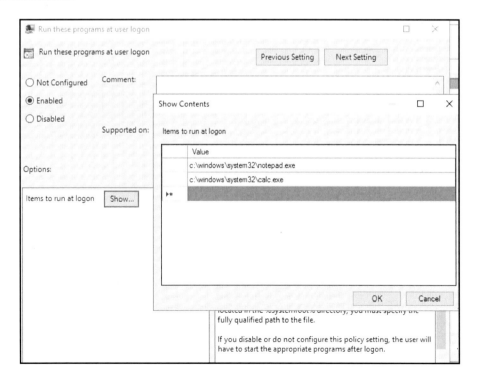

If you look closely (on your own screen, not in the screenshot), you will see a note in the **Help** section of this policy setting—the ability to autolaunch applications upon login is a setting that exists inside both Computer Configuration and User Configuration. Configuring it here on the computer side means that any user who logs into this computer will see those applications open when they log in, configuring it instead on the user side would mean that the application's autolaunch settings would follow the user accounts around to the different computers where they log in. Powerful stuff!

Now that this policy is configured and linked to my LAPTOP1 workstation, when I log into it, this is the very first thing that I see without having clicked on anything. Both Calculator and Notepad have launched and are awaiting my input:

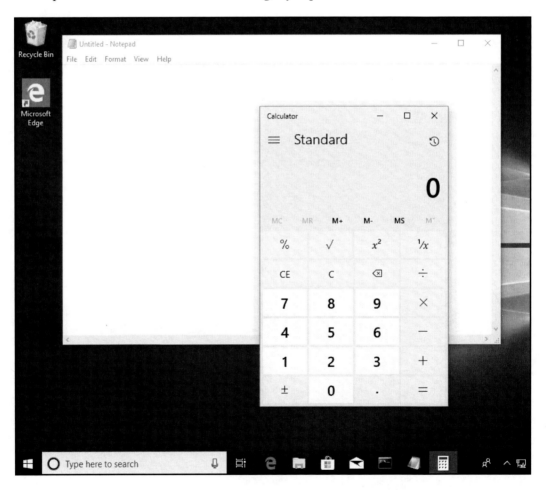

Configuring certificate auto-enrollment

Certificates have been an important part of securing communications for many years, but until recently, most server administrators only ever had to deal with the occasional SSL certificate to protect a website, Exchange, or SharePoint server. These SSL certificates are typically issued from a public certification authority, which meant that you did not need an on-premise **public key infrastructure** (**PKI**). In other words, I am still finding companies even today that do not have a Windows CA server in their environment, and are therefore unable to issue any certificates to their workstations, because they haven't needed to.

There are more and more technologies being released that require workstation or user certificates for one reason or another. Nobody is going to go out and purchase certificates for all of their computers from a public CA, so we build and rely upon our own CA servers in-house, and expect those CA servers to issue all of the certificates that we need on our computers. The problem then becomes, now that I have a CA server running, do I have to manually walk through the wizard on every one of my workstations in order to request a certificate? Certainly not, that would take forever!

Now, configuring a CA server or even configuring the certificate template on that CA server are outside the scope of this book, because those tasks happen on the CA server and not inside Group Policy. If you are interested in learning how to perform these tasks, as well as learning other important certificate-related activities, feel free to check out one of my other Packt Publishing books, called *Windows Server 2016 Cookbook*.

Where GPOs do come into the picture related to certificates is to enable something called **Certificate Auto-enrollment**. As the name implies, auto-enrollment is a way of automatically issuing (enrolling) certificates to your machines within the domain. It is best to think of this policy setting as a light switch that gets turned on for any of the computers to which the policy gets applied. By default, Windows workstations are not set up for auto-enrollment, so even if you configure your certificate templates with auto-enrollment permissions, those certificates will not be issued to your computers. By simply turning on the auto-enrollment light switch, you cause your machines to reach over to the CA server and automatically pull down any certificates for which they have the appropriate permissions.

There are actually a few different places inside Group Policy where you can configure Auto-enrollment, but the newest and best place to configure this policy is here:

Computer Configuration | **Policies** | **Windows Settings** | **Security Settings** | **Public Key Policies**

Inside this section, you want to double-click on **Certificate Services Client - Auto-Enrollment**. Inside this policy setting, change the **Configuration Model** to be **Enabled**. This single change flips the switch and causes auto-enrollment to start happening on any machines to which this GPO applies. Typically, you also want to check both boxes on this page in order to cause the autoenroll process to renew and update certificates automatically whenever those certificates expire in the future. So, in the end, most of the time, we configure the policy exactly like the following screenshot:

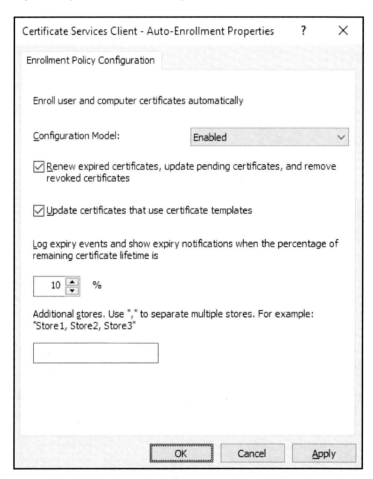

Startup and shutdown scripts – running scripts at the computer level

A common item for companies to put into place on their machines are scripts that run during various times that a user interacts with a computer. Most commonly, we refer to these as logon scripts, but that technically is only one of four different places where a self-running script can be initiated by Group Policy. Scripts are popular with IT departments because you can create a script to be as big or as small as you would like, and get that script to do many different things to the computer or user account.

Using a GPO, you can specify a script to run whenever a computer starts up or shuts down, and you can also specify a script to run whenever a user logs in or logs out. In regard to the *Computer Configuration* section of Group Policy, where we are configuring settings that pertain to the computer account itself, we have the ability to specify **Startup** and **Shutdown** scripts. Implementing scripts with Group Policy is slightly more complicated than the settings we have been configuring so far in this chapter, so let's spend a minute and walk through the process step by step:

1. Build your script. This is outside the scope of Group Policy, but we will assume you have a sample script ready to go. If you want to prove that this is working, you could even create a super simple batch file that echos some piece of information and then does a "pause" so that you can verify you see this activity upon login. Or maybe make a batch file that creates a new text file somewhere on the hard drive, then you could start the computer and go check whether that new file showed up.

2. Copy your script into the appropriate location on your Domain Controller (or into the shared `SysVol` in multi-DC environments). This part can be a little bit confusing, because the folders where Group Policy goes looking for the script don't exist by default. You see, Group Policy needs to be able to pull the script from somewhere centralized, and what better location than inside SysVol, which is where Group Policy files and data are stored anyway?

Startup scripts typically go inside
`\\<Domain>\SysVol\<Domain>\Policies\<Policy GUID>\Machine\Scripts\Startup`, and scripts that you want to run during a shutdown process go inside
`\\<Domain>\SysVol\<Domain>\Policies\<Policy GUID>\Machine\Scripts\Shutdown`.

- What are these `<Domain>` and `<Policy GUID>` things, you ask? Each GPO is stored inside SysVol based on a unique global identifier number—a **GUID.** You can see from the following screenshot that I have created a `Startup.bat` script and placed it inside the default appropriate location within my domain. I expanded the screenshot as wide as I dared for the purpose of printing legibly inside this book, but, even so, some of it was truncated. You get the idea though:the `<Domain>` gets replaced with the name of your domain, and `<Policy GUID>` is the actual GUID identifier for the GPO, to which you are installing this script:

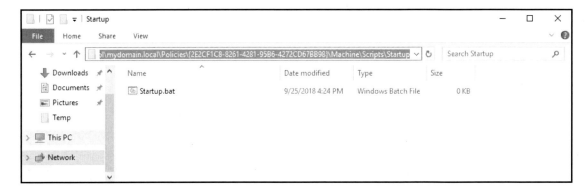

3. I mentioned that this folder structure doesn't exist by default, unless you cause Group Policy to think that you are about to implement a script of some kind, and then Group Policy will go ahead and create these folders. In order to do this, you need to open the script configuration setting inside GPME and click on a button called Show Files. Go ahead and browse to the policy setting, located at **Computer Configuration** | **Policies** | **Windows Settings** | **Scripts (Startup/Shutdown)**. Double-click on either **Startup** or **Shutdown**, as if you were going into this setting to configure it. Down near the bottom of the screen, you will see a **Show Files...** button. Go ahead and click on that button.
4. This button opens up File Explorer to the exact location where you want to place your **Startup** Script! Now you can simply copy your script into this folder.

5. Once your script is in place inside the filesystem, edit the new GPO that you are using to initiate the script, and navigate back to **Computer Configuration | Policies | Windows Settings | Scripts (Startup/Shutdown)**. Double-click on whichever script you are trying to put into place (**Startup** or **Shutdown**), and click the **Add...** button. Then click **Browse...** and select the script file:

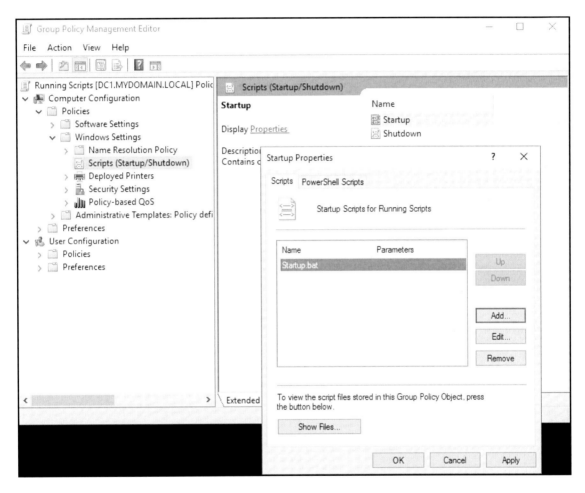

The GPO is now configured to run the script called `Startup.bat` whenever the computer is started. Link and filter this new GPO down to your workstations, and whatever you plug into that script file will run during each start of the operating system.

It is important to note that you don't necessarily have to store your scripts in these crazy file locations. If you wanted to store all of your scripts somewhere else that is centralized, for example inside`\\DC1\SCRIPTS`, that would work as well. You just want to make sure that location is always available and that users/computers have Read access to access those scripts when they start or log in.

Disabling Local Group Policy processing

Let's explore just one more sample policy inside **Computer Configuration**, before we change gears and look at the user side of things. If you remember way back to the beginning of our book, you know that each computer has the **Local Group Policy** settings that can be configured without any domain or Active Directory Group Policy configured. Does anybody ever actually use Local Group Policy? Sure, small environments do. Maybe you have acquired a new company and all of their computers are littered with local policy settings. Or perhaps you have some employees with a propensity to tinker with things, and they have some knowledge in this department. It would be pretty easy for them to dive into their local policy settings to configure their computer in ways that you, as the AD administrator, may not wish to support.

Whatever the reason, it is sometimes necessary to disable Local Group Policy settings from taking effect. Thankfully, this is very easy to do with an Active Directory Group Policy setting:

Computer Configuration | Policies | Administrative Templates | System | Group Policy | Turn off Local Group Policy Objects processing

Simply configure this setting to be **Enabled**, and all Local Group Policy Objects that might be present on the workstations will be blocked from being applied. As seen in the description of this setting, those computers will not process or apply any local GPOs:

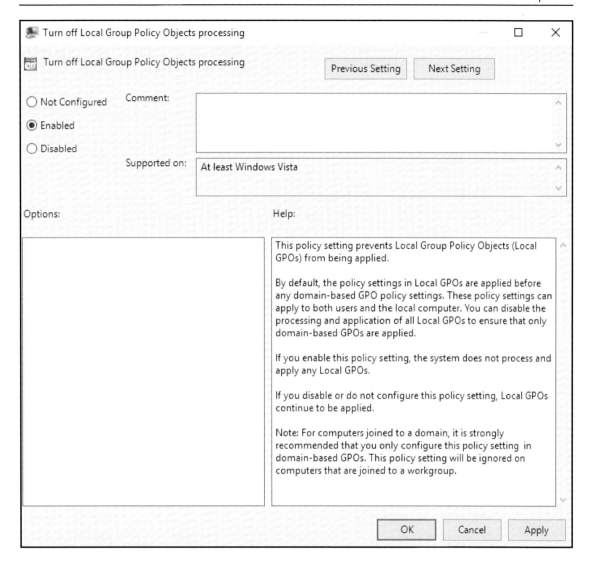

Some folks utilize this setting as a standard practice (even if your machines do not have any local policies), to speed up the Group Policy processing cycle. If you know with certainty that you never want Local Group Policy settings to work on your computers, configure this and the machines won't even attempt to look at local policy settings, allowing that processing time to be better utilized on processing Active Directory Group Policy Objects.

User configuration policies

As helpful as computer configuration settings can be for making sure that certain standards are met on all of the machines inside your domain, the **User Configuration policies** are where the rubber meets the road for user capabilities and functionality. Here, we will cover a handful of configuration settings that are commonly used and very useful when deciding how strict you want to be with your workforce.

Remove the shutdown button

A simple yet powerful GPO setting that is quite common to see in corporate environments is the removal of the **Shut down** and **Restart** functionality of Windows computers. This can be a critical thing inside an **RDS** or **VDI** environment, as you certainly wouldn't want users to have access to shut down a server that is hosting multiple people. Additionally, employees might be used to shutting down their home computers at night, but most companies roll out patches and updates overnight and so typically want their workstations to be turned on during those nights. If you had users shutting down their computers every night, their updates wouldn't install until the daytime hours and could interfere with their work.

In any case, let's check out the policy setting that can be used to restrict my user account from having access to the **Shut down** options inside the **Start** Menu. Create a new GPO, link it accordingly, and edit that GPO with the following setting:

User Configuration | Policies | Administrative Templates | Start Menu and Taskbar

Inside this location, the setting we are going to enable is called **Remove and prevent access to the Shut Down, Restart, Sleep, and Hibernate commands**.

 While you are inside the **Start Menu and Taskbar** options, take a look around at all of the additional settings that are available here. It is quite rare that employees of a company need to be poking around inside the **Start** Menu, so you might as well clean it up by using some of these settings!

Once enabled and applied to a user account, the power functions will be disabled inside the **Start** Menu. I assigned this GPO to the OU where my user accounts are currently sitting, and logging into `LAPTOP1` as my `Jordan` user now proves this to be true. When I open the **Start** Menu and click on the little power icon, all I can see is a friendly message stating that **There are currently no power options available**:

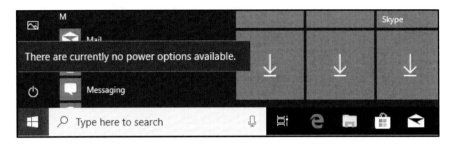

Locking down display settings

Earlier, we had a quick preview of configuring a screen saver to be enabled and password protected, but there are many additional display settings that are common to find inside a **User experience lockdown policy**. Many of those settings are available at **User Configuration | Policies | Administrative Templates | Control Panel | Personalization**, so let's test some of them out.

I am going to enable a bunch of different settings inside here. The following is a list of the setting names that I am inserting into my policy:

- Prevent changing theme = Enabled
- Enable screensaver = Enabled
- Prevent changing desktop background = Enabled
- Prevent changing screensaver = Enabled
- Prevent changing sounds = Enabled
- Password protect the screensaver = Enabled
- Screensaver timeout = Enabled and set to 300 seconds

Now that all of these settings are configured inside my GPO, I log back into LAPTOP1 as myself and will attempt to get in and change some of these **Personalization** settings. Inside **Display** settings, you can see that I am locked out of a number of different places. The options are grayed out and there is a special message near the top of my screen that says **Some settings are hidden or managed by your organization**:

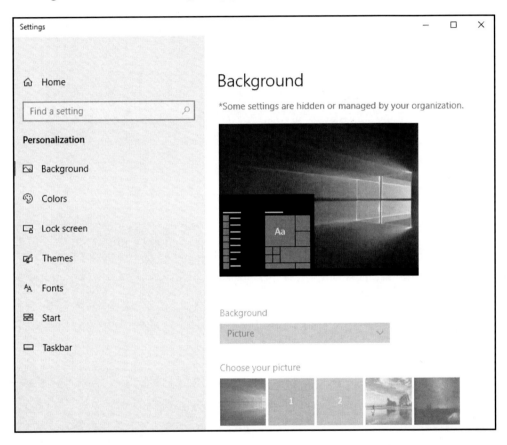

I also told the GPO to block the changing of sounds, so let's take a look at that as well. Typically, if you open the **Control Panel** and then head into the **Sound** section, you will have a screen with four tabs inside it. One of those tabs is called **Sounds,** which is the location where you could normally change and configure which sounds are presented when certain things happen inside Windows. Now that I have issued my GPO settings, which block the changing of sounds for my user account, you can see that the **Sounds** tab doesn't even exist:

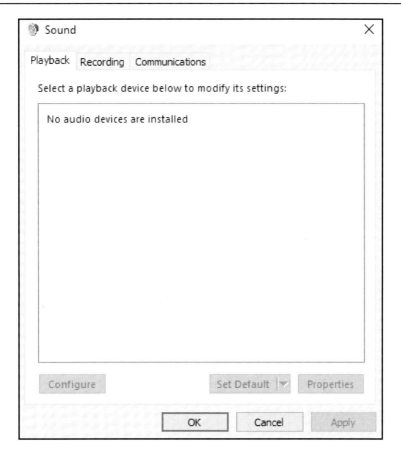

While this example does go somewhat against our standard best practice of keeping the amount of settings inside each GPO to a minimum, since the settings are all in the same location and are all related to one another, in this case I am willing to make an exception and include all of these settings inside a single GPO. Hopefully, at this point, you are starting to realize, if you didn't already, how much of a centralized management solution Group Policy is going to be for your network!

Prohibiting access to the Control Panel and Settings

As you well know, almost anything about a Windows computer can be manipulated through a combination of the **Control Panel** and the **Settings** menu in the newer operating systems. Allowing users to have access to these utilities is a security risk, because they typically have no valid reason for accessing and changing these kinds of settings. Let's find out whether there is a quick way to completely disable access to both the **Control Panel**, as well as **Settings** for your domain-joined PCs:

User Configuration | Policies | Administrative Templates | Control Panel | Prohibit access to Control Panel and PC settings

Look at that! There is a single user configuration setting that looks like it is going to take care of disabling access to both of those management interfaces on the client computers. After setting **Prohibit access to Control Panel and PC settings** to **Enabled**, I log into my laptop and am able to verify those denials. When I try to open the **Settings** window, it simply refuses to open. Nothing at all happens. When I try to force my way inside **Control Panel**, I receive the following error:

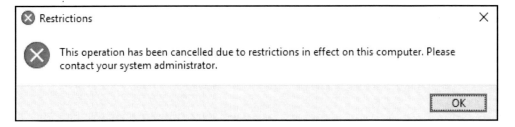

But I'm an IT guy, right? Don't you think I could find some way of circumnavigating this setting, even though my account only has regular user permissions? Nope, not that I could figure out how to do! Even if I try to open some individual setting that typically launches just a part or piece of the **Control Panel** or **Settings**, I am still denied. For example, trying to open directly into **Network & Internet Settings** no longer does anything, just like when I try to open **Settings**. And if I try to do something such as right-click on the desktop and go into my **Personalization** settings, I get a big error message:

This may not be the friendliest of error messages, if I were a regular user I would have no idea why I couldn't get into these settings. I would probably think that something was broken on my computer. But it does block me nonetheless, so I'm going to call it a GPO win!

Logon and logoff scripts – running scripts at the user level

Logon and **Logoff** scripts are basically the same as the **Startup** and **Shutdown** scripts, which we already discussed. The big difference is that **Startup/Shutdown** are computer-level policies, and perform during the operating system startup and shutdown procedures. **Logon/Logoff** scripts, on the other hand, are user-based policies and these scripts run when the users are logging in or logging off. The days of shutting down computers on a regular basis have gone by the wayside, so most of the time when implementing scripts that you want to run during each user session, it is smarter to implement a Logon policy than it is to configure a Startup policy. **Logon** and **Logoff** scripts will be able to follow users from computer to computer inside your domain.

The procedure to implement `Logon` and `Logoff` scripts is the same as **Startup/Shutdown** scripts, with two key differences being the file location for the placement of your scripts, and the settings being configured inside the `User Configuration` node of the GPO:

1. Copy your scripts into their appropriate folder locations inside `SysVol`. `Logon` scripts go inside `\\<Domain>\SysVol\<Domain>\Policies\<Policy GUID>\User\Scripts\Logon`, and Logoff scripts should go in `\\<Domain>\SysVol\<Domain>\Policies\<Policy GUID>\User\Scripts\Logoff`.
   Remember that if these folder locations don't exist or if you aren't sure of the GPO's GUID, simply jump ahead to Step 2 and use that **Show Files...** button to open the exact location where you need to place your `Logon` or `Logoff` script.

2. Edit the GPO inside which you plan to deploy this script setting, and navigate to **User Configuration** | **Policies** | **Windows Settings** | **Scripts (Logon/Logoff)**.

3. Double-click either the **Logon** or **Logoff** policy that you want to configure, and select your script file accordingly.

Group Policy loopback processing

There is quite a bit of information to keep track of in the Group Policy world. You have the four tiers of GP processing (**local**/**site**/**domain**/**OU**), then the two different sets of policy settings available inside GPME (User Configuration settings versus Computer Configuration settings)—we haven't even discussed Group Policy Preferences yet—and then all of our **Scopes**, **Links**, **Security Filters**, **WMI Filters**—the list goes on and on. So, we may as well throw one more wrench into the mix, this thing called Group Policy Loopback Processing.

Loopback Processing is essentially the act of getting User Configuration settings to apply to Computer accounts. Wait a minute, that goes against everything we have learned so far, doesn't it?! Yes. To this point, we have spoken over and over about keeping User settings inside GPOs that are going to be linked to OUs where user accounts reside, and making sure that Computer Configuration settings are inside GPOs that will filter down only to workstation accounts. This makes sense. The problem is that common sense doesn't always fit exactly what we need to accomplish in our environments.

Occasionally, you may want to restrict numerous user settings on a certain set of computers. This is no big deal, you could just create a GPO that has all of your User Configuration settings, and apply it to the users who are going to log into those computers, right? Except what if ALL of your users have the ability to log into those computers? It is most likely that your user accounts are scattered into OUs all across Active Directory, so to ensure those user settings made their way on to these computers, you would have to do a whole lot of linking. Additionally, linking these settings to the user OUs would mean these users would receive the settings wherever they logged in (including their own desktops), and maybe that is not actually what you want.

The real-world situations this is describing are things such as kiosk workstations, maybe public computers that sit out in a lobby for anyone to walk up and utilize. Most often, I see Loopback Policy Processing being used with RDS (Terminal Services) environments. These are prime examples of systems where many, many different user accounts are going to be logged in. It is very common to have more restrictive settings in place for those users inside their RDS session than on their normal desktop computers. Loopback processing gives you the ability to create these locked-down user-configuration GPOs and push them into place on certain workstations, no matter which users are logging into those workstations. In other words, Group Policy Loopback Processing is for specialized computers that you want to treat differently than traditional workstations.

What's really happening?

Normally, when a computer boots and a user logs into it, Group Policy works in that same order. First, it takes a look at all of the GPOs that are linked and filtered to the computer account, and then processes those GPOs—but remember that the computer itself only pays attention to the Computer Configuration parts of the GPOs. User settings are ignored because the computer doesn't care about those. Then later when the user logs in, the reverse happens. All GPOs linked and filtered to the user account will process, putting into place all of the settings from the User Configuration side of the GPO. This is how Group Policy works all day, every day.

When you enable Group Policy Loopback Processing on a workstation, it changes the GPO processing behavior of that computer. It essentially tells the computer to behave as if it were a user. Huh? Don't worry if you're confused, this is a strange concept to wrap your head around. We need to discuss the two different ways that Loopback Processing can be configured.

Merge mode

The first way to utilize Group Policy Loopback Processing is to configure it in Merge Mode. When loopback is configured as such, you will get a merging of GPO settings. During system startup, the computers behave in the normal Group Policy fashion, looking at their GPOs and applying all of their Computer Configuration settings. Then the user logs in, and all of the GPOs that have User Configuration settings go ahead and apply. Again, this is all normal behavior.

The new part is that after user settings have applied themselves, Group Policy then goes back and runs through the GPOs again. It looks back through all of the GPOs that are applied to the Computer, and then processes all of the **User Configuration** settings that are inside those GPOs. See, the computer is pretending that it is a user!

Now you can start to see the benefits here. You likely already have GPOs that are applied to the computer accounts to do computer-ish things. Then, you also have GPOs applied to user accounts to do user-ish things. Now you need to make sure that these special computers always receive the same settings, no matter which user logs in. Rather than try to figure out how you are going to link this GPO to apply to all users, but only to specific computers, you can instead utilize those computer-ish GPOs that you already have, include some User Configuration settings, and the computer will then force those User Configuration settings no matter which user is logging in!

Replace mode

The second way that you can use Loopback Policy Processing is called **Replace Mode**. There is a big difference in the way that Replace Mode works. When a computer boots up, it will run through its normal processing cycle, taking any GPOs that are linked to the computer's OU and putting those Computer Configuration settings into place. However, once it comes time for a user to log into this computer, everything changes. GPOs that are linked to the user and would normally get put into place upon user login are completely ignored!

Instead of user settings getting put into place for the user, the computer becomes the user. Rather than looking for GPO settings that are linked to the user account, the computer will reprocess through the GPOs that are linked to the computer account, and it will then process and apply all of the User Configuration settings that are inside those GPOs. In this way, you can determine what User Configuration settings will be applied to all user accounts who log into any computers where you have this loopback processing enabled.

Remote Desktop Services (Terminal Services)
If you are interested in utilizing Group Policy Loopback Processing to make sure that all users receive the same policy settings when logging into their RDS virtual environments, Replace Mode is usually the way to go. This would cause users to have different experiences whether they are logging into their desktop computer, or their RDS session. If, on the other hand, you want a conglomeration of both settings to exist inside their RDS sessions (with user settings inside the loopback policy getting priority), use Merge Mode.

How to do it?

Implementing Loopback Policy Processing is easier than it sounds. The difficult part is understanding how this setting is going to affect your machines.

Generally, you want to lump your loopbacked computers into one location. So, for example, if you are enabling loopback processing for some lobby/kiosk computers, you could create an OU called **Lobby Computers** and put them all inside. Or, for RDS servers, create one OU called **Remote Desktop Session Host Servers** and make sure all of the RDSH servers make their way inside that OU.

Now create your GPO, and link it to your new OU. This new GPO will contain the User Configuration settings that you want to apply to all user accounts (disable the **Shut down** button, hide the **Control Panel**, set a firm desktop wallpaper, and so on), and this GPO will *also* include the setting to enable Loopback processing. Without enabling the loopback setting, this GPO would do nothing at all, because remember that in normal Group Policy circumstances, when those RDS servers spin through this GPO they are only going to be looking at the Computer Configuration settings, and anything that you plugged into User Configuration would be ignored. By enabling Loopback processing (which is a Computer Config setting), it first enables the RDS server to know it needs to do loopback processing, and then it spins back through the same GPO looking for User Configuration settings. The setting to enable Group Policy Loopback Processing is **Computer Configuration** | **Policies** | **Administrative Templates** | **System** | **Group Policy**.

Here, you are going to **Configure user Group Policy loopback processing mode**. This is the location where you enable loopback processing, and set it to either **Merge** or **Replace** mode:

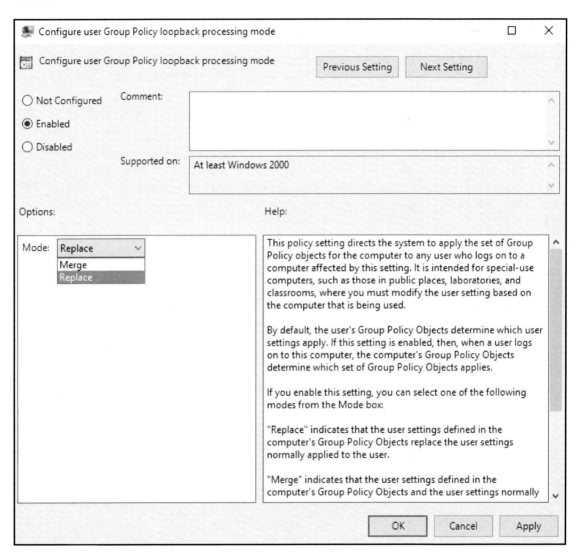

Summary

This chapter was all about the deployment of GP Policy settings. We made the important distinction between managed and unmanaged policies, with some hints about how to quickly tell the difference. We explored Administrative Templates, which is essential information for understanding where our policy settings come from, and what to expect when removing policies from a client computer. Then we got into some real-world examples and deployed numerous Computer Configuration and User Configuration policies within the test lab. We wrapped up the chapter with a talk about Group Policy Loopback Processing, which is a bit of a confusing topic but can be extremely valuable if you run any kiosk-style computers, or if you are working in an environment that offers Remote Desktop Services to its users.

There are some distinct differences between Policy settings discussed here, and Group Policy Preference settings, which we are going to discuss in the next chapter. Turn the page to continue!

6
Group Policy Preferences

Usually, when a company is utilizing Group Policy as a piece of the overall security puzzle for their network, we most often look to Policies in order to fulfill our needs. As you now know, policies enforced by Group Policy are set by the administrator, and remain set no matter how hard the end user attempts to reverse those policies. On the other hand, sometimes what we really want is not necessarily a strict enforcement of particular settings, but a configuration applied to users or computers in order to make the workday more friendly and efficient for those employees. This is where we begin to move over to the **Group Policy Preferences** side of the house, which is the topic we are here to discuss.

The following topics will be covered in this chapter:

- How is a preference different from a policy setting?
- Create, Replace, Update, or Delete
- Green and red marks
- The Common tab
- Implementing preferences
- Summary

How is a preference different from a policy setting?

After creating a new GPO and then heading into Group Policy Management Editor in order to put some settings inside that GPO, you will notice that both the Computer Configuration and User Configuration sections of Group Policy have two main tiers of settings. There are true **Policies**, which we have been working with so far, and then each node also contains a **Preferences** folder, which includes many other settings. You can see the distinction in the following screenshot:

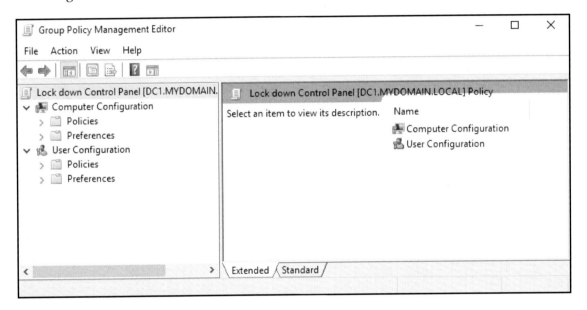

Policies force things to happen, no matter what the user wants. Preferences, on the other hand, are often reversible by the user. So preferences are a good way of configuring settings that will make life easier for the user, but you need to ultimately be OK with the fact that those changes and settings could be changed again manually by the user, if they want to do so. There are some settings that exist in both Policy and Preferences, so this can be a distinguishing factor when deciding how to build your GPO – whether you want to enforce something as a policy, or take the more flexible approach of configuring that setting to a particular default status, understanding that it could later be changed.

You learned in the previous chapter that built-in Microsoft policies, when applied to machines, are stored into special locations in the registry that make those settings both tamper-proof as well as automatically reversible. These policy settings are automatically removed when a GPO no longer applies to a machine or user (if they fall "out of scope" of the GPO), and the user cannot sidestep these policies even if they are pretty tech-savvy.

Preferences stick around! Group Policy preferences (as well as some ADMX-based policies) are not stored in this protected section of the registry and, as such, are able to be usurped. They are put into place on a machine, and those settings then remain in place until they are changed by the user, or until another GPO overwrites them. This means we need to be careful about what we deploy at the preference level, and know that if we want to reverse a preference, we need to make a new preference that changes the setting back to original.

This is ultimately why we call them "Preferences" – you aren't guaranteed that they will be put into place, nor removed from places, when you want them to be. So in general, if there is some setting that you find where you could set it via Policy or Preference, it makes more sense to go with the built-in policy.

By default, Preferences will reapply during every Group Policy background refresh. This differs from policies which only reprocess the GPO when changes are noticed. So keep this in mind when choosing to utilize preferences, because they can increase the amount of work that your machines have to do every 90 minutes during that background refresh cycle. When looking to implement a preference, make sure to search around and find out whether there is a corresponding policy setting that could be used instead. Test both and discover what behaves best in your environment.

Preferences can often be used in place of traditional policy-based logon scripts. Historically, Group Policy administrators would accomplish things such as user configuration settings, mapped network drives, and environment variables by scripting them and configuring Group Policy to run that script each time the user logs in. While this still works today, the running of that script during login is certainly slowing down the logon process. Perhaps the settings you are configuring are items that don't need to be reprocessed during every boot. Maybe they are simple settings that, once configured the first time, can be left alone in the future. These scenarios are use cases where you would prefer Preferences over Policies, which could perhaps even enable you to ditch those old logon scripts.

Create, Replace, Update, or Delete

During the implementation of your first Group Policy Preference setting, you will likely find yourself staring at four different choices. Not all preferences behave this way, but many do. This happens because most preference settings (as well as almost anything you do inside the Windows operating system) is really just a setting or changing of something inside the registry. When telling Group Policy to put registry settings into place, you have the choice of handling that registry key in one of four different ways: **Create**, **Replace**, **Update**, or **Delete**. If you acronym that out, it spells **CRUD**! Hilariously, Microsoft themselves even refer to this selection of choices as "CRUD" in some documentation.

Let's look at an example. In the following screenshot, you can see that I am creating a GPO that contains a new Preference setting. This preference setting is going to plug a new Registry key/value into the registry for my users. We will more thoroughly walk through the steps for creating a new Registry key later in this chapter because that is a fairly common task, but what I wanted to show you right now is that when I create this new Registry item, I have a drop-down list called **Action**. From the list, I get to make a choice of **Create**, **Replace**, **Update**, or **Delete**:

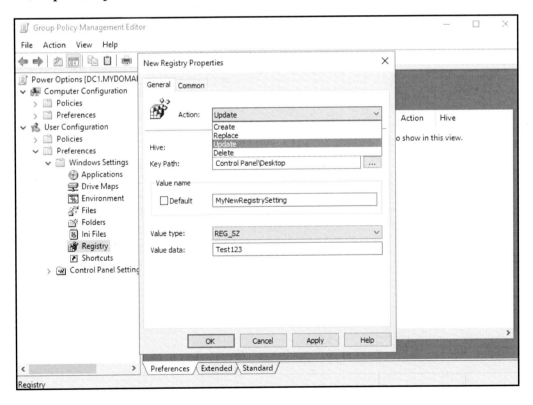

Here are descriptions of the four CRUD actions:

- **Create**: Use this action to create a setting ONLY if it does not already exist. If the setting exists and is set to something else, this preference will then be ignored. In our example, if I were to configure this new registry value for Create, it would only take an action if that value did not already exist inside the user's registry.
- **Replace**: Use this action to remove an existing setting, and replace it with our new setting. The Replace option is a little bit redundant as you will soon see (because Update or Delete are probably more in line with what you are looking for) and, as such, I don't often find preferences that include Replace values.
- **Update**: This is the default action, and is generally the most useful. If the setting that we are configuring doesn't already exist, Update will create it. Additionally, if the setting does already exist on the client machine, it will be updated to reflect our new setting instead. It's sort of like forcing a policy into place, except again remember that preferences are typically able to be overwritten by users, so someone else could still come along and change your preference setting.
- **Delete**: This removes the specified preference settings from the machine. Sometimes you need to make sure that certain settings are gone from a group of machines – this is the way to accomplish that. Deletes are helpful for backing out particular preference settings that you might have been previously enforcing. Remember that Policy settings can typically self-remove when the GPO no longer applies to a machine, but any Preferences that were applied continue to be applied even after the GPO is long gone. If you have applied Preferences to your users or machines and you now want to reverse those Preferences and remove them, you can create a new GPO that contains Preference configuration for the same settings, but change the Action to Delete, and Group Policy will then reach out and do the work for you of forcibly removing those Preference settings. It is always a good idea to test deletion preferences before rolling them out to your workforce, because deleting settings from the registry is a great way to break applications or even Windows itself.

Green and red marks

Sometimes Preferences are individual settings and are very straightforward to put into place. Other times, when you open up a section of the Group Policy editor to take a look at a setting, you will find a collection of numerous settings, sort of like a Preference "package" throwing many different options onto one screen. Here you can see that I have poked my way into some user configuration preferences, and chose to create a new **Folder Options** package. Upon choosing the option to create **New Folder Options**, I am presented with many different options, all of which are underlined in a lime-green color. What in the world do those lines mean? Take a look:

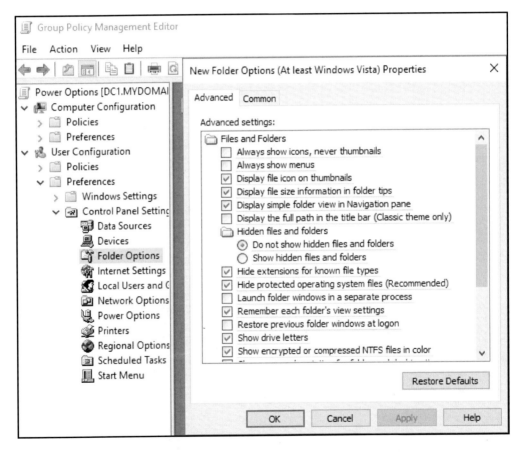

When you come across these preference packages inside your GPO, it is important to understand the lines, and as you'll learn in soon sometimes you will find circles as well. These lines and circles can be green or they can be red, and understanding what these colors mean is crucial to making sure that your GPO does what you intended.

Green and red lines

When a preferences package, is included inside a GPO, when that GPO processes on the computer, every single one of these lines is going to be processed on that machine. The green and red lines are telling you what is going to happen with each individual setting as it gets processed.

Every setting with a green line under it will be pushed to the computer to which this preference deploys. You can change this behavior by switching those green lines to red lines, meaning those settings underlined in red will not be manipulated on the client machine. This is essential to know in cases where you only want to change certain settings within a preference, and don't want to spend extra processing power on changing all of those settings that are underlined in green by default. Once an individual setting is changed over to a red dotted line, it is completely ignored when the GPO processes on the endpoint computer.

How to change them

To change from green to red, left-click on the setting and then press *F7* on your keyboard. This should immediately change the solid green line to a dotted red line, indicating that the setting you have selected will be ignored when the GPO applies to the workstation.

It's easy to accidentally create a preference where you only intend to set one little thing, and then immediately click **OK**, forgetting that what you are actually doing is configuring a whole bunch of settings on that machine! This would happen because even though you didn't specify anything about all of the other settings inside that preference package, they are underlined in green by default. Since this is the case with many preferences, it is a good habit to utilize the *F8* key when creating new preference packages, because *F8* flips all green lines to red lines. Then, once they are all set to red, and therefore not applying to anything, you can selectively re-enable the key settings that you want to put into place.

In fact, here are all of the function keys that can be used within these Group Policy Preference package screens:

- *F5*: Enables all settings listed on the screen (sets them all to be solid green underline)
- *F6*: Enables one setting, the one you currently have selected (sets it to a solid green underline)

- *F7*: Disables one setting, the one you currently have selected (sets it to a dotted red underline)
- *F8*: Disables all settings listed on the screen (sets them all to be dotted red underline)

Any time that you configure a Preference package that includes many settings like this, you will want to take the time to individually assess every single one of those settings, making sure to select the appropriate action you want taken by assigning them either green or red lines. In my Folder Options example, if I only wanted to configure **Show drive letters** and didn't care about anything else, I would walk my way through all of the other options inside this package and set them to red dotted lines. If I forget to do this, every single one of these settings will apply to my machine when the GPO hits. To accomplish this, I opened my new folder options screen, then pressed *F8* in order to disable all settings, and then selected **Show drive letters** and pressed *F6* to re-enable only that one setting. Show drive letters would be enabled by this package, while all of the remaining settings that are shown would be ignored:

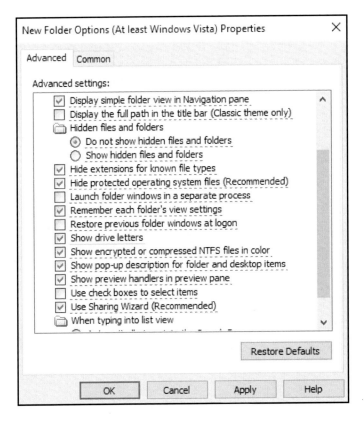

Green and red circles

While most of the red and green marks inside the Group Policy editor are underlining text, you will occasionally find red and green circles hovering around particular settings. Their purpose is exactly the same as the underlines. Sometimes, underlining text doesn't show up well or it is difficult to determine what setting you are manipulating, and so Microsoft switches to circling the settings.

A green circle means that particular setting will process on a machine when the GPO applies, and a red circle means that setting will be ignored. You can see in the following screenshot that these circles show up inside Internet Explorer preferences:

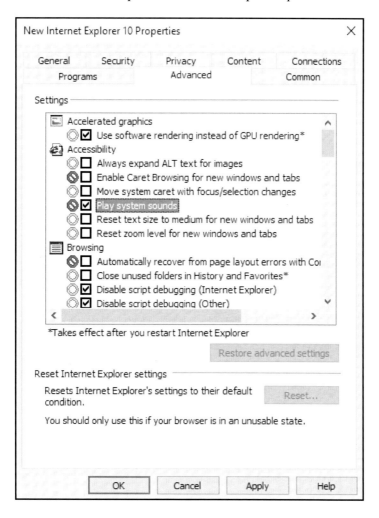

As an exercise to ensure this is all making sense, let's walk through some of the settings shown in the preceding screenshot:

- **Use software rendering instead of GPU rendering** is a green circle, and as such this setting is going to be processed when the GPO applies to the machine. The setting is also checked, meaning that our GP Preference is going to turn this setting **On** inside Internet Explorer.

- **Always expand ALT text for images** is a green circle, so it is also going to be processed. Since the box is unchecked, it means that this setting will be actively turned **Off** when the GPO hits the computer.

- **Enable Caret Browsing for new windows and tabs** is red, so this setting will not be processed by the GPO. It doesn't matter whether the checkbox is marked, because it is going to totally ignore this setting.

- **Play system sounds** is red, also meaning that it will be ignored. I wanted to point this one out because you can see that I have checked the box next to the setting, which makes you think at first that it is going to be applied, but remember that because it is currently circled in red, this means that even though I checked the box, nothing is going to happen with this setting because it will be ignored when Group Policy does its magic.

F5, *F6*, *F7*, and *F8* work with the circles in the same way they work to change the underline colors.

Remember, the red circle or red underline does not mean that the setting is going to be disabled! That would mean that the setting was actually doing something, performing some action. Whenever you see a red underline or a red circle, remember that this means the setting will be ignored completely. If you go ahead and input a value into a red-underlined or red-circled setting, that value has no meaning whatsoever because that particular setting will be completely passed over and ignored.

Internet Explorer tabs

This would be a good place to mention a uniqueness that exists when manipulating Internet Explorer settings with Group Policy. Really, this special consideration exists for any preference packages within which there are multiple tabs of settings, but off the top of my head, the Internet Explorer settings are the only ones that I can think of, so we will focus on these.

When you create a new Preference package of settings that pertain to Internet Explorer, Group Policy Management Editor displays those settings in a neat way; they look and feel the same way they do if you were manipulating the Internet Options on a client computer. Need to enable a proxy server? Visit the Connections tab and input one. Want to change the default behavior of JavaScript on web pages? Head on over to the Advanced tab and make your adjustments. You configure the settings you want to push to your client computers in the same way you would as if you were doing it within the actual Internet Explorer menus. While this is really handy, it also means that as you click through all of those tabs to find the setting that you want to manipulate, you will be seeing a whole lot of green underlines and green circles. You already know why this happens—Group Policy tends to default everything to green. As you also already know, green means take action. Those green-laced settings will be pushed onto the client computers by the GPO.

Any time that you click on a tab inside Internet Explorer settings, whether or not you configure anything within that tab, it enables all of the settings shown within that tab. If you were to create a new preferences package for IE settings and click on the Security, Privacy, and Advanced tabs – even if you did not change a single thing inside any of the tabs – when you click the **OK** button to close that window, all of those settings marked with green are now stored inside your GPO. This is very important to remember as you build IE Preferences!

When dealing with Internet Explorer settings (or any other settings that have tabs), it is smart to head straight to the setting that you want to configure. If you need to poke around a little to find it, go ahead and do that, but then make sure to **Cancel** out of the screen, and then recreate the preference package. On the second go-around, you can then navigate to the exact setting you are looking for, change it, and you won't have touched any other tabs. Any tabs that you don't touch don't pertain to the package and will not be processed. But as soon as you click on a tab, All of the settings inside that tab get pumped into the GPO and are relevant to your package.

Is this a major nuisance? Yeah, it sure can be. But as long as you know about the behavior here, it's easy enough to work with. Keep your fingers close to that *F8* button to set all of the settings on each tab to be red!

The Common tab

Many Preference settings include a tab called **Common**, which contains a set of options that are common between all of the preferences that have this tab. You can see in the following screenshot that I have chosen to create a **New Power Plan**, which is a grouping of preference settings that modify the power options within Windows. Aside from all of the actual power-related settings that exist inside the **Advanced settings** tab (the default screen shown to me when I create a new power plan), there is a second tab at the top called **Common**. Clicking on that tab shows me the five common options available here:

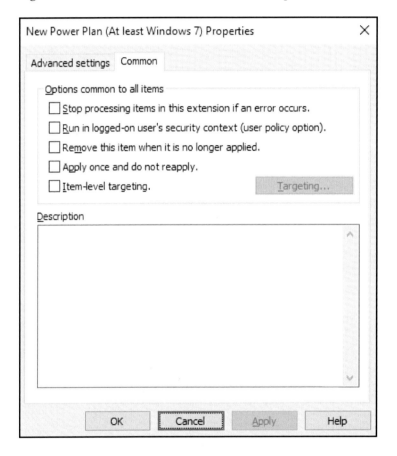

These same five common functions will be available for most preferences that you choose to plug into your GPO. Let's walk through each option now.

Stop processing items in this extension if an error occurs

Just as the name implies, if something goes sideways during the processing of this particular preference, it will abandon ship and stop processing midway through. For example, if your preference is trying to make contact with a particular server (for a drive mapping, file copy, or something of that nature) and can't reach the server, by default the preference would continue with applying the rest of its settings, but checking this box tells Group Policy to bail if any errors are encountered.

Keep in mind that other preference packages or policies that exist in the GPO will continue to work and apply to the workstation; the selection to **Stop processing upon error** only pertains to the settings that are inside this particular little bundle of preference settings.

Run in logged-on user's security context

This option is not available inside computer configuration preference settings, only for the user side.

 If you create a preference package inside **Computer Configuration** and look at the **Common** tab, you will see this option is grayed out.

When selected, this causes Group Policy to apply these preference settings from the security posture of the user who is currently logged in. This is different than typical Group Policy processing, which always runs under the SYSTEM account. While **SYSTEM** has the ability to do pretty much whatever it wants within the operating system (this is why Group Policy is so powerful!), there are some cases where you might want the preference setting to apply from the user's context, and this setting is your method for accomplishing that.

Remove this item when it is no longer applied

As we have already discussed, often preferences will leave themselves in place after a computer or user falls out of scope of receiving that preference setting. For example, if someone changes OUs and therefore no longer receives a GPO that they used to, and that GPO setting contained some preferences, typically those preferences stick around on the machine to which they were applied because Group Policy does not actively remove them. However, checking this box inside the Common tab forces Group Policy to do just that – when the machine moves out of scope, it will remove this preference setting when it is no longer applicable. Usually this is exactly the behavior you are looking for when you check this box, but make sure to think through the ramifications of yanking out preference settings. There is certainly potential to cause some big problems.

Think about a registry key that you have plugged into place by using a Group Policy Preference, and you marked that preference to **Remove this item when it is no longer applied**. In this case, when the GPO no longer filters to you or your workstation, the registry key will be deleted. This behavior might be exactly what you are looking for, or perhaps what your preference actually did originally was to update an existing registry key to a more preferred setting. Your GPO will not know how to set that registry key back to default settings, and by removing the regkey entirely, you could break your application altogether. Or maybe you have modified and would now be removing a registry key that is important to Windows itself. Checking the box to remove this item when no longer applied could actually turn out to be detrimental to your operating system. Just make sure you take the time to think through each scenario when you select this checkbox.

Apply once and do not reapply

This one is also pretty self-explanatory. Default Group Policy behavior is to reprocess Preference settings during every Group Policy background refresh cycle. This means your preferences are redeploying and consuming processing resources on your machines every 90 minutes on average. Sometimes you will deploy settings that really only need to be changed once, and then never touched again. Rather than reprocess these preferences every time that group policy refreshes, selecting the box for **Apply once and do not reapply** will do just that, configuring the setting inside Windows once and then ignoring it in the future. This saves CPU cycles, but if the user contradicts the setting later by performing a manual change, their own configuration will be the one that gets left in place.

Item-level targeting

We already learned about the power of WMI Filters and the ways you can use those filters to make sure that your GPOs only apply to workstations that meet particular criteria. WMI Filters are scoped for the entire GPO, so once they determine `true` or `false`, they either grant or deny the entire GPO and everything inside of it.

Item-level targeting is a very similar idea, but at a very different scope level. Since this Common tab exists on all of your different preference settings, you can have a GPO that is a collection of numerous preference settings, but within each preference, you may individually determine criteria for which destinations these settings are allowed to roll to.

Item-level targeting is also a much more user-friendly interface than WMI Filters. Where WMI Filters need you to know and understand WMI query syntax (or at least be good at web searching for it), Item-level targeting is configured through a graphical interface. You make all of your filtering selections with your good old keyboard and mouse, and make the decisions on what criteria is necessary in order for these preferences to apply within that same interface. It is also easy to require AND/OR/NOT specs to enhance the filtering. In other words, you can easily do things such as, "apply this setting only if the computer is this AND that," "apply this setting only if the computer is this OR that," or even, "apply this setting if the computer is this one thing, but NOT this other thing." Let's walk through an example so you can see for yourself.

This same process can be completed inside whichever preference package you are currently dealing with. For me, I am still inside the new Power Plan that I was creating earlier. All I have done is navigate over to my **Common** tab, and select the checkbox for **Item-level targeting**. Then click the **Targeting...** button to dig into the details.

Here, we build the filtering criteria. Click on the **New Item** button, and make a selection. I am going to choose **IP Address Range**:

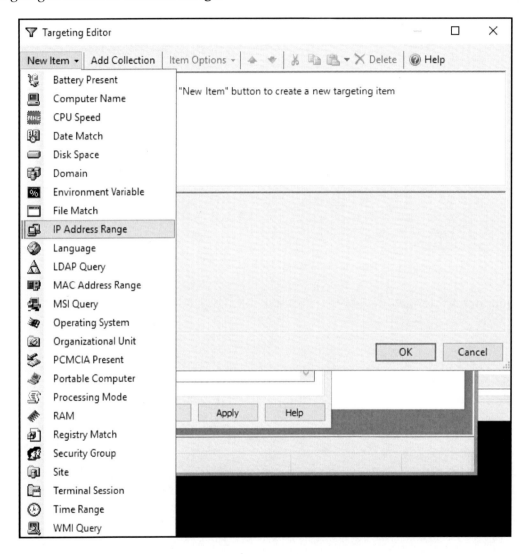

After inputting a range of IP addresses and clicking **OK**, I have now used item-level targeting to filter this preference package only to apply to machines within that IP range. Additionally, I could use a combination of the **New Item** and **Item Options** buttons to add more subnets, or to make exclusions within the ranges I have already specified. For example, here is what my **Targeting Editor** looks like after a few tweaks. I am now including 192.168.1.x as well as 172.16.1.x, but I am specifically excluding 172.16.1.20 through 172.16.1.30, so the handful of machines within that small IP range would not receive my preference settings:

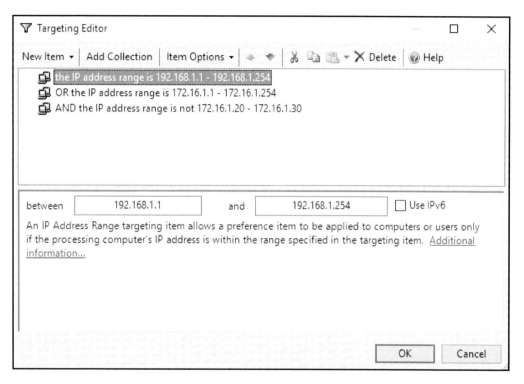

You can see that there are many criteria from which to choose: whether there is a battery present, how much disk space is available, how much RAM a machine has, or even specific machine names or groups to which they are members. There are numerous ways that you could get creative with Item-level targeting to filter the scope of your preference packages.

Implementing Preferences

Now knowing everything that you do about Group Policy Preferences, where they are used, why they are used, and how they are different from Policies, let's build some together. While there is no way that we could cover all available preference settings in a single book, let's pick out a few normal ones and walk through them together to give you baseline preference-creation capabilities as you progress into managing your own Group Policy environments.

Modifying the power options

For a couple of examples and screenshots already in this chapter, I have been talking about this new fancy-pants power plan that I am putting together, without telling you how to find that power plan in the first place. Let's configure our own Power settings by using Group Policy preferences, which we can then roll out to all of the workstations in our organization.

Create a new GPO for your purposes, and link/filter it accordingly. At this point I will assume that you are familiar with that part of the process. Once the GPO is ready to go, right-click on it and **Edit...** that GPO in order to navigate to the following location:

Computer Configuration | **Preferences** | **Control Panel Settings** | **Power Options**

Here, you want to right-click on **Power Options** and choose **New** | **Power Plan (At least Windows 7)**:

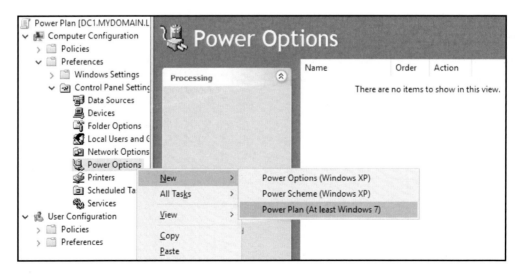

As you can see, we chose to create a new power plan that is for Windows 7 or newer clients. In most environments, this covers all of your workstations. If you still have Windows XP hanging around, well, get rid of it. If that's not an option, then you see that alternative power options exist for configuring those clients as well.

Moving back to configuring our Windows 7 power plan, the first thing we are asked to decide is what CRUD **Action** to take for this preference package. As is most common, I will leave it selected for **Update** so that these power plan settings get rolled out to the client machines and will overwrite any existing power options that the users may have put into place.

Next, I simply choose which preference settings I want to employ on my workstations. If I expand **Display**, then expand **Turn off display after**, I can put timer settings into place. You will see in the following screenshot that the options contained within are underlined in green. Aren't you glad you know what those green lines mean now? I will specify that, while running **On battery**, my screen should turn off after 10 minutes. When **Plugged in**, however, I am going to wait 30 minutes before darkening the monitor:

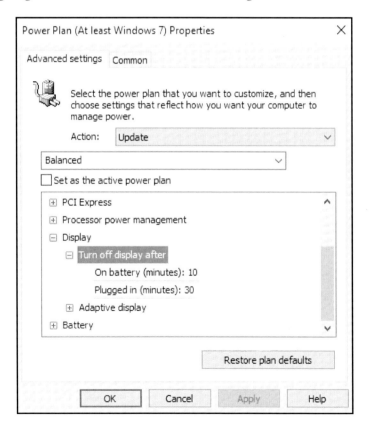

There are many other power options available inside this screen, and you can set as many of them as you would like. For the sake of saving space, since I think you have the idea already, we will leave it at that for the time being. Remember that you can, as with many preference packages, also make use of the **Common** tab at the top of these settings to utilize one or more of those five special configuration settings that we discussed previously.

Power Plan is one of those options that are available in both Computer and User Configuration settings. If you would like to determine power options at the user level rather than the way we have done it here, the alternative location you should visit is **User Configuration** | **Preferences** | **Control Panel Settings** | **Power Options.**

Environment variables

Another configuration you may find yourself needing to push out to client computers are Environment variables. Many applications utilize Environment variables in order to perform certain actions, and you can easily make use of Group Policy to put those variables into place. Once again, this preference is one that you can tag onto **Computer Configuration**, or **User Configuration**. Here are the locations inside GPME:

- **Computer Configuration** | **Preferences** | **Windows Settings** | **Environment**
- **User Configuration** | **Preferences** | **Windows Settings** | **Environment**

After navigating to the **Environment** section, right-click and choose to create a **New** | **Environment Variable**. Here you simply specify CRUD, whether this is a **User Variable** or **System Variable**, and then the **Name** and **Value** of the variable. One of the common environment variables for companies to modify is the **PATH** variable. For example, if I wanted to make sure that a custom directory was included in my PATH variable on my workstations, I could specify it here:

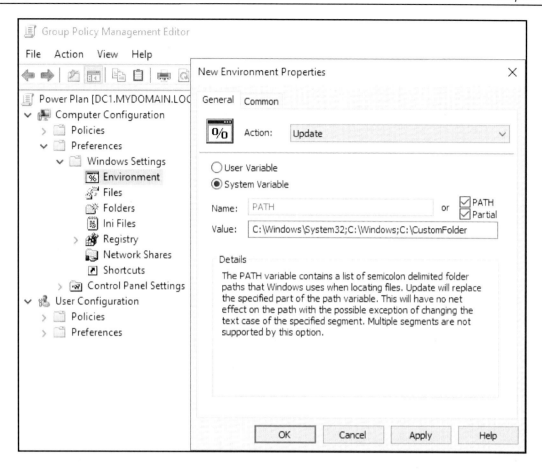

Registry keys

Almost anything inside the Windows operating system (as well as your applications) can be manipulated by creating or updating Registry keys and values. Once again, Group Policy preferences come to the rescue and give us a centralized platform to push these registry settings out to our workforce. You begin configuration of a registry value preference setting in one of these locations:

- **Computer Configuration** | **Preferences** | **Windows Settings** | **Registry**
- **User Configuration** | **Preferences** | **Windows Settings** | **Registry**

Right-click on **Registry** and choose to create a **New | Registry Item**. Just like when creating an environment variable, you specify your CRUD action, whether or not you want to do anything with the **Common** tab, and then input the specifics of your new registry value. Here is an example configuration for inputting a registry value that we often use to manipulate IPv6 on client machines. When this GPO applies to a computer, the new registry key will get plugged in to the system's registry:

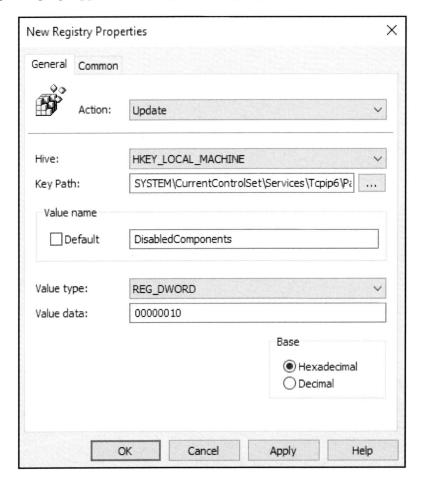

In fact, let's test this one out and verify it is really working. I input this new registry value to my GPO, and I have just linked this GPO to a location where it should be applying to my LAPTOP1 computer. If I log into LAPTOP1 and edit the registry, browsing to the Parameters location inside the registry shows me that the new key is indeed present and accounted for! Check out the following screenshot to see for yourself:

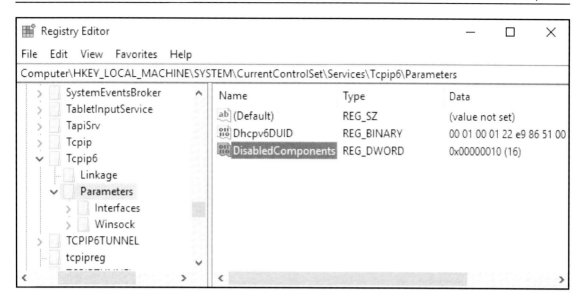

Drive mappings

Mapping network drives is essential to the way that most companies do business. Data is power, data is currency. All organizations create and own new data every day, and they all need a place to store that data. You're certainly not going to let users keep the only copies of their documents on local hard drives, so you of course have file servers to store this data. While the landscape of file storage is ever-changing, especially lately with the move to hyper-converged infrastructure, the fact that your users need drives mapped to those file-storage locations hasn't changed. There are multiple ways that drive mappings could be handled within Windows, including logon scripts that we could run via Group Policy, but let's take a look at a capability that is more natively available inside Group Policy preferences:

User Configuration | Preferences | Windows Settings | Drive Maps

Right-click on **Drive Maps**, and choose **New | Mapped Drive**. All you have to do is specify the network location that the drive needs to be mapped to, and then you can select to utilize a statically assigned drive letter on the local machine, or have the computer grab whatever the first available drive letter is. This option allows some flexibility on a per-machine basis if your users have other network drives created and you don't have them standardized.

I am going to map my S: drive to \\DC1\Sales, a new share that I just finished creating:

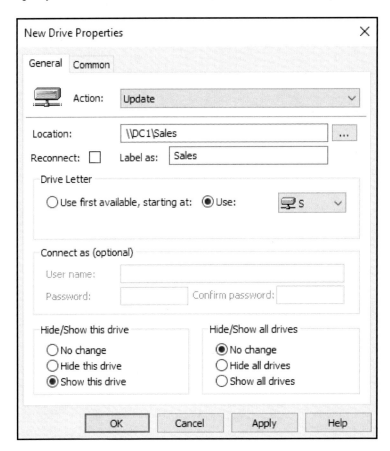

After linking this GPO to my user account and logging in to my laptop, I can now open up **File Explorer** and see the automatically created S: drive mapping to my Sales drive:

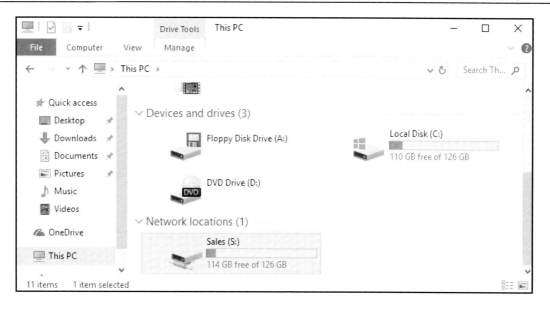

Creating a printer connection

Another task that is a general nuisance for IT folks is the mundane creation of all the printers that your users need to access from their work computers. In a business environment, it is common to make use of a print server of some kind so that you don't have to make individualized TCP/IP connections between all computers and all printers, but even if your printers are all configured to work with a centralized print server, you still need to create connections to those shared printers on each workstation. Group Policy to the rescue again! There is an easy way to identify a printer connection inside a Preference package, and automate the rollout of that printer connection to your users and computers. This is another one of those settings that you can define at the computer or user level:

- **Computer Configuration** I **Preferences** I **Control Panel Settings** I **Printers**
- **User Configuration** I **Preferences** I **Control Panel Settings** I **Printers**

At this point, you're starting to get the hang of configuring new preferences. Once again, all you have to do is right-click on the **Printers** folder, and choose to create a new printer. When creating your printer inside Computer Configuration, you get to choose between **TCP/IP Printer** and **Local Printer**. Utilizing User Configuration settings gives you these two, plus one additional option: **Shared Printer**. This kind of printer selection is only available from within User Configuration settings because access to a shared printer requires user permissions to pass before the printer can be created.

Whichever printer type you are setting up, choose the appropriate option and simply input the configuration settings for the printer. Here is a sample configuration of a Shared Printer:

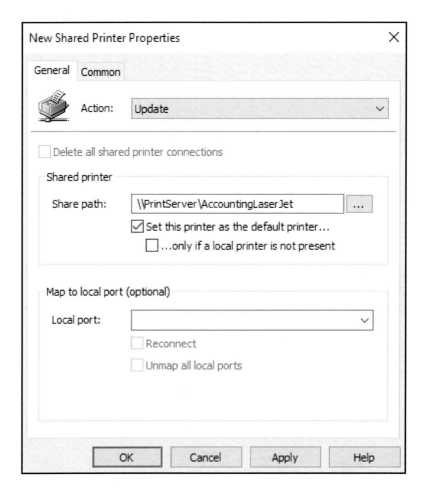

While this is another straightforward and fairly simple option to implement, it can be a big timesaver. Imagine your accounting department needs access to print to a copier for general-purpose documents, a laser printer for better-quality items, plus a special MICR printer when they need to cut checks. Perhaps you have a dozen employees in accounting, and they all need access to each of these printers. Doing this by hand would mean you are setting up 36 printer connections by hand – that could take you most of the morning! With Group Policy, you could input the three printer connections once into a GPO, apply that GPO to your Accounting Computers OU, and go out for breakfast with all the time that you saved.

Forcing an Internet Explorer proxy server

Most of the preferences that we have worked together to put into place have had a similar rollout process. Find the preference setting, right-click and choose to create a new "whatever," fill out one screen, and call it a day. Let's wrap up these examples with a configuration that utilizes a more advanced process, one with multiple tabs full of options. This will help us to put the green/red underline knowledge into practice, by diving into Internet Explorer settings.

The specific item that we want to accomplish today is to use Group Policy in order to force Internet Explorer to pass all of its traffic through a proxy server in our network. The proxy server is already established and waiting for connections; all that remains is to visit IE properties on all of the workstations and specify that they should use that proxy for outbound communications. To accomplish this without having to touch each of the computers, create a new GPO, and visit the following location:

User Configuration | Preferences | Control Panel Settings | Internet Settings

Right-click here and create a new package for whatever version of Internet Explorer you are trying to use. You'll see in this menu that you have separate options for IE versions 5 through 10. Due to changes in Internet Explorer between these versions, you have to utilize different packages of settings in order to properly configure them. If all of your workstations are running the latest versions of everything, great! Then you only need to configure an Internet Explorer 10 package, like we are going to do right now. If you still have some down-level clients with older versions, you will simply have to walk through this process two or more times to duplicate our settings for however many versions of IE you have out in the wild:

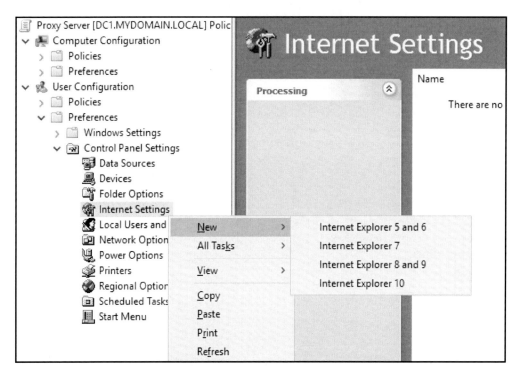

After selecting **Internet Explorer 10**, we are immediately presented with the **General** tab of Internet Explorer properties. You will notice some green underlined settings already on this page. Remember that since we saw green with our own eyes, that now means that the settings underlined in green on this page will be manipulated by our GPO when it applies. Even though we did not touch these settings for **Startup** behavior and **Browsing history**, the settings that we see on the screen will force themselves into place unless we do something about it.

Therefore, I am going to press the *F8* key, which changes all of the settings on this page to be underlined in red. This means that these settings will be ignored when the GPO processes, and whatever settings are in place on the workstation already for **Startup** and **Browsing history** will remain intact:

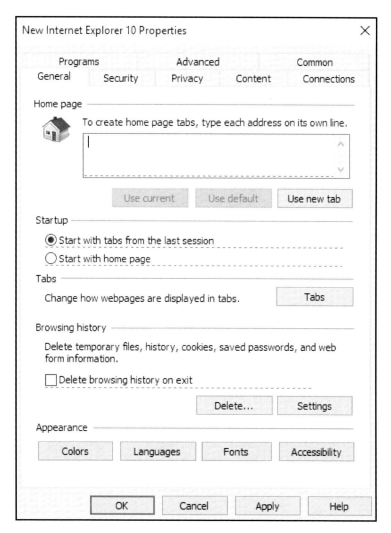

Now we need to decide what to do next. Remember that if I click through all of these tabs hunting and searching for my proxy server settings, I will be enabling all kinds of settings with green underlines and green circles, which is definitely not what I want to do. Instead, I should have already done my homework at this point and made sure of where exactly I need to go, in order to configure proxy server settings. Thankfully, I do know exactly where this setting is, on the **Connections** tab:

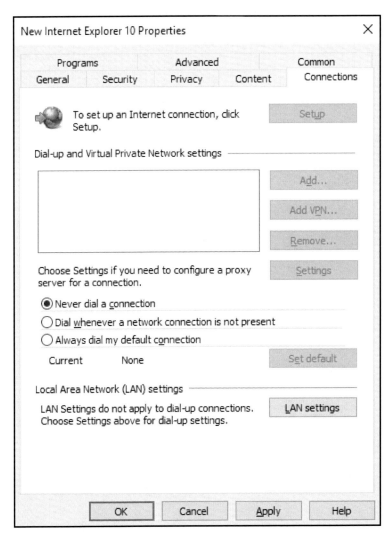

Here we see some green underlines again, so I will press *F8* one more time on this screen in order to also change the default behavior of all settings on this tab to be "ignored" (red underlined). Now I am ready to input the actual proxy server settings. Those are located inside the **LAN settings** button, so go ahead and click there. Once inside LAN settings, I press my *F8* key one more time to set everything to red by default, and then, as I select the proxy server options that I do want to configure, I click on those individual options and press the *F6* key to re-enable (green underline) only the options for **Proxy server**. This ensures that only the Proxy server setting is going to be updated on my client machines, and none of the other settings that reside within this tab:

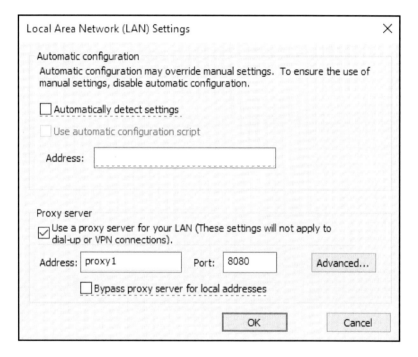

The final step is to test out this new Preference package. I have linked the new GPO to my Testing OU, where LAPTOP1 currently resides. Logging back in to that machine, I launch Internet Explorer, visit **Internet options** inside the **Tools** menu, and navigate to the **Connections** tab. Clicking on the **LAN settings** button, I can see that the proxy server option is checked and the name and port of my proxy server are correctly specified:

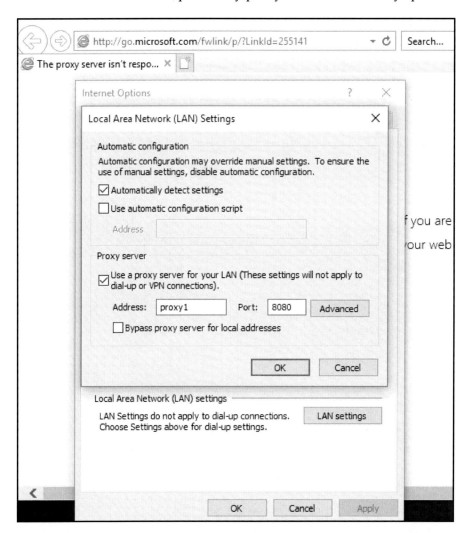

Summary

This chapter was all about Group Policy preferences, which have some considerable differences when compared to traditional Policies inside GP. Understanding the differences between Policies and Preferences will certainly enhance your administrative capabilities of Active Directory and Group Policy within your own network. We had a little bit of fun with CRUD, then moved on to Kindergarten coloring class by learning the differences between green and red as we discussed the color-coded underlines and circles that show up all over Group Policy Preference packages. We also covered all five available options inside the Common tab, which are common to pretty much any Preference that you may choose to employ. Wrapping up, we walked through some real-world examples of Preference settings that you can start using today to enhance the security and usability of your domain-joined workstation computers. In the next chapter, we will take a look at using Group Policy as part of your overall security strategy.

7
Group Policy as a Security Mechanism

Group Policy can and should be used inside any Active Directory domain environment for many different duties. While certainly useful for deploying settings and applications, and for making life easier on your users, in my opinion, those things are far from the most important focus area for Group Policy.

To me, security is the single most important aspect of the capabilities provided to us inside the Group Policy engine. Password policies, firewall rules, application blockers, the list goes on and on. Since Group Policy is basically all-powerful and able to manipulate almost anything on any workstation joined to your domain, it makes all kinds of sense to utilize this platform as your primary mechanism for securing the entire Windows infrastructure.

The following topics will be covered in this chapter:

- Password rules and regulations
- A plethora of security settings
- Windows Firewall with Advanced Security
- Manipulating Local Users and Groups
- Denying access to Command Prompt
- Prohibiting user software installation
- Disabling IPv6 via Group Policy
- User Account Control (UAC)
- Blocking USB drives

Password rules and regulations

We have already spent some time in this book updating password criteria for our domain. To accomplish this, we edited the built-in **Default Domain Policy** GPO, as it exists in any instance of an Active Directory domain and contains password settings by default. I bring up this topic once again to point out the fact that this prebuilt policy, Default Domain Policy, really is the best place to maintain password settings for most companies.

This mindset differs from that of any other settings. My general advice for the Default Domain Policy is "don't touch it!" You should not be throwing settings into that policy for the fun of it. In general, whenever you want to push out new settings with Group Policy it should really be from inside a brand new GPO. The exception to this rule is password-related settings. When increasing the security of your passwords, it certainly is possible to incorporate password settings into a new GPO but that GPO then automatically starts stepping on the toes of Default Domain Policy.

While this is not necessarily bad, remember that GPOs have to prioritize themselves over each other all the time, so it could easily lead to confusion down the road. If you have password settings inside the Default Domain Policy, and more password settings hiding inside a new GPO as well, what happens when you go on vacation and another administrator at your company suddenly needs to figure out how to change password complexity requirements? I hope your took your laptop along on that Bahamas trip. Maintaining password rules and regulations in multiple locations will turn hairy, so it's best to leave them all in one place. Unless you have a very good reason to divert, that one place should really be the Default Domain Policy GPO.

A plethora of security settings

Before walking through any specific security settings, if you are the type of person who just wants to dig in and try it for yourself, let's take a minute and point out a few common locations inside GPME that contain multitudes of security-related settings. There is no way that we can cover all useful settings inside one chapter, so I encourage all of you to dig around inside these locations and find many additional configurations that will fit into your overall security strategy. As with most GPO settings, there are many options that can be configured inside either Computer Configuration or User Configuration, depending on your target audience for the GPO. Our primary location for security settings is, aptly named, inside the **Security Settings** folder, **Computer or User Configuration** | **Policies** | **Windows Settings** | **Security Settings**:

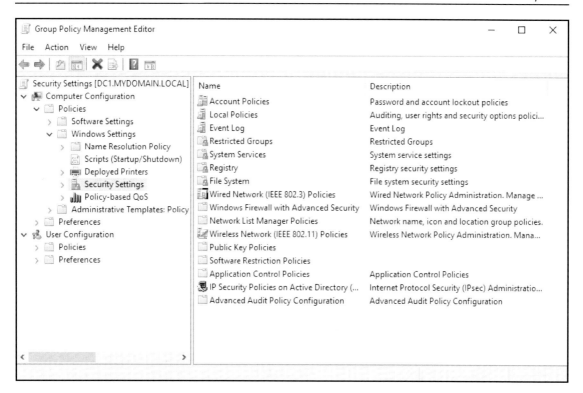

While **Security Settings** contains many items to sift through, there are also administrative templates and even preferences that contain settings that can enhance the security of your computers. Here are a few of those locations:

- **Computer or User Configuration** | **Policies** | **Administrative Templates** | **Control Panel**
- **Computer or User Configuration** | **Policies** | **Administrative Templates** | **Start Menu and Taskbar**
- **Computer or User Configuration** | **Policies** | **Administrative Templates** | **System**

Now that I am looking through some of these folders, there are security-related settings everywhere!

The moral of the story is this: if there is a particular task that you want to accomplish, or a specific piece of the Windows operating system that you want to lock down, there is a great chance that a Group Policy setting exists to do it. Browsing around inside these lists will give you a lot of great ideas for new ways that you can lock down your machines.

Windows Firewall with Advanced Security

The primary purpose of this security chapter is to get our hands dirty with implementing some real-life scenario settings that you can turn around and use in your own networks today. What better way to begin our lessons than with manipulating the Windows Firewall? Or more specifically, what we are modifying via Group Policy is the advanced portion of the firewall, appropriately called the **Windows Firewall with Advanced Security (WFAS)**.

In the latest versions of Windows 10, this console has been renamed to be **Windows Defender Firewall with Advanced Security**. This change reflects the increase in capabilities of Windows Defender and all of the ways that it ties in with the operating system. Fear not, it is the same console with a new name. Throughout this chapter you will hear me reference Windows Firewall, Windows Firewall with Advanced Security (most commonly shortened to WFAS), and Windows Defender Firewall with Advanced Security. They all mean the same thing.

I use Group Policy for many things, but I would bet that my most-often-visited location inside GPMC is the WFAS configuration section. Unfortunately, the Windows Firewall has a bad reputation hanging around from years ago. It used to be fairly true that Windows Firewall was difficult to manage, unreliable, and altogether fairly low in value. So what did all of us IT folks do with Windows Firewall? Disable it. I find many companies where that is still the mentality today. Create a policy to disable everything about Windows Firewall, and call it a day.

While we will be actually covering the information you would need to disable the firewall, because sometimes there is a legitimate need to do so, what I am here to argue is that WFAS is now an incredibly capable and secure platform. As a general rule, it should be enabled on all of your workstations and servers! WFAS really is an enterprise-ready firewall tool that you can trust to keep your machines safe.

Location of WFAS policy settings

Every Windows computer has WFAS enabled by default, and contains a standard set of inbound and outbound firewall rules that are in effect. Essentially, it "allows all outbound" and "blocks all inbound" by default, though that is just a vague and unspecific way of saying it and isn't completely accurate, as there are actually a myriad of rules that work together to make it feel this way. When you enable certain services and options inside Windows, the operating system is often creating new WFAS rules in the background that enable those functions to work properly.

Since every computer has some firewall rules out of the box, that must mean that WFAS has a ruleset that is stored outside of Group Policy, right? Exactly right. WFAS has a local configuration store that can be seen and edited from inside the Windows Firewall with Advanced Security console individually on every Windows computer you have. To launch that console, you can search for it inside the Start menu, open the **Control Panel Windows Firewall** settings and click **Advanced settings**, or my favorite way of doing it—simply type WF.MSC into **Start | Run**, **Command Prompt**, **PowerShell**, or just about anywhere else:

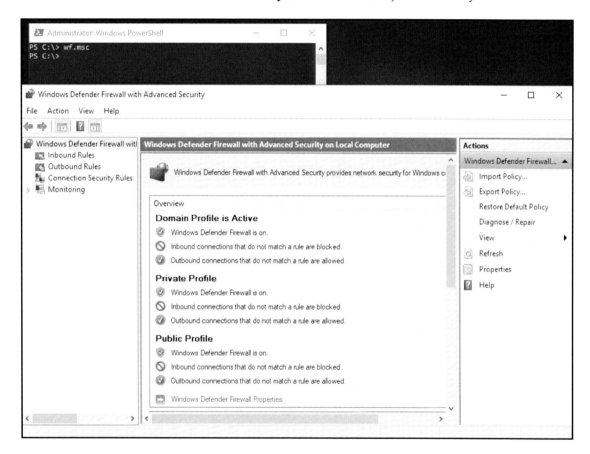

So, you could manipulate the WFAS settings individually on every computer, but who's got time for that? Instead, we can tap into these settings with a GPO. The reason I wanted to point out the local WFAS configuration is because by default it will continue to coexist with your Group Policy firewall rules. The computers do not throw away their local WFAS policy in order to accept the Group Policy settings, rather they remain intact and the GPO settings are added on. We do have the ability to change this behavior as you will learn shortly, but for now it is important to understand that when you create GPOs with firewall settings, some of those settings (such as on/off settings) will overwrite the local WFAS configuration, but many of the GPO settings (such as inbound/outbound rules) are really just adding new information to WFAS, and the local rules will all continue to exist.

Clicking on **Inbound Rules**, we can see all of those predefined firewall rules that are already inside my local WFAS configuration:

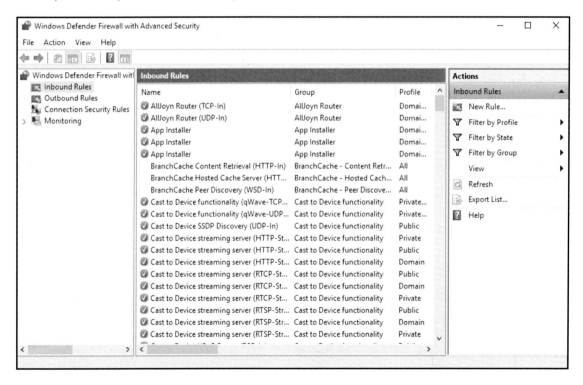

Here is the location inside GPME that you will need to visit in order to modify and create WFAS rules:

Computer Configuration | Policies | Windows Settings | Security Settings | Windows Firewall with Advanced Security | Windows Firewall with Advanced Security

In the previous screenshot, I made sure to have the Inbound Rules section open so that you could see all of the firewall rules that are plugged into my operating system right out of the box. Now looking at the WFAS settings inside GPME, we notice that **Inbound Rules** is completely empty. This again follows the idea of GPO settings being add-ons to the firewall config. Your existing local WFAS rules and regulations will continue to exist on the workstations, and settings implemented by our GPO will be added in alongside:

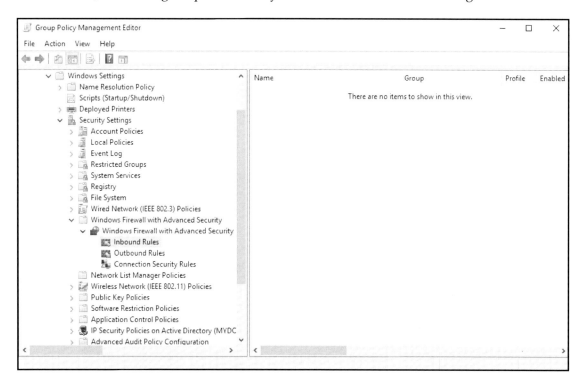

General settings

When configuring your Firewall Configuration GPO, the first section of settings you find are the general settings for how the firewall behaves. These are the settings available right on the **Windows Firewall with Advanced Security** screen. The most common thing to do here is to enable or disable the firewall altogether, which we will be performing with some step-by-step examples shortly.

Inbound Rules

Inbound Rules is the location you visit when you want to create specific incoming firewall rules. It is easy to get mixed up in thinking about inbound and outbound rules, and which one you are really looking for. Always think about these terms from the client computer's perspective.

When these rules get pushed out to your workstations and are then sitting inside WFAS, inbound rules are for manipulating the traffic that is coming inbound toward that client computer. These are by far the most common types of rules to be configuring for your systems. Since Windows Firewall tends to block inbound traffic by default, you will find yourself most often creating inbound rules that are configured to allow traffic into your machines. This is even more true of server operating systems, as there are many legitimate reasons why you might allow inbound traffic to a Windows Server than to a client computer.

Outbound Rules

Alternatively, Outbound Rules are all about protecting traffic that is leaving your client computers. Typically, when interacting with Outbound Rules, you will find yourself creating block rules. This may be useful when you have a special section of the network where you do not want users to have access (though this could also be done by blocking the traffic inbound at that location on the network itself). Another reason to create some Outbound Rules would be to restrict certain ports or protocols from flowing outbound from your workstations. Perhaps you have a set of computers that are Internet Kiosk machines, whose only purpose is to allow users to walk up and utilize a web browser. Generally, for web traffic, you only ever need outbound TCP ports 80 and 443, so you could use WFAS rules to block all outbound traffic other than ports 80 and 443, allowing internet browsing but blocking other things that the users may try to do.

Connection Security Rules

Connection Security Rules are not utilized nearly as often as Inbound and Outbound Rules, but CSRs are vastly more powerful. These types of rules are useful for setting up more advanced restrictions about how computers can communicate. This section of WFAS has a lot to do with IPsec protecting traffic between endpoints, making sure that certain endpoints can only communicate with certain other endpoints, or perhaps for requiring certain kinds of encryption between those two devices.

One of the places where I touch on Connection Security Rules is when configuring the Microsoft remote-access technology, `DirectAccess`. Inside the `DirectAccess` configuration, there are Connection Security Rules at play that negotiate IPsec tunnels between the DA clients and the DA server, which are the secure tunnels used to transport data over the internet. These rules are sort of the secret sauce that allow the automatic VPN-like connectivity for users working remotely. IPsec can also be used to secure communications within your LAN, for example requiring an encrypted traffic stream between your accounting computers and their server that contains super-sensitive payroll data.

Forcing Windows Firewall to always be enabled

Users can be pretty savvy, which sometimes means they will make changes on their corporate computers that you would prefer not to support. Group Policy is used to protect systems and maintain concurrency of settings that you want enforced. One of the ways we can do this is to ensure that the Windows Firewall is always enabled and working. You might not even be protecting against human activity, sometimes applications (or malware) will attempt to make changes to the firewall settings, perhaps even disabling it, and you may want to protect against that behavior.

Create a new GPO and navigate your way back to our WFAS location, **Computer Configuration** | **Policies** | **Windows Settings** | **Security Settings** | **Windows Firewall with Advanced Security** | **Windows Firewall with Advanced Security**:

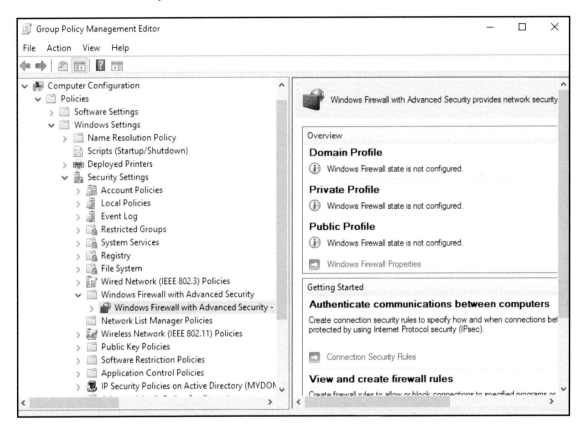

On the right-hand side of the screen, take a look inside the **Overview** section. Here, you will see the three Windows Firewall profiles (for more information on these profiles, see the *An aside about WFAS Profiles* section). Currently, all three firewall profiles are listed as `Windows Firewall state is not configured`. Go ahead and click on the **Windows Firewall Properties** link.

You will now be looking at properties of the **Domain Profile** tab, click on the drop-down menu titled **Firewall state** and select **On (recommended)**. Now visit the tabs for **Private Profile** and **Public Profile**, and select the exact same option in all three places:

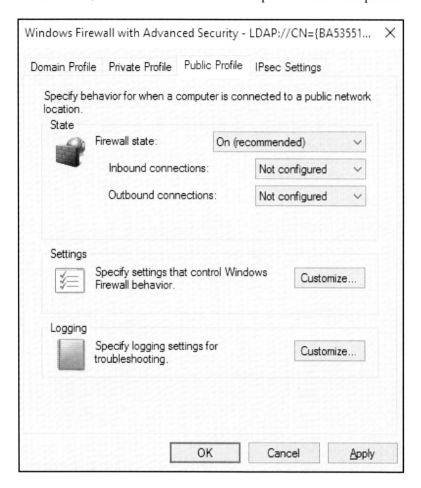

That setting is the only thing required to ensure that the firewall is enabled on my workstation. I have now linked this new GPO to the OU where my LAPTOP1 machine sits, and opening up the WF.MSC console on LAPTOP1 shows me that my firewall is enabled. When I click on the link to attempt to turn my firewall off, you can see that the drop-down box is grayed out and there is a message at the top of my screen stating **For your security, some settings are controlled by Group Policy**, which is perfect:

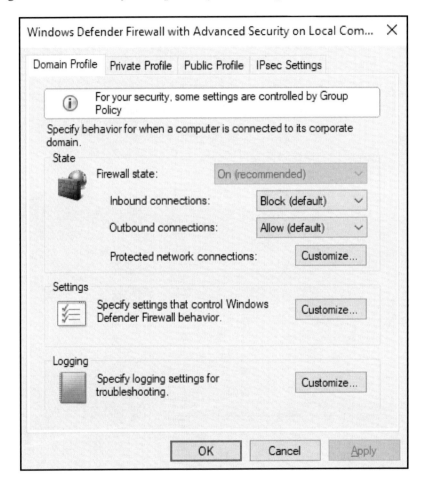

An aside about WFAS Profiles

Let's take a quick minute and direct our attention to those three firewall profiles, so that we can discuss what they mean. You see, every time your Windows computer makes a connection to a network, and if your firewall is enabled, the firewall will flag that network for one of these three firewalling profiles. You have probably seen the pop-up window that often appears when connecting to a new network, asking you whether this is a home, work, or public network. Sometimes computers are configured not to ask you this, and then they typically just lump all new networks into the Public category. The service in Windows that handles this distinction between networks is called **Network Location Awareness** (**NLA**).

When you make this decision, what you are really doing is telling Windows Firewall how to handle this network. You will see that when we create setting configurations or rules for WFAS, we always have to specify which of these three firewall profiles we want our rules to apply toward:

- **Domain Profile**: This is the firewall profile most often engaged when you are plugged into your corporate network. That is because any time that NLA can discover a Domain Controller for the domain to which your computer is joined, it will automatically assign the Domain firewall profile. In essence, you could treat the Domain Profile as your "inside the network" profile.

- **Private Profile**: Whenever NLA does not discover Domain Controllers, it then pegs the network as either a Private or Public profile. In the discovery box that is presented and asks you what kind of a network you are connecting to, if you choose either **Home** or **Work** you will then be assigned the Private Profile. The **Work** selection is a little bit confusing because you might think that would assign the Domain Profile, but it does not. Domain is only ever in effect if one of the Domain Controllers is able to be contacted by NLA. In general, people consider Private networks to be slightly more trusted (perhaps using fewer firewall rules) than Public networks.

- **Public Profile**: If you chose **Public** from the list, or if you ignored the popup and didn't select anything at all like I usually do, then any new network that you plug into will default to falling into the Public Profile category. Typically, you want to consider Public Profile to be the least secure kinds of networks, where you would want the most stringent firewall rules and regulations to apply.

When creating our new GPO that forces Windows Firewall to always be enabled, we had to configure that setting in three different screens because the three firewall profiles are handled separately. You could easily have a mix where you enabled the firewall whenever your connected network was Public or Private, but perhaps disable the firewall when you are connected to your corporate LAN, where the Domain profile would then be engaged.

Firewall profiles are assigned to a particular NIC inside Windows, so it is definitely possible for a computer or server to be assigned multiple firewall profiles at the same time. If that server has multiple NICs installed, and they are connected to different networks (such as one on the internal network and the other inside a DMZ), you may find yourself with both the Domain and Public profiles being active at the same time. The WFAS rules defined for Domain would apply to traffic coming or going from the internal NIC, and WFAS rules defined for Public would be actively protecting the DMZ NIC.

Disabling Windows Firewall by policy

We just finished forcing all Windows Firewall profiles to be enabled by policy, so why don't we now do an about face and try the opposite. Sometimes there is a business case for disabling the built-in Windows Firewall on all workstations. While I do not personally recommend this approach, perhaps you have a third-party firewall tool for which you forked over a lot of cash, and aren't ready to give it up yet. Multiple firewalling tools on the same machine sounds like it would be super safe, but in reality they get nasty with each other and cause all kinds of problems as they fail to coexist. So, let's pretend we now have the need to forcibly disable Windows Firewall on the client system—all three firewall profiles.

We do not need to walk through all the steps again, simply create a new GPO (or modify the existing one), and set all three firewall profiles to **Off**. Once this GPO filters down to the client machines, the Windows Firewall will be completely disabled on those workstations:

Creating a rule to allow inbound traffic

The Windows Firewall restricts inbound communications by default, which is a great thing. Our machines are almost always connected to the internet these days, so we need to do all we can to keep the bad guys out. What this means in practice, however, is that often when you have a legitimate need to make a remote connection of some sort to a laptop, server, or whatever, it will be denied by default. Sometimes, the firewall plugs in rules automatically. For example, when you enable RDP on a Windows Server, it automatically plugs an Inbound Rule into WFAS on that server to allow incoming port 3389 traffic, because Windows knows that it will be necessary to make successful RDP connections to your server.

Other times, WFAS is not intelligent enough to make these decisions, and we need to manually input rules in order to make things happen. Let's work together to push out a rule that allows some incoming traffic. For our example today, we are going to create a rule that applies to our client machines which allows ICMPv4. ICMP is the traffic that happens when you try to ping an IP address. IT folks are used to pinging resources to figure out whether they are online, or whether a particular IP address is in use on the network. These days, you cannot always rely on a ping reply to tell you whether something is actually sitting on that IP address. As you can see in the following screenshot, I am logged into my DC1 server and from here I am attempting to ping LAPTOP1. My LAPTOP1 machine is online and working on the network, and you can see that my ping command does resolve LAPTOP1 to the proper IP address, but the pings are timing out:

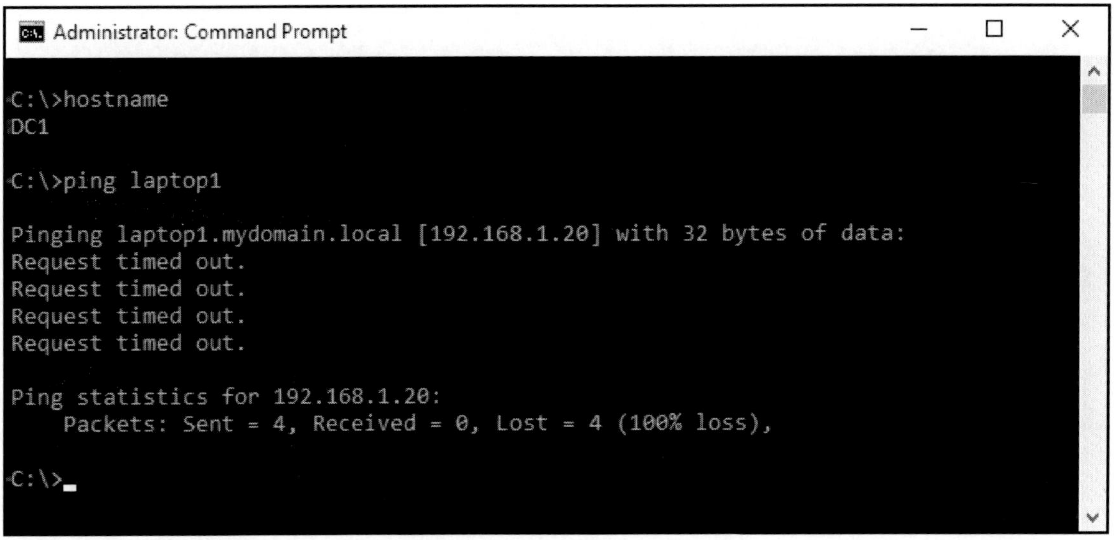

```
Administrator: Command Prompt                          —    □    ✕

C:\>hostname
DC1

C:\>ping laptop1

Pinging laptop1.mydomain.local [192.168.1.20] with 32 bytes of data:
Request timed out.
Request timed out.
Request timed out.
Request timed out.

Ping statistics for 192.168.1.20:
    Packets: Sent = 4, Received = 0, Lost = 4 (100% loss),

C:\>
```

It appears `LAPTOP1` is offline, but it is actually up and running right now. This happens because WFAS does not allow pings (ICMPv4) by default. Let's use a GPO to change that behavior, because I like to ping stuff!

I am going to edit the same GPO that I used to enforce that my Firewall was turned on. Navigate to the following location:

Computer Configuration | **Policies** | **Windows Settings** | **Security Settings** | **Windows Firewall with Advanced Security** | **Windows Firewall with Advanced Security** | **Inbound Rules**

Here you will see a lot of blank space. Right-click in this blank space, and choose to create a **New Rule...**

On the **Rule Type** screen, you decide what kind of a rule to build. Here is a quick summary of these types:

- **Program**: Use this to apply a firewall rule to a particular application on the system. I almost never use this option.
- **Port**: Definitely the most common option used personally, selecting **Port** here allows you to define which ports the rule that we are creating will allow or deny.
- **Predefined**: This is a list of all kinds of services inside Windows that have predefined port numbers or ranges. If you want to allow something to work, but are not sure what ports or functionality that resource requires, browse this list to see whether there is a predefined entry for it. I tend not to trust the predefined entries, I would rather make a more specific rule that is applying only to the ports or protocols that I tell it to.
- **Custom**: If any of the other three do not fit the bill, choose **Custom**. This is the case for my ICMPv4 rule, as I do not see that as an option inside any of the other locations. So I will choose **Custom** and click **Next**.

You now have another chance to apply this rule only to particular programs. I want my rule to apply to the entire system, so I will leave it marked for **All programs**, and click **Next** again.

Now for the fun part, deciding what kind of traffic this rule applies to on the **Protocol and Ports** screen. The default option is **Any**, make sure you change that dropdown to be your desired item. If you were to create an **Any** rule, you could suddenly allow all incoming traffic on all of your workstations! I want to enable inbound **ICMPv4**, and so I make that selection from inside the **Protocol type** menu:

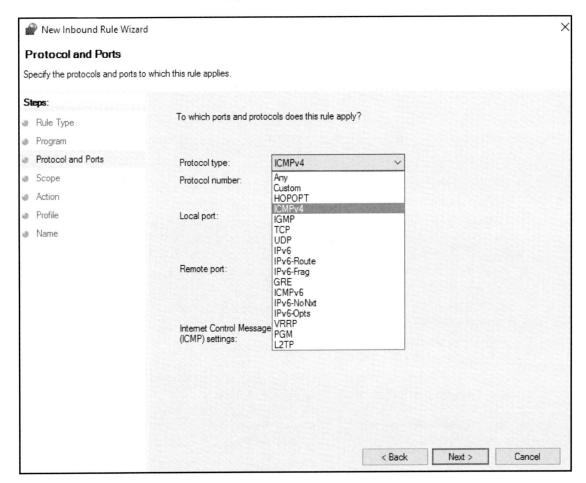

Moving on to the **Scope** step, we are going to click **Next** to accept the defaults. I want my ICMPv4 rule to allow ping replies from any machine. We will later utilize the **Scope** screen in more depth, when we create an outbound rule.

Action is pretty self-explanatory, we are creating a rule that allows this ICMP traffic and so we need to **Allow the connection**.

Profile are those three firewall profiles listed once again! When you create firewall rules, whether inbound or outbound, you can choose to apply these rules to one, two, or all three of the firewall profiles. If you had a need to allow certain things while computers are sitting inside the corporate network, you could apply those rules to only the **Domain** profile.

However, if you wanted a more locked-down experience when those machines (maybe laptops) move outside of the corporate network, then the firewall would apply either the Private or Public profiles, and perhaps you have a different set of firewall rules that takes over when that distinction is made. I do not want my machine responding to pings when it is sitting at a user's house or in their local coffee shop, only when it's inside my LAN. So I am going to select only the **Domain** profile here:

```
        New Inbound Rule Wizard

Profile

Specify the profiles for which this rule applies.

Steps:
                                    When does this rule apply?
  Rule Type

  Program

  Protocol and Ports              ☑  Domain
                                       Applies when a computer is connected to its corporate domain.
  Scope

  Action                          ☐  Private
                                       Applies when a computer is connected to a private network location, such as a home
  Profile                              or work place.

  Name                            ☐  Public
                                       Applies when a computer is connected to a public network location.
```

Finally, make up a **Name** for your new WFAS rule, and this new rule is now sitting inside our GPO, ready to be assigned to client computers. After waiting a few minutes for this new setting to roll down to LAPTOP1, if I open WF.MSC on that machine and look inside the **Inbound Rules**, I can see that my new firewall rule successfully came down from the GPO and added it in at the top of my rules list (again, the remaining rules sitting inside this folder are the default rules that ship with Windows):

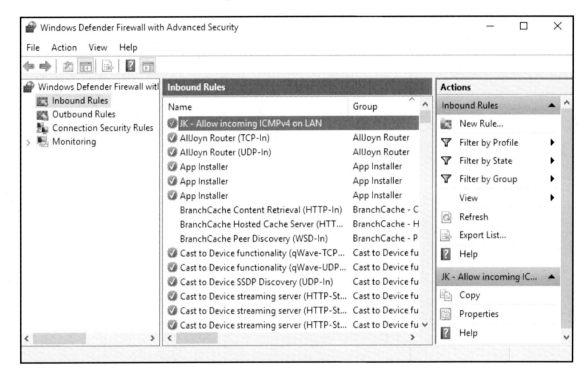

Once inside the Inbound Rules folder, that ICMPv4 allow rule should take immediate effect. Logging back into DC1, I can now successfully ping LAPTOP1:

```
Administrator: Command Prompt                        —    □    ×

C:\>hostname
DC1

C:\>ping laptop1

Pinging laptop1.mydomain.local [192.168.1.20] with 32 bytes of data:
Reply from 192.168.1.20: bytes=32 time<1ms TTL=128
Reply from 192.168.1.20: bytes=32 time<1ms TTL=128
Reply from 192.168.1.20: bytes=32 time<1ms TTL=128
Reply from 192.168.1.20: bytes=32 time<1ms TTL=128

Ping statistics for 192.168.1.20:
    Packets: Sent = 4, Received = 4, Lost = 0 (0% loss),
Approximate round trip times in milli-seconds:
    Minimum = 0ms, Maximum = 0ms, Average = 0ms

C:\>
```

Ping is such a common troubleshooting command that many companies utilize Group Policy to push this same kind of **Allow ICMPv4** rule out to all devices inside their networks. Computers, servers, tablets, anything that can receive GPO settings. You may want to think about doing the same.

Creating a rule to block outbound traffic

By default, the Windows Firewall allows pretty much everything to travel outbound. Usually when discussing firewall rules, you are crafting inbound rules so that you can continue restricting what is able to reach in and touch your machine, but there are certainly times when limiting access on the outbound could be helpful.

Let's pretend that I have a special subnet on my network that I do not want any of my Graphic Design colleagues poking around inside. We are going to use a WFAS Outbound Rule inside of a GPO to ensure they can't. The process here will be very similar to that of creating an inbound rule, except that we are going to scope this rule to a specific remote location, and will be using this rule to block traffic rather than allow it. Create the new GPO, edit it, and navigate to **Computer Configuration | Policies | Windows Settings | Security Settings | Windows Firewall with Advanced Security | Windows Firewall with Advanced Security | Outbound Rules**.

Right-click to create a **New Rule...** and we are once again going to choose **Custom** for our **Rule Type**. On the **Protocol and Ports** screen, leave the default setting for **Any** defined in the **Protocol type** drop-down list. We are choosing **Any** here because we are going to block all traffic that is destined to this special subnet.

Next up is the **Scope** tab, and this is where we are going to divert from how we created the inbound rule earlier. We do not want to block access to everything in the network, only traffic destined for our special subnet. That subnet is `172.16.100.0/24`. On the Scope tab, manipulate the **Which remote IP addresses does this rule apply to?** section of the screen so that our subnet is defined inside that field. You do this by using the **Add...** button and typing in the subnet address:

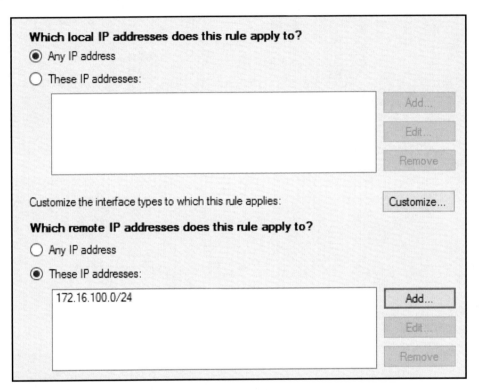

On the **Action** screen, make sure to select **Block the connection**. Walk through the remaining steps for configuring the rest of the firewall rule however you see fit. Once this WFAS rule is in place and applied to the machines via Group Policy, those computers will no longer be able to contact any of the IP addresses within that subnet.

As I mentioned, you could certainly block this access at a different level as well. Perhaps on the servers that live within the `172.16.100.0/24` subnet, create inbound rules that block people from coming in. Or perhaps you even have a physical firewall that sits in between the clients and this special subnet, and you could limit access that way. The purpose of this exercise was to get you thinking about utilizing outbound block rules in ways that you may not have in the past.

As a real-world example, over the last few months I have had three separate occasions where I was working on a server with multiple NICs, and I needed to block just one of those NICs from from being able to contact the domain. The primary "internal" NIC of that server needed access to everything inside the LAN, but the second NIC needed to be secluded away from the domain. To do this, I had to block access from that NIC to all of the Domain Controller servers in the environment. We ended up using an outbound deny rule inside WFAS on the server, modifying the Scope tab so that the local address the rule applied to was only the IP address listed on that special NIC, and the remote IP addresses listed for the rule was a listing of all Domain Controllers in the environment. By using WFAS in a perhaps unorthodox way, we were able to accomplish our goals without having to involve the network team or make any router/physical networking equipment changes.

What about conflicting rules?

Usually, when configuring firewall devices (physical, dedicated firewalls), you always have to factor in rule conflicts and rule-order priority. What if your list contains rules that overlap or fight with each other? What if you create a rule that allows traffic from your clients to the entire network, but then another administrator creates a rule that only allows traffic to certain parts of the network? What happens? Who wins?

In the WFAS world, everybody wins. (I promise I am not a millennial!) Unlike most firewalls, the rules presented inside WFAS are not sequential, those listed at the top have no higher priority than those listed at the bottom of the list. Instead, all rules inside WFAS are added up and applied cumulatively. If there are multiple rules that configure different levels of access to the same devices, it does not matter because they all get joined together. All of the rules apply.

The one potential conflict that does still exist is if there is an allow rule that directly conflicts with something inside a block rule. If this happens, the block rule always wins.

Configuring GPO to clear local WFAS rules

As you now know, there are WFAS rules that exist inside Windows by default, and by plugging new rules into GPOs we are adding new rules into that already-extensive list of predefined rules. While this usually works just fine, sometimes it feels a mess inside there, and wouldn't it be nice if we could create one standard set of firewall rules for everybody? Wouldn't it be great to know that there were no locally-configured, predefined rules in play, and that only the ones we define through Group Policy exist on the workstations? This is the last setting that I want to point out in our discussion on WFAS. There is an option hiding away in there that forces the local WFAS rules out, and only places the GPO-sourced rules back into play:

Computer Configuration | Policies | Windows Settings | Security Settings | Windows Firewall with Advanced Security | Windows Firewall with Advanced Security

Back on this primary screen of WFAS settings, click on the link that says **Windows Firewall Properties** – the same place we visit to enable or disable the firewall profiles. Inside these properties, you will see a section called **Settings** and a button that says **Customize...**:

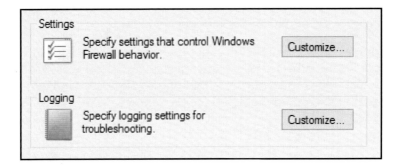

Make sure to check out the Logging section of this screen as well, in the event that you ever need to enable logging of the firewall for troubleshooting purposes.

After clicking on the **Customize...** button that is listed in the **Settings** section, you are presented with a handful of options. One of those options is **Rule merging**. This is where you can decide what to do with the locally-configured WFAS rules on your computers. By using the drop-down box next to **Apply local firewall rules** and setting this to **No**, when this policy applies to your workstation, it will clear out all of those locally-configured WFAS rules and the only ones remaining will be the ones that have been put into place by Group Policy:

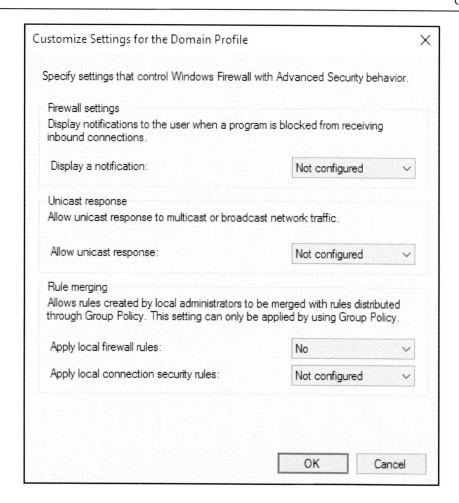

Manipulating Local Users and Groups

An enormous portion of any company's overall security posture is making sure that users have proper rights and permissions. You want everyone to be as restricted as possible, while still allowing them to perform the work they need to accomplish for their jobs. When a user logs into a Windows computer, they receive security permissions inside Windows based on what local group or groups they are members of. Out of the box, Standard users have the most restricted rights, Power Users are able to perform some heavier-duty tasks, Administrators have full control within Windows—you get the idea. There are multiple tiers of permissions baked into the operating system.

When your Windows computer is joined to a domain, there are some inherent changes automatically made to these groups. For example, the Domain Admins Active Directory group is generally added into all of your computer's local Administrator group. Therefore, when you log into a domain-joined computer with a user account that is part of the Domain Admins group inside AD, you will automatically receive Administrator rights on each workstation or server that you log into.

Sounds great, right? Except that administrative permissions are way too powerful for most users. It is even a best practice these days to keep your IT administrators away from having Domain Admin rights all the time. It is too easy to make mistakes that way. Instead, we can utilize some of those in-between levels of permission, putting user accounts or groups into the local security groups, to divvy up permissions in a more comprehensive way.

You certainly do not want to have to visit every one of your servers and workstations in order to manually plug user accounts into their appropriate groups, so we turn to Group Policy. As an example, I have a new Active Directory security group called Server Administrators. I do not want these folks to have full Domain Admin rights; that would be too extensive. Instead, I simply want to make sure that all Server Administrators can successfully RDP into any of the servers running in my environment. To accomplish this, I want to add the Server Administrators AD group into the Remote Desktop Users local group on all of my Windows Servers. When finished, any user who is joined to Server Administrators inside AD will immediately have rights to RDP into any server.

To perform this task, create a new GPO and scope it so that it applies to all servers in the environment (this is, of course, only necessary for my example—you go ahead and scope your GPO however you see fit).

Edit the new GPO and head over to **Computer Configuration | Preferences | Control Panel Settings | Local Users and Groups**. Then right-click in the blank space and choose **New | Local Group**.

As you can see here, you have the ability to create truly new groups as well, if you ever have the need to do that. What we want to do today, however, is **Update** the existing Remote Desktop Users group, so I am selecting that from the **Group name** drop-down list. There are options to rename the group if you wanted, and to delete existing members from the group if you want to ensure that your selections on this screen were the only ones remaining after the GPO finishes. I do not care so much about those extra options for this particular task, so I will simply tell it that I want the **Remote Desktop Users** group to be **Updated** to include the **Server Administrators** group, as you can see here:

Now when logging into one of the servers in my environment, opening the Local Users and Groups shows me that yes indeed, Server Administrator has been automatically added into the existing Remote Desktop Users local group on that server, and folks in that group have permission to RDP into it:

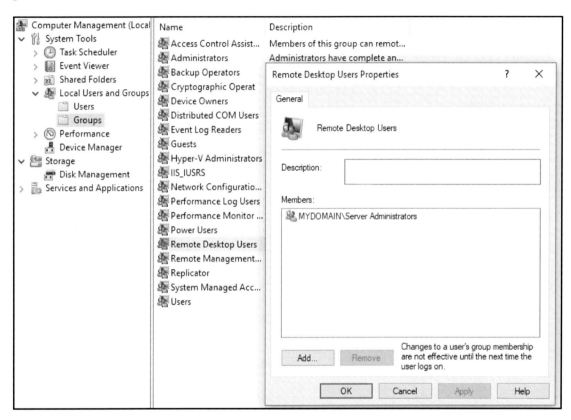

 These Group-Policy-based local users and groups settings can also be used for managing individual user accounts. This could be useful for manipulating the password of a local account that exists on all workstations, resetting that password on all machines in one fell swoop. Or perhaps you need to create a new local user account that you want to push out to all of your devices, that is also easily done.

Denying access to Command Prompt

While I personally love Command Prompt and almost always have an instance of it open in order to launch administrative tools, in general it is true that Command Prompt is a security nightmare. If any user somehow stumbles their way into an elevated Command Prompt window, they can do literally anything inside the Windows operating system. So as a matter of security common sense, if there is not a legitimate need for Command Prompt to be used on workstations in your environment (and I very much doubt that there is), disable it! This is a quick and simple policy, but one that is almost always a great addition to a well-rounded security package:

User Configuration | Policies | Administrative Templates | System | Prevent access to the command prompt:

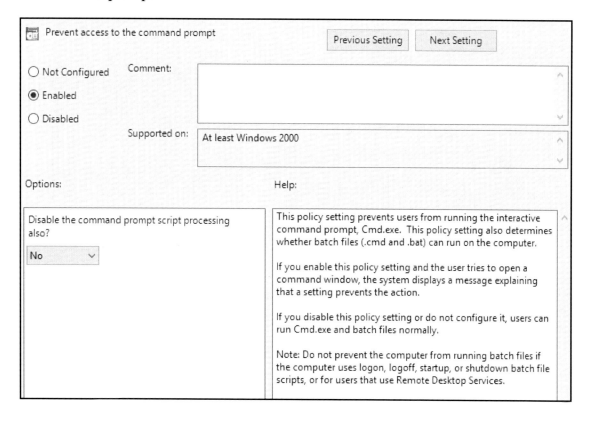

Set **Prevent access to the command prompt** to **Enabled**, that's it! CMD.EXE is now blocked wherever this GPO applies. You will also notice that there is a separate selection within that setting regarding scripts and whether they should continue to be allowed to run. If you are utilizing batch-style logon or logoff scripts, you will want to make sure script processing remains enabled. Otherwise, this GPO will break your scripts.

Once enabled, attempting to launch Command Prompt from my user login now results in the following message:

Remember that this is a **User Configuration** policy, and as such you will be scoping your GPO to apply to user accounts, not computers. For example, I just mistakenly linked this GPO to my testing GPOs OU where my LAPTOP1 machine sits, and then sat here wondering why I could still access Command Prompt on that machine. Doh! What I actually needed to do was link this GPO to my accounting users OU, which is where my test user account resides. After making the change, I was immediately blocked from accessing cmd.exe.

 Check out one more security policy setting that is available inside this same location; in fact, it should be listed immediately below the policy setting, which disables Command Prompt. This one is called **Prevent access to registry editing tools**, and is also a great one to configure for most user accounts.

Prohibiting user software-installation

It is very common to find software on your managed desktop computers that you (the admin) did not put there, because users are very good at figuring out ways to install applications and software that they use at home. Sometimes, this is with good intentions, utilizing an online tool to help their productivity at work, but other times—perhaps most of the time—what you find are apps installed for entertainment purposes. Maybe a user has installed the Chrome browser because your company-issued Internet Explorer is too restrictive for their tastes, or you sit down to troubleshoot a computer only to find a personal Dropbox application or Spotify running in the systray. I am not saying these applications are bad – in fact, I use all three. The scary part of this scenario is that the user was able to download and install these applications in the first place, without administrative input.

There are actually many different places inside Group Policy where software installation restrictions can be put into place, some are vastly more complex than others. If you're interested in diving into one of the more complex ways (which in the end will provide you with more granular control over your restriction policies), make sure to do some additional reading on these topics:

- **Software Restriction Policies**: `https://docs.microsoft.com/en-us/windows-server/identity/software-restriction-policies/software-restriction-policies`
- **AppLocker**: `https://docs.microsoft.com/en-us/windows/security/threat-protection/windows-defender-application-control/applocker/applocker-overview`

While these technologies can offer comprehensive options for deciding what can or cannot be installed, or even what applications can or cannot be opened on a computer, they are both complex topics that require a bit of research before you will be ready to make use of them. Today we are here to discuss a simpler and more straightforward approach to denying software installations:

Computer Configuration | Policies | Administrative Templates | Windows Components | Windows Installer | Prohibit User Installs

Once enabled, the **Prohibit User Installs** option is a quick and easy way to stop per-user installs from happening. When an application is installed at the computer level, it is available to all users and so everyone would still have access to run the programs that you have installed at the administrative level. The difference in this setting is that users would be unable to install applications inside their user context, those apps that do not require administrative rights to install and run. Without this setting in place (or one of the other restriction technologies), you will most certainly find applications on your workstations that you did not place there. By enabling **Prohibit User Installs**, you at least take some initial steps to keep games, entertainment software, and other potentially malicious programs away from your corporate machines.

Disabling IPv6 via Group Policy

IPv6 is the future! Well, not exactly. While IPv6 is pretty important to internet traffic, because we are legitimately running out of addresses in the IPv4 world, a company's internal network is a different story. I have heard the warnings about moving to IPv6 for many years, and yet it is extremely rare that I run into any network that is actually using it inside of their buildings. Why is that? Because it is just not necessary in most cases. IPv6 has always been touted as having enough address space so that every device in the entire world could have its own globally-unique IPv6 address, but the implication in that statement is that companies would actually allow their devices to be connected directly to the internet using these globally-routable addresses. The level of trust required here is simply too great. Instead, we hide our internal networks behind firewalls and NATs, just like we always have, and it continues to function fine and dandy. It is my guess that this trend will continue for many, many, many more years.

What is my point? Most corporate-owned computers do not need IPv6 in any way, shape, or form. Unfortunately, IPv6 is still a mysterious black box to many IT groups, so it actually makes pretty good sense to disable it, if you are not using it anyway. You see, the IPv6 stack in Windows is pretty smart, maybe a little too smart, and whenever your IPv6-enabled computer sees other IPv6-enabled computers on the same network, they will start to create networks among themselves. While this is not inherently a bad thing—it is actually very useful for home networks—in a restricted domain environment, it can create communication pathways that are outside the scope of your IPv4-based network protection systems. Most network admins want to ensure that they know about all the traffic flowing to and from their computers, and IPv6 is often viewed as rogue in that scenario.

If you are not using IPv6, let's disable it. Thankfully this is easily done via Group Policy. One simple registry key, called `DisabledComponents`, will allow us to tweak the IPv6 stack inside the operating system in myriad different ways.

To create a new Registry key via Group Policy, create a new GPO and navigate to **Computer Configuration** | **Preferences** | **Windows Settings** | **Registry**.

Right-click here to create a **New** | **Registry Item** and we want to create the following registry key:

- **Action**: **Update** (unless you want a different CRUD)
- **Hive**: **HKEY_LOCAL_MACHINE**
- **Key Path**: **System\CurrentControlSet\Services\Tcpip6\Parameters**

We are creating a **DWORD** called `DisabledComponents`:

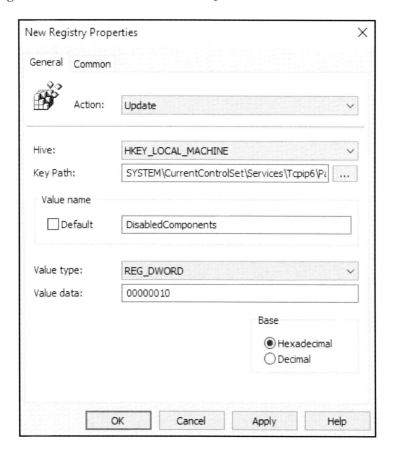

Value data is where you get to decide the specifics about what you are disabling/squashing inside IPv6. The following are the configurable options for this registry key. You can see in the previous screenshot that I have configured mine to 0x10, which blocks native IPv6, but allows the IPv6 transition-tunneling adapters to continue working. I am doing this because I often work with the remote-access technology `DirectAccess` and this requires the transition-tunneling adapters to be active on my laptops:

- Prefer IPv4 over IPv6 = 0x20
- Completely disable IPv6 = 0xFF
- Disable IPv6 on all nontunnel interfaces = 0x10
- Disable IPv6 on tunnel interfaces = 0x01
- Disable IPv6 on nontunnel interfaces (except loopback) and on IPv6 tunnel interfaces = 0x11

More details on these options are provided here: `https://support.microsoft.com/en-us/help/929852/guidance-for-configuring-ipv6-in-windows-for-advanced-users`.

After creating the regkey, pushing it out to some computers via GPO, and then restarting those computers, IPv6 will now be configured to meet your corporate needs.

User Account Control

Noooo, it's that annoying pop-up screen again!

This little credential prompt seems so annoying, yet it can save your bacon. UAC is an invaluable tool that halts installation processes, or the launching of applications into a mode that has elevated privileges. For example, I tried to open an administrative PowerShell prompt and was presented with the preceding screenshot.

UAC is an in-your-face reminder that something big is about to happen. When an application installer gets launched, you want to make sure it is something you actually intended to install, right? I have witnessed webpages try to launch malicious installers on computers, only to be stopped by UAC. By simply pressing No on this screen, you stop whatever activity was about to happen. There is also plenty of danger in opening up an administrative window, so Windows uses UAC to double-check with you that opening this all-powerful utility is really what you intended to do.

If a user is logged into a computer as an administrative account and is prompted for UAC, you simply click **Yes** or **No** on whether to allow the action to happen. You already have admin rights, it is simply confirming that you really want this process to run. When logged in as a standard user account, UAC gets quite a bit harder to push through. As in the preceding screenshot, you need to provide administrative credentials to proceed.

This safety net is very useful. For example, when setting up computers for friends, family, and neighbors (I am sure you are the neighborhood IT person, too), I always try to talk to those folks into having two accounts on their computer—one that is a regular user, which is the profile they always log in with, and then a second account that is a member of the administrators group. This way, whenever they try to install something (or when some other process attempts to install something), UAC prompts them to enter those administrative credentials before allowing the installer to continue. I spend much less time cleaning viruses and reinstalling Windows for people now that I have started this practice of keeping people away from having inherent administrative rights.

Ultimately, UAC is enabled by default and does a pretty good job at keeping users from doing things they should not be doing. If this is working well for you, you do not need to use a GPO here at all. But if there are settings within the UAC options that you want to tweak, such as making it more or less difficult for your users or even administrators to make changes, let's explore the settings available to us inside Group Policy.

Configuring UAC via GPO

Computer Configuration | Policies | Windows Settings | Security Settings | Local Policies | Security Options

There are many options inside the **Security Options** folder, which are worth checking out at some point. This is also the location where you can do neat things such as rename the built-in local administrator and guest accounts, modify *Ctrl + Alt + Del* behavior on login, and decide whether the Shut Down option is available from the login screen. The settings we care about for UAC are near the bottom of the list, beginning with the words **User Account Control**.

I do not feel that we need to cover all of the possible options for UAC, let's just point out some of the more commonly used ones.

User Account Control – Behavior of the Elevation Prompt for Administrators in Admin Approval Mode

Default behavior of UAC, even for administrative accounts, is to prompt the Yes/No dialog box, but not force the user to re-enter credentials. By configuring this GPO setting, you can additionally require that even admin accounts will have to re-punch their password before getting through a UAC prompt. Or, you can see here that you could alternatively **Elevate without prompting**, which squashes the UAC prompt and lets you make system admin changes without having to pass through UAC. Be careful here! While convenient, this is not a generally recommended way to go.

User Account Control – Behavior of the Elevation Prompt for Standard Users

This is the same idea as our previous setting, but now we are talking about affecting UAC permissions for the majority of your users—anyone who is a Standard User. Default behavior is to prompt the user for administrative credentials, as we saw when I tried to open an elevated PowerShell window.

Here you will also find an option that says **Prompt for credentials on the secure desktop**. This setting changes the look and feel of the UAC prompt to something that is Windows-specific. This allows you to give a sense of assurance that the UAC prompt is really from Windows, and is not a fake prompt being presented by a malware application. The third option here is to **Automatically deny elevation requests**—if your intentions are to build a secure, locked-down desktop where users should not have to make system changes or install software, why even allow the prompt at all? Just default-deny anything that the user tries to do outside the scope of their standard user rights.

Let's give this one a shot and see what happens. I have incorporated **Automatically deny elevation requests** into my GPO and assigned it to my LAPTOP1 computer. When I log back in as a standard user and attempt to open that same elevated PowerShell prompt, I no longer receive the prompt for admin credentials. Instead, I get a message informing me that I have been blocked:

User Account Control – Detecting Application Installations and Prompting for Elevation

Here, we can specify whether UAC prompts when application installers are launched. By default, it does prompt in this scenario, but there are some cases where you may want to disable this piece of UAC. By disabling only the installer-initiated prompt, you would continue to receive UAC prompts when a user tried to open an administrative window. This option is useful in cases where you are using some kind of software-push technology that attempts to install software onto the computers from a centralized location. You would not want UAC blocking this automated process from installing corporate-sanctioned software, so perhaps this UAC Group Policy setting could be used to allow those installers to be successful.

What is a little bit funny on this setting is that what UAC really watches for is executable files that start with `setu`, `instal`, or `update`. It is not really a smart logic that blocks all installers, but simply watches for appropriately-named files that signify installer or update packages. Malware does not typically take the approach of naming their files with these words, so while this is a good option to assist with software package pushes, relying on UAC to block all software installations is not foolproof.

User Account Control – Running All Administrators in Admin Approval Mode

By disabling this setting, you effectively disable UAC. While this is generally a bad idea, some of you will be visiting these UAC settings to figure out how to "turn off that stinkin' pop-up message," and this setting will accomplish that for you.

Blocking USB Drives

You have probably heard about the, "Whoops! I dropped my USB stick in the parking lot" penetration test that was performed years ago. If not, here is the short version: pen testers configured a bunch of USB memory sticks so that as soon as those sticks were plugged into a computer, they would immediately run some malicious code that the user was completely unaware of. Anybody who used one of these USB sticks would think it was a blank volume, waiting for them to store documents, pictures, whatever they needed. In the background, however, the USB stick would "phone home" and record when it was plugged in, proving that code can be executed by simply plugging in one of these USB drives.

Then... the pen testers dropped a bunch of these USB sticks in a company's parking lot. This is recalled strictly from my own memory, but the numbers were pretty staggering. I want to say that 80-something percent of users who found USB sticks walked right inside the office, and plugged them into their corporate, domain-joined computer to see what was on them. "What's the big deal?" you ask, "How bad could a little USB stick really be?"

I remember sitting in a Microsoft TechEd session once where our presenters convinced an attendee to bring their brand new Microsoft Surface to the front of the room, and to plug their USB stick into it. After reassuring him that they would remove the malware when the demonstration was finished, he reluctantly (this was an IT professional, after all) went ahead and plugged in the memory stick. Within seconds, I mean like three seconds, we were staring at a live video stream of him up on the big screen in front of the room. That USB stick had installed itself, established a connection with a server out on the internet, taken over his camera and was live-streaming his face to the web. Oh, and the software also made sure to disable the little light next to his camera, so other than seeing himself larger-than-life on the screen, he would have absolutely zero idea of what was happening to his computer. They could have done so much more, that little tablet was completely owned and theirs for the taking at that point.

Do not plug in USB drives unless you know for sure what is on them!

It is "cool" these days for businesses to hand out memory sticks full of marketing materials, rather than dumping business cards and paper product sheets in your lap. You should take those free USB sticks and throw them straight in the trash. Do not plug them in, do not think that you can be fast enough to format them before they do anything bad to your computer. It's not worth the risk.

Unfortunately, this is something that many IT folks don't even know, let alone end users. So, we need to proactively protect our computers from this vulnerability. The easiest way to do this is to wholesale disable USB drives from working, via one single policy setting inside Group Policy:

User Configuration | Policies | Administrative Templates | System | Removable Storage Access:

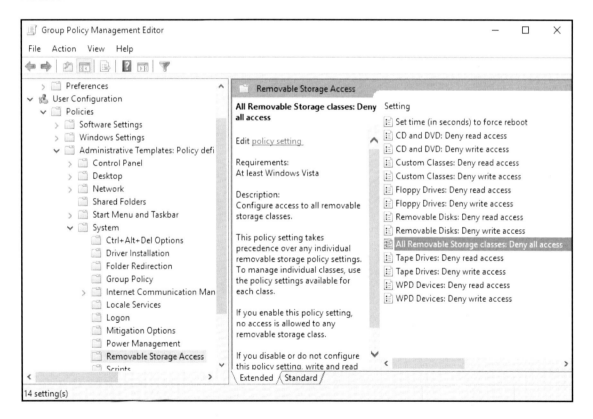

You can see that there are many different options here, if you wanted to selectively disable only floppy drives or CD/DVD drives. Even tape drives are listed! But, seriously, who uses those things anymore? Even CD/DVD drives don't come in many computers these days, we simply don't need them most of the time. So let's take the most secure approach and configure just a single setting: **All Removable Storage classes: Deny all access**. This blocks all drives identified as "removable storage" and gives us the best chance at protecting against those rogue USB devices, while still maintaining the ability to use our USB ports for things such as keyboards and mice.

Summary

There are many, many more security-related settings available inside Group Policy; it's simply impossible to cover all of them. Now that you have some baseline knowledge of how to implement these policies and where the security settings are stored in Group Policy (all over the place!), the possibilities are endless for coming up with creative new ways to lock down your systems. To me, creating a secure environment is the number one reason to utilize Group Policy in any domain environment, and I think that the majority of companies out there would increase their use of GPO security settings tenfold if they took the time to sift through the options and figure out what they really want from a desktop lockdown policy.

In addition to some sample ad-hoc settings that are useful to incorporate into almost any environment, we spent quite a bit of time discussing the WFAS. This updated firewall console is enterprise-class, and ready to protect your systems. Using Group Policy to configure WFAS in your environment should definitely be on your to-do list.

Now we find ourselves wandering into the less exciting land of Group Policy Maintenance. Nobody wants to spend time maintaining their Lamborghini; they would rather be out driving it! But alas, without some care and planning the wheels will eventually fall off. Let's go change the oil.

Group Policy Maintenance

8

As we begin to wind down this discussion on Group Policy, we close the chapters regarding the cool capabilities and functionality that exist inside this technology, and turn our attention to ensuring that Group Policy continues to run well in our environments. While maintenance tasks are always less glamorous than creation-type tasks, it is every GP administrator's duty to know how to perform the jobs outlined here.

The following topics will be covered in this chapter:

- Documenting Group Policy
- Searching Group Policy
- Starter GPOs
- Backing up and restoring GPOs
- Implementing ADMX/ADML files
- Delegating permissions to manage Group Policy

Documenting Group Policy

You do not need to write your own book about how Group Policy works in your environment, but the further you get into your journey of implementing GPOs in your organization, the more you will wish that you had followed some good documentation practices from the start. We already discussed naming GPOs according to the settings contained within, as this good practice alone will help tremendously when looking back on these GPOs a year down the road.

Additionally, there are some other things that you could be doing on a regular basis whenever you create a new policy that will help you to flesh out documentation for your AD environment. These items will be particularly useful for any other administrators that log into the domain and attempt to diagnose or otherwise figure out the purposes behind your policies.

Commenting inside GPOs

As we have moved through Group Policy and taken a look at numerous screenshots, you may have noticed some comment fields. Primarily used inside the GPOs, these comments can prove to be invaluable to other administrators who are filling your shoes for a day. Commenting inside policies will also become useful to your future self when you find yourself opening up a policy 2, 3, or 10 years down the road and wondering why in the world you implemented those settings in the first place.

Let's take a look at the places where we can insert comments into GPOs. Launch the GPMC with me, and expand out the `Group Policy Objects` folder so that we can view all of the GPOs that we have created throughout this book. Then, **Edit** a GPO to launch GPME. I am going to edit my GPO called `Auto-launch Notepad+Calc on login`. This policy is already aptly named so that anyone who looks at this policy will be able to guess exactly what it is doing, but we'll flesh out a comment in here anyway to give even more information.

The option to add comments is listed inside each policy setting. So, in order to add a comment appropriate for my policy, I will need to re-navigate to the location of my **Run these programs at user logon** setting, and double-click on that setting in order to edit it. This is exactly the same screen where we went to create this policy in the first place, so you can see how it makes the most sense to add in these comments on day one, immediately when creating the policy and plugging settings into it.

I am simply going to populate the **Comment** field with a little bit of useful information. I like to include the date and my initials with the comment. That way, other administrators who log in here and take a look at your policy will have a clear idea about who created this, when they created it, and for what purpose. It is also helpful to include your initials here for searching purposes, which we will review later in this chapter:

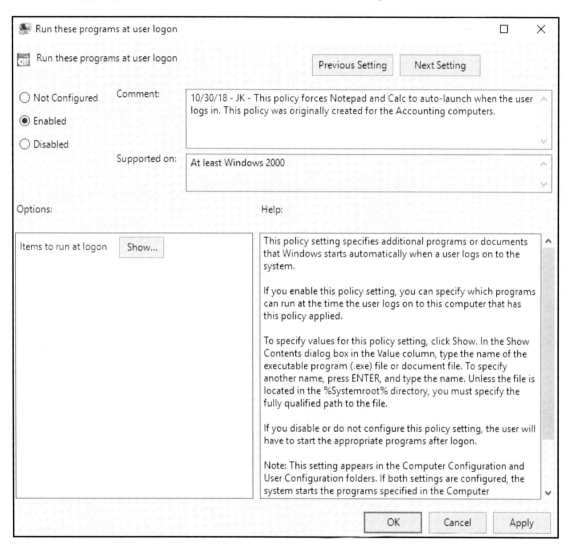

Generating a GPO report

Another incredibly useful documentation feature inside GPMC is the ability to export a report for any given GPO. There are two different places from which you can generate this report. On the left tree of the screen, you can simply right-click on any GPO (or even a link to a GPO), and choose **Save Report...**:

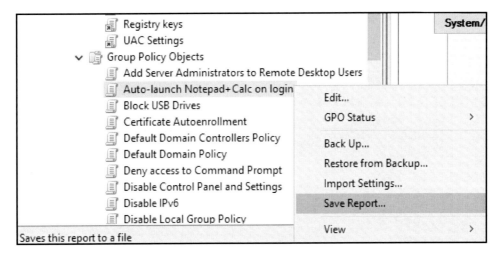

Alternatively, if you are already looking inside the **Settings** tab for any given GPO, you may also right-click anywhere inside the **Settings** screen and choose the option to **Save Report...**.

Whichever location you use for clicking on this option, all you need to do is specify a location and name for saving this report, and select whether you want it to be an **HTML File** or **XML File**. I like the look and feel of these settings inside HTML, so I am going to select that option:

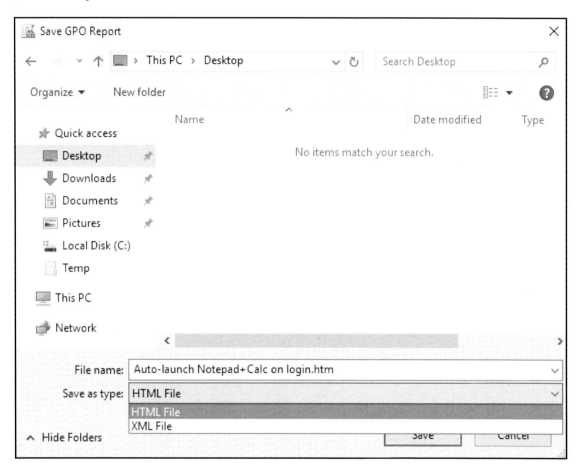

Now, double-click on the report file in order to open it, and view the data stored inside. The generated report contains information from the **Details** tab inside the Group Policy, so you can quickly discover whether user or computer configuration settings were disabled. It also shows all of the active links related to this policy. **Security Filtering** settings and **Delegation** are listed next. Finally, down at the bottom of the report are all of the settings stored inside this GPO. With the information provided inside this little report file, you could completely recreate your GPO from scratch in the event that it was ever accidentally deleted or modified:

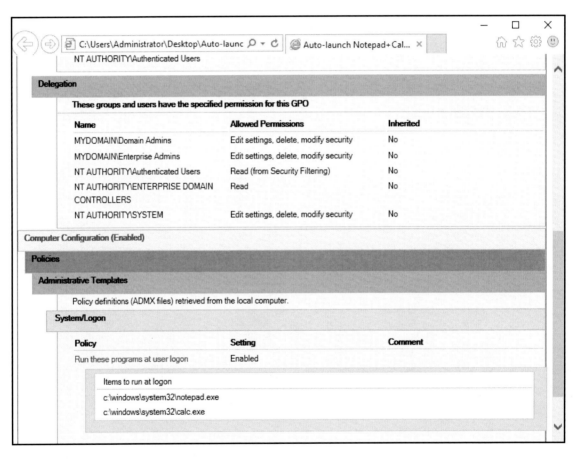

It may be smart to store these reports somewhere centrally. If you take two seconds and create this report immediately after creating any new policy, you will always have a backup "paper" copy of every single one of your GPOs and the settings contained within. You could also create new reports after any change to an existing GPO. In the event of a catastrophic failure of Active Directory or a recovery gone wrong, where you lose GPOs and their settings, you could then utilize these reports in order to rebuild the environment.

Searching Group Policy

We live in a search-driven world. Almost any answer to any question is available at our fingertips, with 5,770,000,000 results presented to us in 0.50 seconds. Are we losing a human element in today's IoT-focused world? Absolutely. Need to change brake pads on your new car? Maybe it used to be the case that you would pick up the phone and call your father or grandfather for some advice, or even to invite them over to help out. Now, there is a good chance that at least 30 different people have YouTube videos walking you through changing those pads, every step of the way. Does your child have an interest in sewing? A common-sense wealth of knowledge on this subject may be your own grandmother or a neighbor down the street, but taking that approach requires time and effort, and it is just easier to find online tutorials that you can start right now, from your cellphone.

I think this is terrible. However, the technology behind the change in behaviors is enormously impressive, and I use it all the time. Online searching is how we "do life" now. If you start using Group Policy to its full extent, I guarantee that you will visit search engines often in order to quickly track down which settings are best suited for your purposes. There is also a search functionality built right into Group Policy, and it is important to know how to utilize these searches to quickly find GPOs or settings in your own environment.

Searching for GPOs

First, let's search for GPOs. Right now, our test lab is small enough that it is pretty easy to identify and find whatever GPO we are looking for within a few seconds of clicking around, but the more you utilize Group Policy, the larger that list of GPOs will grow. Pretty soon, you will forget what policies you put into place. Do you need to implement some new Internet Explorer settings? Do you really want to immediately create a new GPO, when it is possible that there is already an existing GPO full of IE settings? Maybe it would make more sense to modify the existing policy, rather than create a new one. But, did you name that policy starting with `Internet Explorer`, or something such as `Security for IE`, or maybe even `Much ado about IE settings`? Hmm, if we look inside the Group Policy Object's alphabetically-organized folder full of GPOs, we might be here for a while trying to decide whether we have an existing policy that deals with IE settings.

Instead of doing that, simply right-click on the name of your domain (or forest) inside GPMC, and select **Search...**.

There are many criteria from which you can search through Group Policy. You can search for GPO Names, links, security groups, even by GUID if you happen to know it. I would guess that the most common search criteria is **GPO Name**, so I will utilize that one. I am going to search for any **GPO Name** that **Contains** the word settings.

After specifying that criteria, press the **Add** button to add that to the **All search criteria** box, and then click the **Search** button. We see in the following screenshot that four of my GPOs have names that include the word settings, and right from this screen I could even click the **Edit** button to head straight into one of those policies:

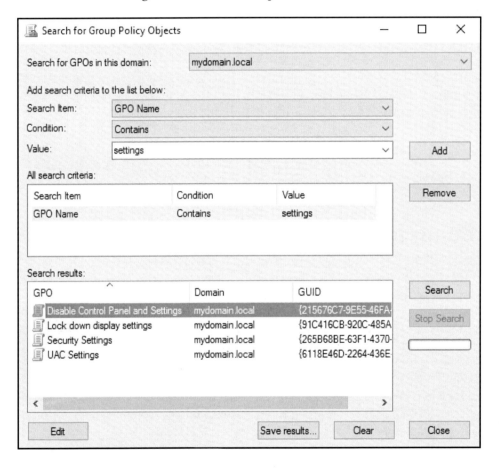

While this search functionality is extremely useful for identifying GPOs that you have named properly, indicating the use of the GPO as part of the name, the capabilities of this search screen for looking inside of GPOs is limited. You cannot simply throw in a keyword and search for any settings that might contain that keyword. But, you can still do some searching inside the GPO configuration settings. For example, by clearing our search results and now searching for **Computer Configuration – Contains – Registry**, we are now viewing search results of all the GPOs that are accomplishing registry changes on our client machines.

When searching for something inside **Computer Configuration** or **User Configuration**, you are not able to type in the field to specify your own **Value** criteria. Instead, you are limited to a predefined drop-down box that lists the searchable options, of which **Registry** was a value I could choose:

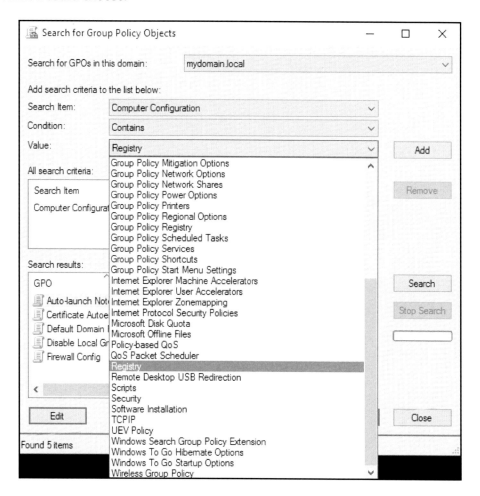

Filtering settings

While searching for criteria about the GPOs is helpful, searching for criteria *inside* of GPOs is even better. There is an ability to hone in on particular settings within a GPO. This is really more akin to filtering than it is to searching, but is still useful. This is probably the most powerful search function inside Group Policy, because GPO settings is a vast wilderness that contains thousands and thousands of possibilities. Rather than resorting to an online search engine, let's find out what results can be obtained by using the built-in filtering capabilities.

 It is important to note that filtering settings within a GPO only works for **Administrative Templates**. It's a bummer that this same capability is not ported over to **Software Settings** or **Windows Settings**, but alas I guess we will take what we can get.

Filtering for **Computer Configuration** and **User Configuration** will be separate entities. If you create a filter inside **Computer Configuration** so that its **Administrative Templates** are only showing you filtered results, moving over to the **User Configuration** will not be filtered in any way, unless you configure a second filter inside that node.

To get started with creating a filter, edit one of your GPOs. Once inside GPME, navigate to the `Policies` folder of either `Computer Configuration` or `User Configuration`, and then right-click on your `Administrative Templates` folder in order to select **Filter Options...**:

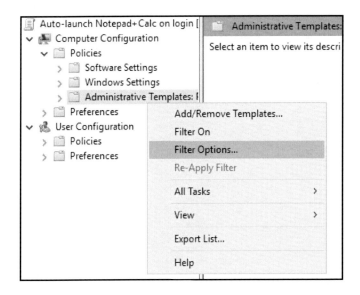

Filtering by keywords

In my own experience, searching for particular keywords is the most useful feature here. This is particularly true if you have a certain task in mind. For example, what if we wanted to take a peek at what settings exist regarding roaming profiles? You could turn to the internet and look it up that way, or you could create a filter inside GPME to discover all settings that contain the words `roaming profile`.

Here is a screenshot of filter criteria that are going to narrow down my scope to only policy settings that contain the words `roaming` and `profile`:

Much of this screen is self-explanatory. Under the **Enable Keyword Filters** section, you can see that I have typed the keywords that I want to search for, and told it that any results need to include **All**, which means only show me results where the settings contain both words. There is another option there for **Any**, but that would then also show me all settings that contained `roaming` or `profile` separately, and that would likely give me many results that I am not interested in. Then, underneath the keywords that I typed, I have options to search for these words inside the **Policy Setting Title**, inside the **Help Text** that is contained within the setting, or even within the **Comment** field inside those settings. If you want to search for all instances of `roaming profile` across any of these text fields, select all three checkboxes.

There are a few drop-down menus across the top of the **Filter Options** screen that we should take a minute to discuss:

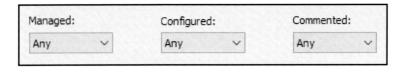

- **Managed**: This will filter results based on whether the policy setting is managed. We learned earlier that "managed" means the setting resides inside one of those special registry locations, and as such managed policy settings are able to automatically remove themselves when a GPO no longer applies. Selecting **Yes** here will display only managed policy settings, and selecting **No** shows only settings that are non-managed. I have chosen **Any**, so that I will see both managed and non-managed settings in my filtered results.
- **Configured**: Configured is an indicator as to whether the policy settings to be displayed have been configured at all by an administrator inside this GPO. If you select **Yes**, you will only see settings that have already been configured in the policy. **No** will display only settings that have not yet been configured, and **Any** displays both configured and non-configured policy settings.
- **Commented**: You probably have this one figured out already; this dropdown will configure the filter based on whether a comment exists inside the policy settings. Choosing **Yes** would only show you results for settings that have comments typed into them. **No** will show only settings that have no comments, and **Any** will display both commented and non-commented policy settings.

When searching for settings based on keywords, it is most common to leave all three of these dropdowns set to **Any**.

After clicking **OK**, I am not presented with search results as you might expect. Instead, I am taken back into the main GPME screen for editing my GPO, except that I notice it has changed. Prior to setting up my filter, I would have had much more information listed here under **Administrative Templates** – now there are only a few folders. I also notice that these folders now have a little gray funnel icon tagged onto them. This is your indication that you are viewing a filtered set of data. The GPME is now presenting to me only the Group Policy settings that have passed my filtering criteria. If I expand the folders available, I will notice that all of the settings are in some way related to roaming profiles, which is cool:

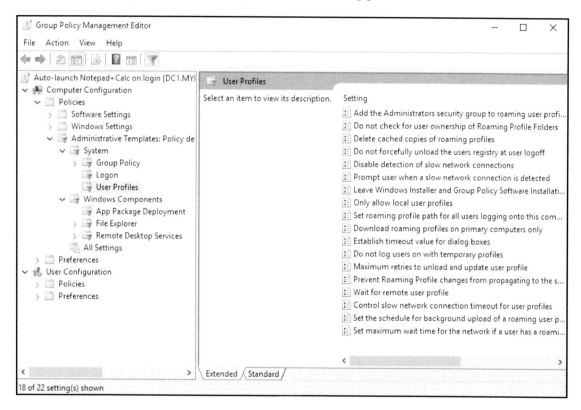

Filtering by your own comments

Let's look at another filtering example, and at the same time prove to you that typing comments into your Group Policy settings is a beneficial use of your time. Heading back into **Filter Options**, let's now remove our keyword specifications and instead create one simple filtering requirement. Change the drop-down menu for **Commented** to say **Yes**:

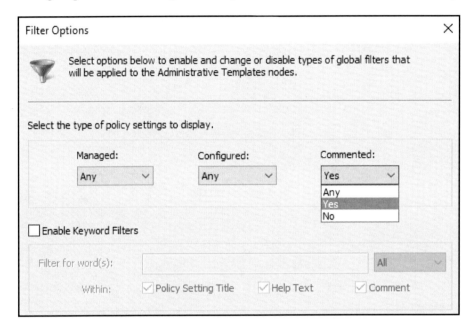

This filter will display for us only policy settings that have had comments added to them by us, the administrators. You can see those results in the following screenshot, and as you will notice there is only one policy setting being displayed to me inside my **Computer Configuration | Administrative Templates** – the **Run these programs at user logon** setting that I am using inside this GPO. This is the only policy setting inside `Administrative Templates` (within this GPO) that has a comment attached to it:

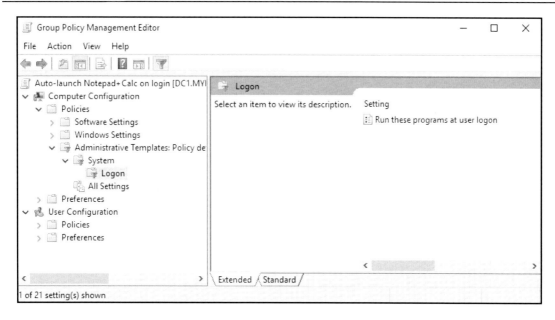

There is also the option to combine the comments selection with a keyword search. By choosing **Commented=Yes**, and then specifying a **Keyword Filter** that says JK with the **Comment** box checked, I am telling the filter to display for me settings that are commented, but only where the **Comments** section includes JK (these are my initials):

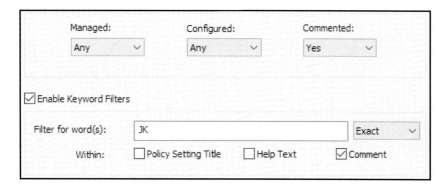

This is one of the reasons that I always type my initials into comment fields. If another admin stumbles upon my settings, they know who put it into place. Additionally, if I wanted to filter a GPO and find all settings that I put into place, by having my initials plugged into the **Comment** field on all of those settings, they are easily searchable.

Filtering by settings that have been modified

Often, you will find yourself with a task to modify a GPO, only to put off this simple, little task for days because you do not feel like poking through all of the available Group Policy settings in order to find the setting that needs to be adjusted. Well, procrastinate no more! There is a super-simple way to filter GPME so that it only displays the settings that have already been modified inside your GPO.

Pick any GPO from your environment, and **Edit** that guy in order to open GPME. Then, right-click on **Administrative Templates** (yes, once again it is unfortunate that these filtering options only exist for **Administrative Templates**), and choose **Filter Options...**.

Only one simple change is needed to filter GPME to display only already-modified settings. Click on the **Configured** box, and select **Yes**. Now, click **OK**, and your GPME window will immediately be filtered to show you only **Administrative Template** settings that have been modified. All of the other thousands of untouched settings will be hidden away so that you can very quickly and easily look through what has already been configured in this policy, and make changes to those settings if necessary.

Clearing the filter

Clearing out the filter that you just created is very simple, but it is important to do because once a filter is set on a GPO, it tends to stick around until you manually turn it off. For example, I closed GPME after I was done poking around inside my Notepad+Calc policy, and then re-edited that GPO. Once opened, I was still only seeing bits and pieces of the policy, until I realized that my filter was still enabled even though I had exited and come back into that policy.

To clear your search results filter within a GPO, simply right-click on the `Administrative Templates` folder that you have filtered, and deselect the **Filter On** option:

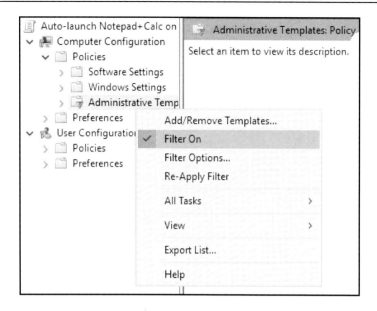

If you need to re-enable your filter, do the opposite. Rechecking the **Filter On** option immediately turns the filter back on. It remembers your last filter criteria from the **Filter Options** screen, so there is no need to resubmit that criteria.

Starter GPOs

In your work with Group Policy so far, you have probably noticed the phrase "Starter GPO". Every time that you click to create a new GPO, one of the options on that screen is to select a **Source Starter GPO**, but the option is initially grayed out. What is that thing?

Starter GPOs are sort of like GPO templates. You, as the primary Group Policy administrator, have the ability to create these special GPOs, called **Starter GPOs**, and then when junior-level administrators need to build out a GPO containing settings, they can look through the list of Starter GPOs and select one of these preconfigured policies that you put together. This gives you the ability to hand off the grunt work part of creating policies, while ensuring that the settings you always want configured are implemented inside the GPOs from the start. You are providing them with a starting point, so they do not have to reinvent the wheel of knowledge that you already took time to put together inside the Starter GPOs.

When that junior administrator goes to create a new GPO, they select a Starter GPO, and all of the settings baked into that Starter GPO get plugged into their new GPO automatically. It is also helpful for them if you provide comments alongside the settings that you configure, as those will also come through from the Starter GPO into their real GPO.

Creating a Starter GPO

To begin working with Starter GPOs, you first need to enable them in Group Policy. Open up GPMC, and look on the left-hand side for the folder called `Starter GPOs`. Click on that folder, and you will see one big button for you to click on that says **Create Starter GPOs Folder**:

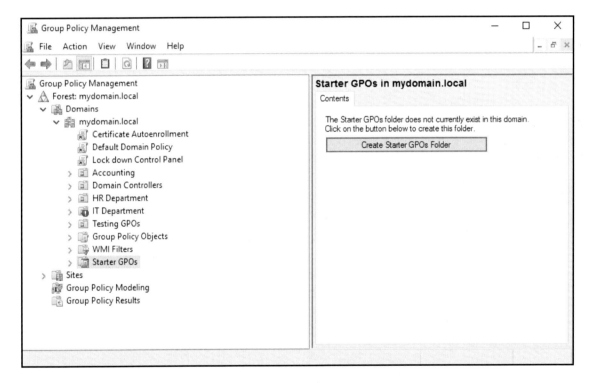

Clicking this button immediately enables you to create and use Starter GPOs in the environment. You will notice that two Starter GPOs show up automatically (or possibly more, if you are running an older version of the GPMC). These default Starter GPOs state that they are the **System** type, which is simply your way of identifying them as the Starter GPOs that were pre-built for you. Any new Starter GPOs that you create yourself will show the type as **Custom**.

To create a new one, right-click on **Starter GPOs** and select **New...**:

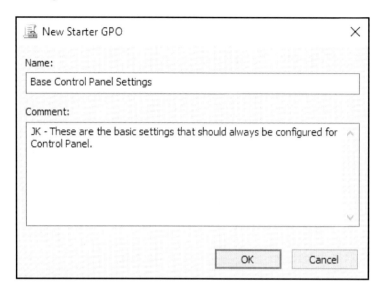

Provide this new Starter GPO with a **Name** and a **Comment** (again, this will be helpful for other admins to know what you were thinking when you created this object), and then click **OK**. Your new Starter GPO now exists inside GPMC, but currently it has no settings inside of it.

Editing a Starter GPO

It makes sense that our next step when dealing with Starter GPOs is to edit that policy and give it some settings. Editing a Starter GPO is exactly like editing any other GPO, except that you will find you are restricted to only the settings contained inside the `Administrative Templates` folders, as you can see in the following screenshot.

Right-click on the new Starter GPO that you just created, and choose **Edit...**:

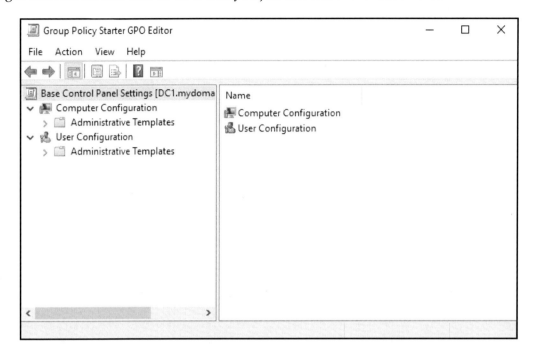

Using a Starter GPO to build finalized GPOs

Now that we have a Starter GPO that contains some settings, I am going to pretend that I am the apprentice to the Group Policy administrator, and need to build my own GPO. There are a couple of different ways that I can invoke a new GPO that builds off of a Starter GPO. One way is to navigate to the `Starter GPOs` folder, find your Starter GPO, right-click on it, and select **New GPO From Starter GPO...**:

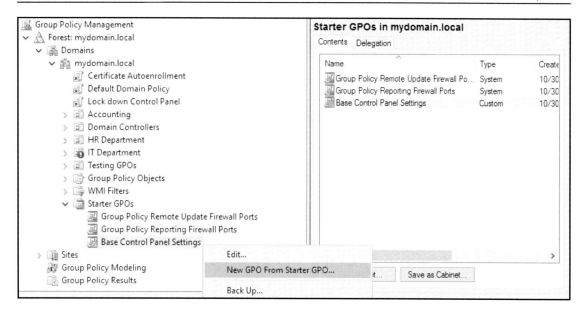

Alternatively, junior administrators can right-click on the main **Group Policy Objects** folder and select **New** just like they would with any other GPO. The first screen that is presented asks for a **Name** input for the new GPO, and gives you the opportunity on this same screen to specify a **Source Starter GPO**. You can see in the following screenshot that I am creating a new GPO called **Accounting Control Panel Settings**, and have chosen to utilize the Starter GPO called **Base Control Panel Settings**:

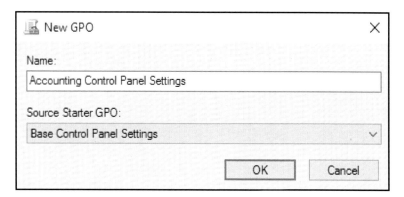

As soon as this new GPO is created, if you take a look at the **Settings** screen, you can see that the handful of settings that were included in the Source Starter GPO, in this case **Base Control Panel Settings,** have already been implemented into the new Accounting GPO:

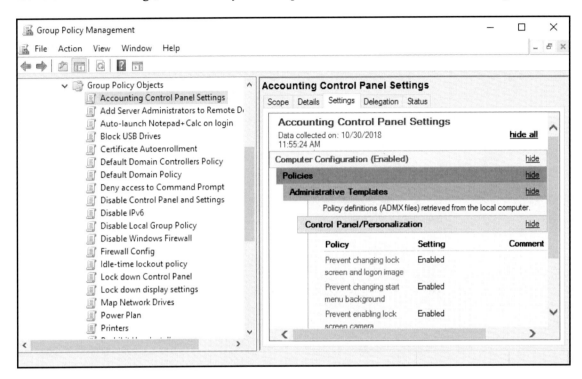

Backing up and restoring GPOs

Backups are critical inside any environment. To most users, this means storing extra copies of their documents in case they are lost, but those of us who work in IT know that backups mean so, so much more. It's not just about keeping multiple offsite copies of data in case that data is lost or damaged; backups are also a key piece to any disaster-recovery scenario. When a server goes down, you need a plan (and a backup) to deal with restoring that server. When a system gets hacked, you need a plan and a backup in order to wipe and restore that machine. It would be great if we had one big Backup Now button for a domain and everything inside of it, but the reality is that each piece of technology we use inside our networks has special considerations when it comes to backups.

This is especially true when it comes to Domain Controllers and the data that resides on them. Not only do physical Domain Controller servers have special backup requirements, but more and more companies are running virtual Domain Controllers and those have some interesting gotchas when trying to keep copies of those virtual machines. As you know, Group Policy data is stored on your Domain Controller servers. Since most companies run multiple Domain Controllers, and Group Policy data is automatically replicated among all DCs, simply having multiple servers in the mix offers some redundancy for Group Policy built right into the solution. If you are keeping good backups of those Domain Controllers, even better – you now have built-in redundancy as well as copies of the actual data that could be restored in a pinch.

Backups and restores in Group Policy are, therefore, more like rollback capabilities than they are actual data-recovery capabilities. At least, this is true in practice. You create backups of GPOs in order to create rollback points in case the change you are about to make goes sideways. Or, perhaps you make it standard practice to create a new backup of any GPO that you touch for any reason. GPO backups are incredibly small; you can keep many copies of all your GPOs and not have to worry about disk space for storing these backups.

Keeping backups of GPOs then allows some interesting scenarios. If an administrator makes a change within a GPO and it creates a negative result, you can simply roll that GPO back to the previous settings. Additionally, if someone accidentally (or purposefully) deletes a GPO and that causes problems, you can very quickly slap that GPO back into place with a very fast, very simple restoration wizard. It would be a rare occurrence that you would actually have to run a full operating system recovery process on a Domain Controller server, but could be an everyday task to restore an individual GPO. Let's take a few minutes and make sure that we are familiar and comfortable with backing up and restoring Group Policy Objects.

Backing up GPOs

You can see file-based information about your GPOs inside `SYSVOL`, and some people mistakenly believe that keeping a filesystem-level backup of that folder is all that they need to consider their GPOs backed up. While this file data could be useful, it is not the full picture. Log into your Domain Controller, and take a look at the following location: `C:\Windows\SYSVOL\sysvol\mydomain.local` (if you have configured your Domain Controller with something other than `C:\Windows` as `%systemroot%`, then navigate there instead).

Here, you will see a folder for `Policies`, one for `Scripts`, and one for `StarterGPOs` (if you followed along in *Using a Starter GPO* to build finalized GPOs and enabled Starter GPOs in your environment). This is the file structure data used by Group Policy. Opening up the `Policies` folder shows us a bunch of strange-looking GUIDs, and each one is a folder for one of our GPOs:

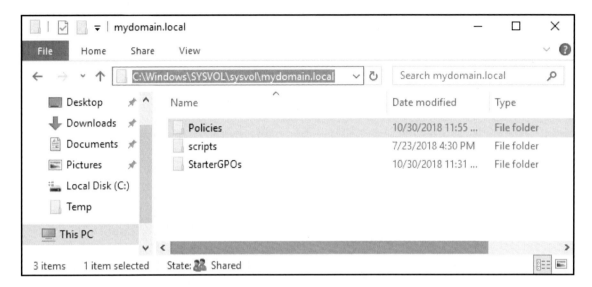

The process of backing up a GPO combines this Group Policy Container information stored in `SYSVOL` with Group Policy Template data inside Active Directory. These two pieces of information are combined into backup files that are saved wherever you specify during the backup process. Here is a list of the types of data that are saved when backing up any GPO:

- **The GPO settings**
- **The GPO permissions** (visible on the **Delegation** tab of the GPO)
- **WMI Filter Links**: Only information about which WMI Filters were linked is stored, the WMI Filters themselves are not stored when you back up a GPO. The actual WMI Filters need to be backed up separately, which we will cover later in this chapter. This is necessary because WMI Filters are not stored inside Group Policy Objects, but rather stored alongside them in Active Directory.
- **GPO Link Locations**: While GPO Links are indeed stored inside a GPO backup, the process of recovering a GPO does NOT restore GPO links. We will also discuss this in more depth when we cover the restoration of GPOs.

Permissions needed to back up a GPO

In order to backup GPOs, you need sufficient rights to open and view the information inside GPMC. Additionally, you will need read permissions on each GPO that you want to back up. Typically, those who are backing up GPOs are already running in the context of a Domain Admin, because that enables you to do anything inside Group Policy – but in the event that you wanted to delegate away the task of backups, it is important to know the necessary permissions.

Backing up a single GPO

Backing up a single GPO really could not be easier. Open up GPMC, and navigate to the primary `Group Policy Objects` folder. Once expanded so that you can see all of your GPOs, choose one and right-click on it. Then, click **Back Up...**:

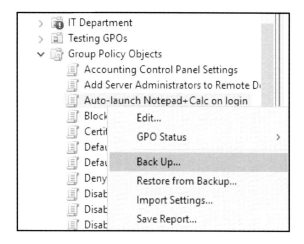

Simply specify a **Location** where you want to store this backup, and a helpful **Description** that can later be seen by anyone who may be trying to restore this GPO:

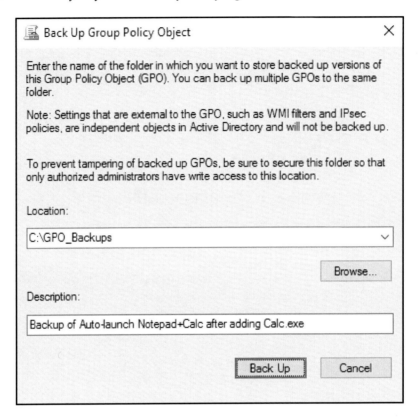

It is usually a good practice to store your GPO backups in a single location. This is true even when you have multiple backup copies of the same GPO. When you create a GPO backup, the output backup file begins with a unique, random GUID (this is different from the GPO's actual GUID inside AD). This means that even if you store 100 backup copies of the exact same GPO inside the same folder, they will not overwrite each other, and you will have the ability during restoration to choose from any of those backups. In the following screenshot, you can see my C:\GPO_Backups folder after I have run a few GPO backup jobs. Some of these are backups of the same GPO, but are stored separately because of those unique GUIDs that are generated:

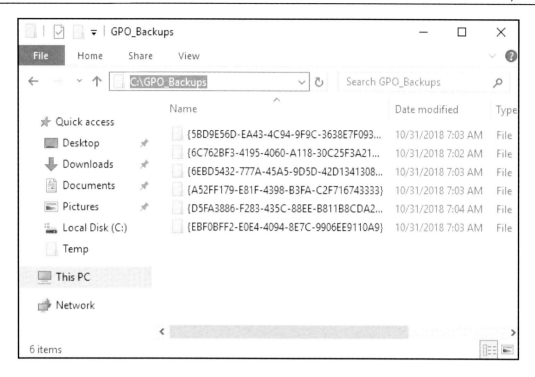

Backing up all GPOs at once

Right-clicking and choosing to back up an individual GPO is very quick, but it would still be an enormous pain in the neck if you were trying to back up all 697 GPOs that are in use within your domain. Thankfully, there is a very fast and easy way to create backups of *all* your GPOs at once.

The easiest way to make backup copies of all your GPOs is to right-click on the `Group Policy Objects` folder, and select **Back Up All...** from the menu. Here, you simply populate the screen asking for the backup **Location** and **Description**, and when you click the **Back Up** button, you can step away, grab a coffee, and wait for it to finish. That's it!

Just like with individual GPO backups, you can **Back Up All** into the same directory as many times as you want. All of the backup copies of the GPOs will remain unique because of those random GUID numbers being generated during the backup process. This allows you to retain all kinds of historical rollback points for your GPOs:

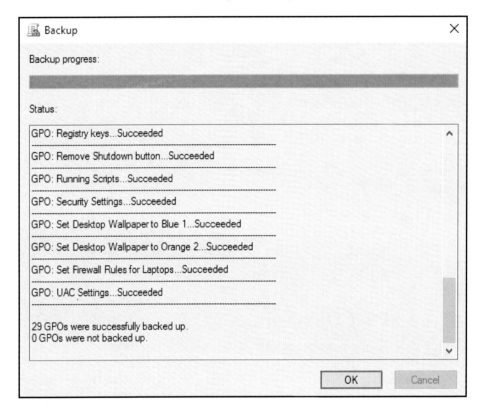

Restoring GPOs

Whenever discussing the restoration of data from a backup, it is always the goal that you never actually have to enact these steps. Recovering backup data is generally associated with disaster-recovery, which is not a situation that any IT professional wants to find themselves in the middle of. However, there are two different reasons why you might find yourself needing to restore a GPO, and one of them is something that can actually be quite common. Restoring a GPO could become necessary in the event that a GPO is lost, deleted, or somehow corrupted. In these cases, you are still in that disaster-recovery boat, wanting to recover the GPO in order to restore order to the force.

The second, and much more common, reason to restore a GPO is to roll it back to a prior point in time. Let's say you have a working GPO, and want to add an extra setting into it. You take a backup of that GPO before you make the change, and then edit the GPO to introduce the new setting. Let's also pretend that you forgot to test this setting out on some laptops before rolling it out to production, and now you discover that this new setting is causing a big issue. There are two different paths you could follow. One would be to re-edit the GPO and remove the setting that you just plugged in, but depending on the setting (or settings), you might have to spend quite a bit of time poking around in here to negate all the things you put into place. Alternatively, you can simply recover the GPO to its previous state, based on the backup that you took right before you made the change.

This second scenario is one that you may have to utilize numerous times during your role as an AD/GPO administrator.

Permissions needed to restore an existing GPO

Backing up GPOs requires minimal levels of permissions on those GPOs, but more are needed in order to recover a GPO. This makes sense, since we are talking about writing into Active Directory, or even overwriting existing GPO settings. To be able to restore an existing GPO, one that is still sitting inside AD but that you want to roll back to a previous point in time, you will need to have the permission entitled **Edit settings**, **delete**, **modify security**.

Permissions needed to restore a deleted GPO

If you are facing the challenge of recovering a GPO that was completely deleted and no longer exists inside Active Directory, you will need slightly higher rights to accomplish that. You will need to have the same access permissions as someone who is able to create new GPOs, because that is essentially what you will be doing when you walk through the process of recovering that deleted GPO. It creates a new one, and pumps the settings back into it.

To create new GPOs, or to restore deleted GPOs, you need to be a member of a built-in Active Directory Security Group that is called **Group Policy Creator Owners**. We will learn a little bit more about this group in the *Delegating permissions to manage Group Policy* section.

As always, if you have access to a user account that is part of the Domain Admins or Enterprise Admins groups, you will have all the permissions you need to do anything inside Group Policy, including the restoration of deleted GPOs.

Two ways to restore a GPO

There are two different mechanisms inside GPMC that can be used to restore a GPO.

The first is a simple right-click of the GPO that you want to restore, and choosing the option called **Restore from Backup...**.

This invokes the **Restore Group Policy Object Wizard**, which is a pretty fast and simple walk-through. Specify the location of your backup files (if you always back up to the same folder, it auto-inserts this information), and then the wizard will display all of the different versions inside this backup folder that exist for this specific GPO. You can see in the following screenshot that I have selected to restore my Auto-launch applications GPO, and there are three different rollback points listed. You can easily determine which is the newest by the **Time Stamp** displayed for each backup copy, as well as being able to review the notes that I typed when I was performing these backups. You can even use the **View Settings...** button to open up the HTML report of what is inside this GPO. That is an awesome feature:

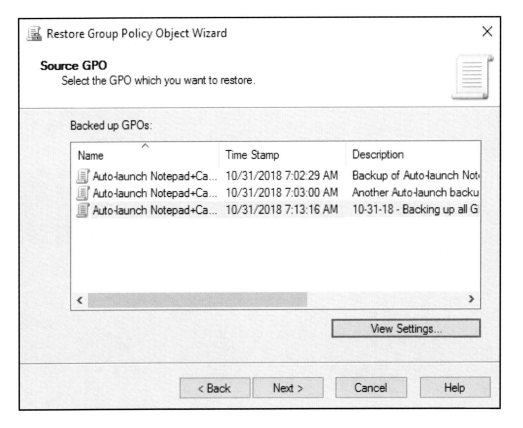

After selecting the version of backup that you want to restore, click **Next** and **Finish** and the GPO is immediately rolled back to the previous settings.

Managing backups

The second, and more comprehensive, way to restore GPOs is by launching the **Manage Backups** tool. You do this by right-clicking on the `Group Policy Objects` folder, and selecting **Manage Backups...**:

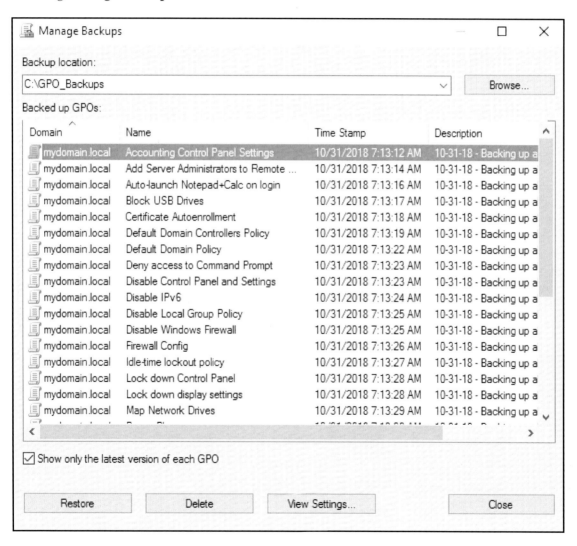

Here, you can see all of the backup files and versions that are sitting inside my `C:\GPO_Backups` folder. This tool is definitely the way to go if you need to restore multiple GPOs. All that you need to do is select a backup copy, and click the **Restore** button. This rolls the GPO back to the settings defined inside the backup. As you can see, the **View Settings...** button is also available in this tool, and there is a neat checkbox to **Show only the latest version of each GPO**. If you are confident that the latest backup you took is the one you want to roll back to, selecting this box really narrows down the number of objects that are presented to you inside this screen.

When trying to restore a GPO that has been deleted from Group Policy, the **Manage Backups** tool is the right place for you. By browsing through the backup files for the GPO that was deleted, you can very quickly and easily restore the GPO right from this interface.

Relinking restored GPOs

When you recover a GPO that was still in existence, all of your links should still be fine and dandy. But, if you have restored a GPO that had previously been deleted, we now need to do some damage control. GPO Links will have to be re-established manually. Why doesn't this happen automatically as part of the GPO restore process? Well, what if link locations changed between the date of your last backup and your date of GPO restoration? Or, what if the GPO was deleted because it was causing problems? You would not want the restore process to immediately relink and therefore start causing those problems all over again. So, the restoration process leaves it on our shoulders to relink the GPO after it has been recovered. Thankfully, there is information stored right inside the backup files about what links existed at the time the backup was taken. You can view this information by doing the following:

1. Right-click on **Group Policy Objects** and choose **Manage Backups...**.
2. If it's not already selected, browse to the location of your backup file.
3. Select the GPO that you restored or are planning to restore, and then click **View Settings...**.
4. Inside the presented HTML file, browse to the **Links** section. This shows you all of the links that were active when this backup file was created, and you can use this information to manually re-establish links to OUs in your environment after the restore is complete:

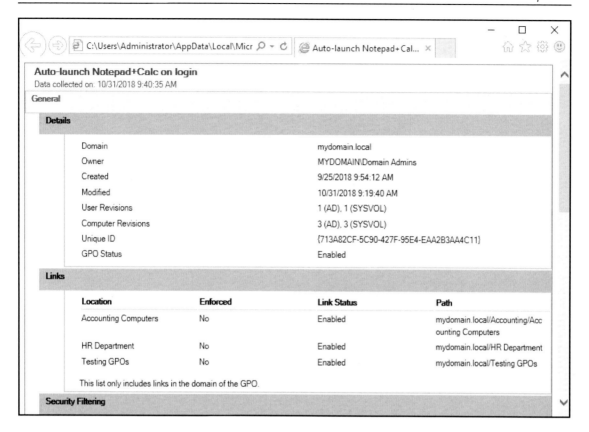

Exporting and Importing WMI Filters

While I love the idea of WMI Filters, I am going to be honest: not many people use them. Chances are that you do not need to worry about backing up or restoring WMI Filters, because chances are that you do not utilize them in your Group Policy filtering. However, if you are one of the brave few that use this powerful capability, it is important to note that WMI Filters are not backed up or restored through the conventional GPO backup/restore processes. They are handled separately, and have their own wizards to walk through in order to back them up, or to restore those backups. Technically, what we are really doing is exporting and importing those filters.

Very similar to backing up GPOs, all you need to do is right-click on the WMI Filter that you want to save, and choose **Export...**.

This generates a `WMI Filter MOF files (*.mof)` and all you need to do is choose a place to store this file, give it a name, and click **Save**:

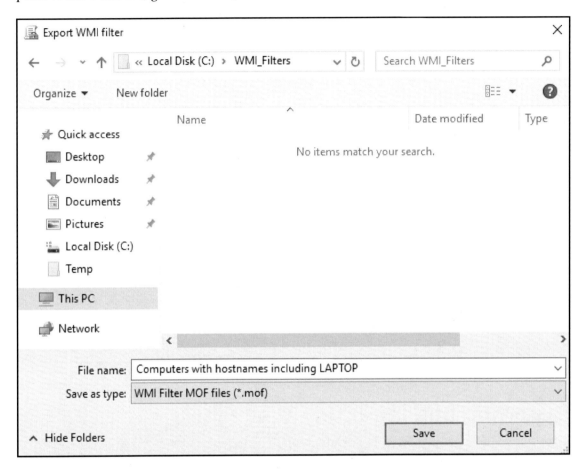

The WMI Filter is now exported out to this file for safekeeping. In the event that you lose or mistakenly delete a WMI Filter from inside GPMC, the process for bringing it back is even easier. Right-click on the `WMI Filters` folder, and choose **Import...**

Select the MOF file that you want to import, and you will then have a chance to review the WMI query that resides inside this saved file. If everything looks good, click the **Import** button and this WMI Filter is now restored to Group Policy and ready to be used for filtering:

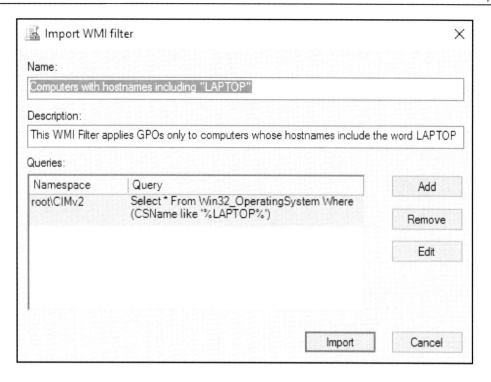

Implementing ADMX/ADML files

You already know a little bit about ADMX and ADML files – that they are used when new settings need to make their way into the Administrative Templates section of the Group Policy Editor. Now, we need to figure out how to actually use them in our environment.

There are a few different reasons that you may need to work with ADMX files to modify your templates. One is when making Group-Policy-management platform changes. Each new Windows operating system that releases comes with some new settings and functionality inside of Group Policy. For example, the GPMC inside Server 2016 has more capabilities than a GPMC running on Server 2012 R2. If you would rather continue using your Server 2012R2 for GPMC management duties, rather than spinning up a Server 2016 (or Windows 10 client) for this purpose, you could grab the ADMX files from a Server 2016 and copy them over to receive the new functionality. Another reason to become familiar with using ADMX files is that software vendors (including Microsoft) will sometimes release customized ADMX/ADML files for administrators to use in order to modify and interact with some of their software offerings. Third, you may need to create your own template settings in order to customize homegrown applications.

Whatever your reasoning for using ADMX files, let's work together to put some into place so that you are familiar with the process.

Importing a new ADMX file

Let's jump right in and import one of these files to give us some new settings inside Group Policy! One of the things I commonly do in this area is import settings from Microsoft for a tool called the **DirectAccess Connectivity Assistant** (**DCA**). This is a piece of software that Microsoft developed, but one for which they do not have settings built into Group Policy out of the box. Instead of configuring the DCA tool individually on each workstation, Microsoft provides an ADMX file available for download that allows the configurable settings to be injected into Group Policy. From there, we can easily pump these settings into a GPO, and roll them out to everyone that way.

For the moment, we are going to continue focusing on our existing test lab environment, which is composed of a single Domain Controller. This means that all Active Directory files are stored locally on that server. The process for working with ADMX files changes slightly when inside a domain with multiple DCs, but starting here will be good background information to better understand this process.

The location for placing ADMX files

The beauty of ADMX/ADML files is that the process for importing them is as simple as making sure those files exist in the proper locations. After copying your files into the correct places, the next time that you launch GPMC they will be automatically available inside the interface.

On a single Domain Controller, the location for copying our new ADMX file is `C:\Windows\PolicyDefinitions`.

 Technically, the location is `%systemroot%\PolicyDefinitions` – if your Domain Controller has something other than `C:\Windows` defined as `%systemroot%`, you'll need to drop the file inside that location instead.

You will see many ADMX files listed inside this location. Yes, this is where all of the existing settings inside GPMC's `Administrative Templates` folders are being pulled from:

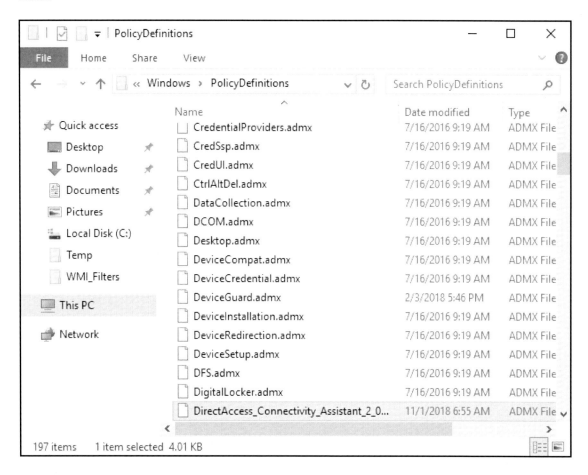

The location for placing ADML files

Before ADMX and ADML files existed, this process was handled by older ADM files. In those days, there were fewer files overall, but each file contained much more data. Now, ADMX files are language-neutral, so they contain an accompanying ADML language file. The ADMX file contains details about the settings that can be changed by this policy, while the ADML file contains all of the text strings and descriptions (such as the text listed on the Explain tab inside each setting) that correlate to those settings. This makes it possible to port settings over to multiple languages. Every ADMX file should have a corresponding ADML file, and each language has a folder listed inside `PolicyDefinitions`. For example, here in the US, we typically utilize the following location for placing our English ADML files:

`C:\Windows\PolicyDefinitions\en-US`

Again, `C:\Windows` is really whatever your `%systemroot%` definition points to.

Once both the ADMX and ADML files are in place, open up GPMC and edit a GPO. Now, when navigating into **Computer Configuration** | **Policies** | **Administrative Templates**, we can see a brand new folder listed here that is full of `DirectAccess Connectivity Assistant` settings:

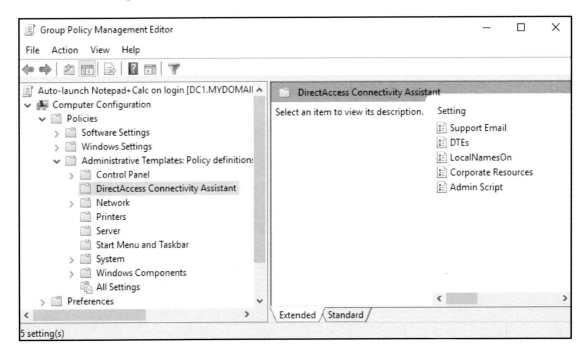

The process we just followed only adds the new template files to the machine where we physically copied the files. If there are multiple Domain Controllers and multiple potential GPMC management workstations in your environment, they will NOT automatically receive these updates. Keep reading to learn about centralizing templates via the Central Store!

The Central Store

By default, these ADMX and ADML files are stored and managed independently on each machine that interfaces with Group Policy. Basically, anywhere that you launch GPMC is going to pull files from that machine's own hard drive. Let's face it, many of us still log into a Domain Controller every time that we need to modify something inside GPMC, and so if you were to handle the distribution of ADMX/ADML files on your own, you would be looking at the task of copying these files onto the hard drives of each of those servers. Then, combine that with any other administrative workstations you have that are using the RSAT tools in order to launch GPMC from Windows desktop operating systems, and suddenly the easy task of pushing out a new `Administrative Template` becomes a burden.

Thankfully, there is a much, much easier way to roll these settings out to all of your management machines! Group Policy information is stored inside Active Directory, and Active Directory is ingrained into almost every aspect of our domain-centric environments. We can make use of something called the Central Store in order to roll these new template settings out to all management machines at the same time. The Central Store allows us to put the ADMX and ADML files into place just once, and all of those settings are then distributed to all Domain Controllers automatically. Once the Central Store is created, all management machines (Domain Controller or otherwise) look to it in order to find these new template files.

Creating the Central Store

Creating the Central Store is a very easy process and is something you can accomplish from any Domain Controller in your environment. Simply create two new folders inside your `SYSVOL` catalog, and the next time that any GPMC inside your environment opens up, it will automatically check for the existence of these folders. Once discovered that the folders exist, GPMC will automatically pull any ADMX and ADML files from this `SYSVOL` location into their local Group Policy Editor.

When you're logged into a Domain Controller, create the following `PolicyDefinitions` folder for ADMX files:

`%systemroot%\SYSVOL\sysvol\mydomain.local\Policies\PolicyDefinitions`

Create accompanying language folders for each language you want to support, such as the following:

`%systemroot%\SYSVOL\sysvol\mydomain.local\Policies\PolicyDefinitions\en -US`

In the preceding locations, make sure to swap out `mydomain.local` with the name of your own domain.

That's it! GPMC pulls information from this `SYSVOL` location whether you are launching it from another Domain Controller, or from a Windows desktop running RSAT tools. This makes rolling out new `Administrative Templates` (and maintaining consistency among them) so, so, so much easier!

Verifying Central Store is working

Now you are thinking, "Sure, Jordan, you had us create a couple of folders on a server. Whoop dee doo! Now you want us to believe that by creating two folders we have somehow unlocked some "Central Store Magic," without performing any other actions?" Fair enough, I understand your skepticism. We did not press any **Apply** or **Commit** buttons, we did not see anything change, and we did not get any kind of verification prompt telling us that we have made such a significant adjustment to the way that `Administrative Templates` work. I guess I'll need to prove it to you. Now that we have added our folders, let's relaunch GPMC and verify that Central Store is enabled. Prior to adding the new folders, I remembered to take a screenshot from inside the GPME, where you can see that the Administrative Templates tell us that they are being `retrieved from the local computer`. This tells us that the displayed settings are coming from ADMX files stored on the hard drive of this machine. Again, this is the way it looked before I created the two new folders:

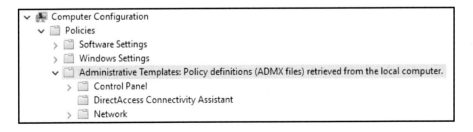

When I visit this same screen after creating those two folders inside SYSVOL, I now see different results. In fact, I will even open GPMC from a different machine – my LAPTOP1 Windows 10 machine where I have the RSAT tools installed. I created those SYSVOL folders on my Domain Controller, yet opening up GPMC on this remote workstation and navigating to Administrative Templates now reports that Policy definitions (ADMX files) retrieved from the central store:

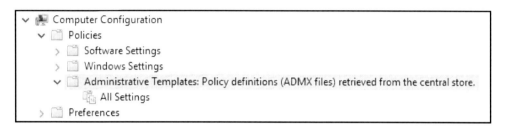

Importing new ADMX/ADML files into the Central Store

Uh oh! You may have noticed a big difference between the previous two screenshots. When I was pulling ADMX files from my local hard drive, I had a bunch of settings in there. Now that I have changed over to using the Central Store for ADMX files, my Administrative Templates folder is empty!

This is because the new folders we created are also empty. We simply need to populate our new Central Store folders with the existing ADMX and ADML files. They are still sitting on the hard drive of my Domain Controller, so go ahead and make the following file copies on a Domain Controller:

- Copy %systemroot%\PolicyDefinitions
  to %systemroot%\SYSVOL\sysvol\mydomain.local\Policies\PolicyDefi
  nitions.
- Copy %systemroot%\PolicyDefinitions\en-US
  to %systemroot%\SYSVOL\sysvol\mydomain.local\Policies\PolicyDefi
  nitions\en-US.

Looking inside GPMC, we now have all of our `Administrative Templates` back in the console, and can also see that they are still being pulled from the Central Store:

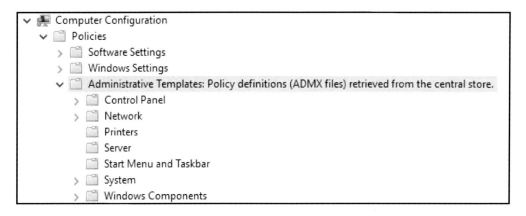

I have left my `DirectAccess Connectivity Assistant` ADMX/ADML out purposefully, so that we can prove that in the future, whenever you need to import a new ADMX/ADML file combination, the only thing you have to do is copy them into their corresponding folders inside the Central Store's `SYSVOL`. After copying the files into their Central Store folders, those new template settings will then be available to access from any GPMC inside your domain. If I re-copy my DCA's ADMX/ADML files into their corresponding `SYSVOL` folders, opening up GPMC from `LAPTOP1` immediately shows me those new settings:

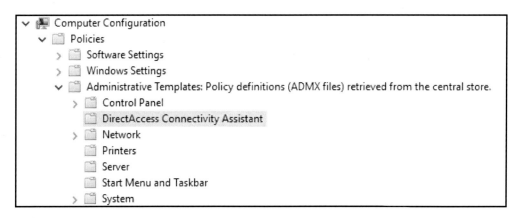

Delegating permissions to manage Group Policy

There are many different tasks that need to be accomplished on a daily basis inside Group Policy, and different levels of administratorship (if that's a word) are needed for these tasks. Domain Admins and Enterprise Admins are the only folks who have access to do everything inside Group Policy, so let's explore the ways that permissions for individual tasks can be delegated to others.

Delegation to edit GPOs

By default, only Domain Admins, Enterprise Admins, or the original GPO creator have access to modify a GPO. Sometimes, you may discover a need to have a junior-level administrator make some tweaks inside a GPO, but perhaps that admin does not have one of these permission levels inside Active Directory. The **Delegation** tab inside each GPO can be used to enter some additional edit permissions, giving a non-admin or even a group of people the access they need in order to modify a GPO that has already been created.

You can see in the following screenshot that I have opened the **Delegation** tab of my Accounting Control Panel Settings GPO, where I can view the current permissions for this particular GPO. Using the **Add...** button, I am able to specify my **Junior AD Admins** group, and give them permissions from this drop-down menu:

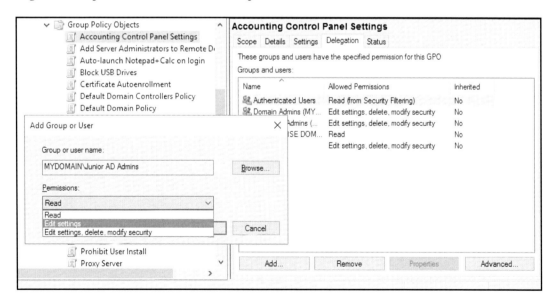

I have chosen to give this group **Edit settings** permissions on my GPO. This will allow anyone who is a member of the **Junior AD Admins** group to change settings inside the GPO, but will continue restricting them from being able to delete the GPO or modify security settings related to this GPO.

Delegation to link GPOs

Another permission that is common to delegate is the ability to link existing GPOs. This does not grant the users access to create their own GPOs, but rather just to view existing GPOs and link them only to OUs for which they have linking access. You generally want to make sure that only trusted administrators are able to create new GPOs. This delegation allows you to retain control over the creation process, but allows the head of the Accounting department the ability to assign/link those GPOs to the groups of Accounting users or computers that they deem fit.

GPO permissions are generally set inside GPMC's Delegation tabs, but this linking permission really has more to do with OU security than it does with GPO security. As such, the tool that needs to be utilized to configure GPO Link Delegation is **Active Directory Users and Computers** (**ADUC**).

Inside ADUC, find the OU that you want to modify. Then, right-click on that OU and choose to **Delegate Control...**:

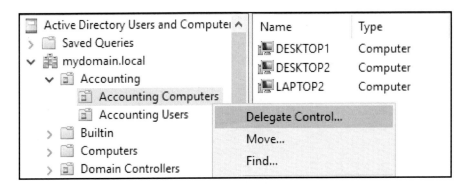

Walk through the **Delegation of Control Wizard**. You are first asked about which users or groups for whom you are delegating control, to which I input my user named Accounting Boss. Next is where we need to decide what tasks you are going to allow this user to accomplish. In order to grant the ability for Accounting Boss to link GPOs to this Accounting Computers OU, I am going to select **Manage Group Policy links**:

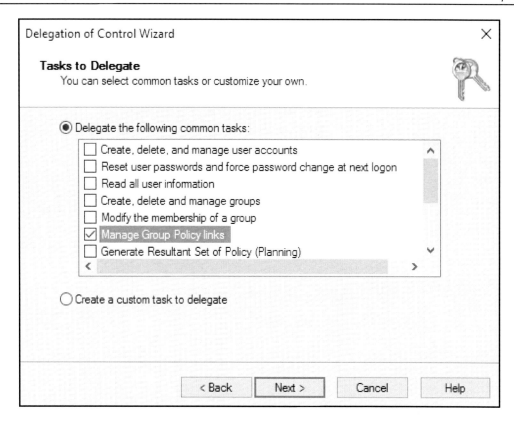

As you can see, there are many other common delegation duties that can be checked inside this wizard. This is an interesting way to divvy up permissions inside your Active Directory management tools and grant people access to specific tasks, without needing to give them Domain Admin rights.

After finishing the wizard, Accounting Boss now has permission to link GPOs to the Accounting Computers OU.

Delegation to create new GPOs

Some of you are skimming over this delegation section, because you assume that anybody who ever needs access to perform these functions inside Group Policy will always have access to a Domain Admin account. While being a member of that group would indeed grant them access to do whatever they need inside Group Policy, let me tell you right now that the days of us having Domain Admin rights are almost over. The ideas of **Just-In-Time (JIT) Administration** and **Just-Enough Administration (JEA)** are gaining popularity, necessarily so because Domain Admin rights are simply too broad and powerful these days. Stolen Domain Admin credentials could certainly turn out to be detrimental to your business, as would the case of an IT professional who leaves the company on bad terms. It is common to discover environments where even senior IT administrators struggle to gain access to do the things they need on servers in their own domains, because their default permissions are being limited and they need to submit requests for specific delegation of controls in order to do their jobs.

Creating new GPOs is a task that typically falls onto AD administrators, but if you need access to this and do not have a Domain Admin account, there are two ways through which you can be granted access to create new GPOs:

- Add your account to the Active Directory security group, called **Group Policy Creator Owners**. This is a predefined group that exists by default in any Active Directory implementation. Adding users to this group inside ADUC automatically grants them rights to be able to generate new GPOs inside Group Policy.
- Alternatively, inside GPMC you can click on the primary **Group Policy Objects** folder, and then navigate to the **Delegation** tab. Here, you see a list of folks who have permission to create new GPOs. Domain Admins and Group Policy Creator Owners are already defined here, which explains why anyone in these groups already has the ability to create new GPOs. Rather than adding users into one of those existing groups, you could simply add their user accounts straight into the **Delegation** tab, as I have done in the following screenshot for the user account called Laura:

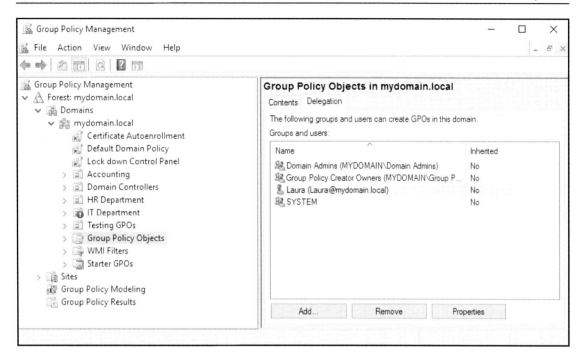

Additional delegation capabilities

Almost every place you can click inside the GPMC console has a tab called **Delegation**. The capabilities provided inside the Delegation tab differ whether you are looking at the properties of a GPO, a GPO Link, the primary Group Policy Objects folder, the root of the domain, the WMI Filters folder, or Starter GPOs. Each entity inside Group Policy has a unique way that permissions can be assigned and delegated.

Inside most Delegation tabs is a button, called **Advanced...**, that allows you to dig even deeper into specific allowances or blocks that can be performed. If you find yourself tasked with creating a permission that does not appear to be an option on the primary Delegation tab, make sure to check inside Advanced delegation properties before giving up the search completely.

Summary

Maintaining Group Policy is a chore that every Active Directory administrator will have to tackle at some point in their careers. You will learn that you can make life much easier on yourself and future admins by documenting all settings and configurations as you build out the environment. In fact, quite a bit of this chapter relates to good practices that make future work inside Group Policy flow more smoothly and efficiently. Utilizing Starter GPOs certainly saves some time and effort on your part, and delegation of control is all about removing items off your plate so that you can focus on bigger-picture things. We also spent time learning about the backup and restoration options available for our GPOs, as these will certainly be critical pieces of our security stance, and absolutely need to be recoverable in the event of a failure. ADMX and ADML files are always a tricky bit for admins new to Group Policy administration, so we covered those as well.

Even if you maintain your domain perfectly and never make any mistakes, someday you are bound to run into an issue that you cannot easily explain and that you will need to dive in and troubleshoot. Turn the page to continue on with our next chapter, which is all about troubleshooting in your Group Policy environment.

Group Policy Troubleshooting

9

A chapter on Group Policy troubleshooting? Am I implying that things can go wrong during the processing of Group Policy Objects? Am I insinuating that Group Policy administrators may not be perfectly planning out every single setting that they put inside every single GPO? How insulting to both Microsoft and to you admins!

Alas, nothing and nobody is perfect. Even in the smallest of environments, if you use Group Policy to deploy settings, you will eventually need to troubleshoot some aspect of this process. Most of the time, Group Policy issues are caused by human error. It is very easy to deploy settings to the wrong workstations or users, or forget to set filtering, or link something before you have fully tested it. It is also easy to create conflicting settings packages, or to deny permissions and forget about them, only to cause you grief down the road. There aren't many checks and balances inside the Group Policy mechanism; the technology trusts you as the administrator to know what you are doing, and to do it properly. It will allow you to shoot yourself in the foot, and it will take down your entire network if you tell it to do so. When things go south, we need to know where to start and what tools are available to us for tracking down problems inside the Group Policy engine.

The following topics will be covered in this chapter:

- Troubleshooting tools and procedures
- GPO version numbers
- Checking the replication status via GPMC
- Detecting slow links
- The trouble with FRS
- Group Policy results wizard
- Group Policy modeling

Troubleshooting tools and procedures

When in a bind and needing to troubleshoot something inside Group Policy, there are numerous commands and tools at our disposal. Group Policy is an interaction between multiple systems. As such, you will almost never be troubleshooting from a single place. If attempting to diagnose the addition or disappearance of settings on a client workstation, you will likely be touching that local machine to see what's going on. Once you have a handle on what is or is not happening with the client, chances are that you will discover that some kind of change must have been made within the server infrastructure, which caused the symptoms you are now experiencing on that client machine. So you will probably find yourself logging in to a Domain Controller, or at least launching GPMC from your management workstation, to check out that side of things.

And don't forget about the network in between. All of the Group Policy magic happens successfully because the underlying network is transporting all of the data and packets back and forth between those servers and client computers. Sometimes this network is the super-stable LAN, and sometimes it is weaker, slower remote connections, such as MPLS circuits or VPN links. There are a number of things that could go wrong between client and server. Here are some of the most common general things to look for when troubleshooting a Group Policy interaction.

GPUpdate

We discussed the specifics of GPUpdate and the various switches that can be used with it in Chapter 3, *Daily Tasks in Group Policy*, but it is very important to mention it in this chapter as well, because this is probably the most commonly utilized Group Policy troubleshooting tool. If ever you are in a situation where you believe GPO settings are not making their way down to a user or computer, the very first thing to test is a simple gpupdate /force command, where we can watch in real time as the client workstation attempts to reach out to a Domain Controller and process any Group Policy settings that are waiting for it. Any other troubleshooting would be premature if you have not first attempted to GPUpdate.

If GPUpdate presents you with errors, now you have a defined path for continued troubleshooting. Errors in GPUpdate can point out network connection problems, or permission problems, or even clue you in when a particular policy setting is waiting for a logoff or reboot.

When `GPUpdate` comes back with a successful status, chances are that Group Policy is processing successfully, and the issue you are tracking is sourced elsewhere. But keep in mind that a restart of the client operating system is never a bad idea. There are some changes, such as moving a computer from one OU to another, that are not immediately recognized by the workstation. Moving a computer to a new OU will often change the GPOs that are being applied to the workstation, but those GPO changes will only happen once the computer knows about the new OU membership. Rebooting is the fastest and easiest way to force a client to recognize new OU or group membership. Group Policy always processes during operating system boot, so doing a quick restart will both ensure that changes inside Active Directory are picked up by the machine, as well as force Group Policy to reprocess and reapply.

"Have you tried rebooting?" is and has always been question numero uno when calling any help desk, with good reason. There are many symptoms inside Windows that are mysteriously fixed after a reboot, and sometimes Group Policy falls into this boat as well. I will say that Windows 10 is far superior to its predecessors. In Windows 10, you really don't have to reboot very often, but when you're working on an issue and trying to determine what's going askew inside GPO-land, falling back on the good ole reboot is never a bad idea.

GPResult and RSOP

Once again, I find myself mentioning tools that we have already taken the time to describe previously in this book, but with good reason. We have left the specifics of these commands in `Chapter 3`, *Daily Tasks in Group Policy*, where they belong, but they are worth another honorable mention because `GPResult` and RSOP data is often the key ingredient needed when determining a GPO filtering problem. Let's take a look at the output of each command for an idea of what helpful information is provided to us.

RSOP

Running RSOP on a client workstation presents us with all of the Group Policy settings that are being installed onto this machine. This allows admins to poke through these settings and determine whether they are appropriate, or whether they are causing any grief. Depending on what you do or do not find, this could help steer your troubleshooting:

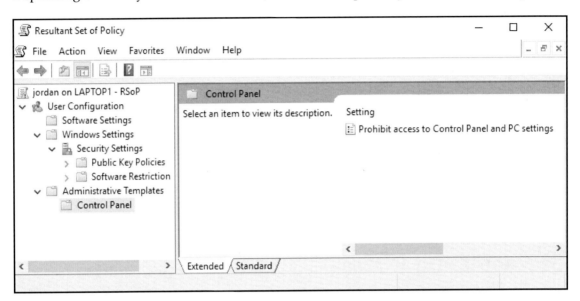

GPResult

GPResult does just what the name implies – it is a command that runs on the client machine to display results of some of the things going on with Group Policy. Primarily we use this command to verify whether a particular GPO is successfully applying to a computer or user, but there is quite a bit more information inside the GPResult output that is interesting to take a look at.

Here is a screenshot of gpresult /r from my LAPTOP1 machine, currently logged on as the Jordan user:

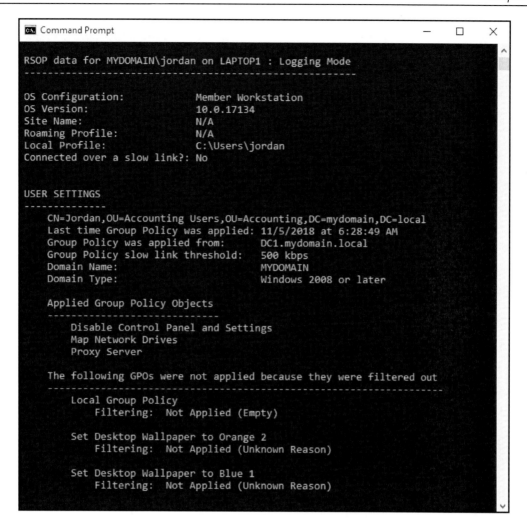

Here are descriptions of some of the useful information listed inside `GPResult`:

- **Connected over a slow link**: We will discuss slow links later in *Detecting Slow Links* section, but sometimes when troubleshooting users who are connected remotely, determining whether they are connected via a slow link can be essential information.

- **Group Policy slow link threshold**: Another useful piece of info regarding slow-link detection is the current threshold that Windows uses for determining whether the user is on a slow or fast link.

- **Last time Group Policy was applied**: As it states, this will show you the date and timestamp of the last successful Group Policy refresh. When troubleshooting whether settings are processing correctly on a client computer, this stamp can be noted, then reviewed again after running a `GPUpdate` command. If the timestamp has updated itself, you know Group Policy is processing information successfully and in real time.

- **Group Policy was applied from**: It displays which Domain Controller was pulled from the last set of Group Policy information. If you are getting unexpected results on your workstation, perhaps one of your DCs is out of date, or out of sync with the rest of the environment.

- **Applied Group Policy Objects**: In my experience, this is the most commonly visited section of `GPResult` data. Here you will find a list of the GPOs that have been applied to your machine or user account. This is your verification on whether a particular GPO is being successfully applied.

- **The following GPOs were not applied because they were filtered out**: This is not simply a list of all GPOs that did not apply to the user or computer (because that could be an enormous list), but a list of GPOs that would have successfully applied, except that some kind of specific filtering criteria blocked them from applying. When you see GPOs listed in this section, it means the user or computer account does reside in an OU to which these GPOs would have normally applied successfully. However, something about the GPO settings has stopped that from happening. There are three different reasons as to why they could be blocked:

  - **Denied (Security)**: The user or computer has been specifically denied permissions to apply this GPO. This happens when a GPO's Security Filtering is configured to only apply to a certain set of users or groups, and your user or computer is not part of that group. Therefore, the policy would have applied to you based on OU membership, but not based on the additional filtering criteria defined inside Security Filtering. This would also happen if you have modified the Delegation tab of a GPO in order to create a specific Deny rule, disallowing particular objects from receiving these GPO settings.

- **Not Applied (Empty)**: This is displayed when a GPO attempted to apply to you, but there were no settings to apply. This could mean that the GPO is set to Disabled, or it could mean that just half of the GPO is set to Disabled. Remember that we have the ability to disable either User Configuration or Computer Configuration settings on any given GPO, and if the GPO is actually empty without settings or half of that GPO is blocked, you may see it listed as Empty.
- **Not Applied (Unknown Reason)**: This is a catch-all for any other reasons why a GPO might not be applying. I find that this most often happens when Block Inheritance is affecting the application of these GPO settings. Such is the case for the preceding screenshot.

User or computer results – not usually both

Most of the time, when running either RSOP or GPUpdate, you are trying to track down something specific, and you probably have a pretty good idea of whether the things you are looking for reside inside User Configuration settings, or Computer Configuration settings. You will notice that when you run RSOP or GPUpdate, you generally only get one side of the story. For example, running either of these commands from a non-administrative Command Prompt that is running in the logged-on user's security context, you will only get results that are specific to that logged-on user (this was the case for both my RSOP and GPResult data in the earlier screenshots). RSOP will even give you an error message informing you that the user does not have rights to view the computer-level information. Since these regular user accounts do not have the permissions needed to query Computer-level criteria, RSOP and GPUpdate will only display the information that is relevant to the user account and **User Configuration** settings.

Alternatively, when you need to view information about **Computer Configuration** settings, a regular user account will not have permission to see this data and you would naturally launch an elevated Command Prompt from which to re run the command, right? While this will correctly display for you the RSOP and GPResult information related to the computer account and Computer Configuration settings, it is important to note that any user data displayed inside this output is now relevant for whatever administrator's credentials you used to open the elevated Command Prompt. Since the Command Prompt is no longer running in the logged-on user's context, you can't view that user's information inside the RSOP or GPResult output.

If you need to review both **User Configuration** and **Computer Configuration** settings, you will likely need to run your commands twice, once from each security context (administrator versus standard logged-on user).

GPO permissions

After taking a look over the GPResult data, you may still be struggling to determine the cause for a GPO whose settings simply will not apply to your workstation. Another possible interference to the GPO application process is GPO Permissions. Remember that any person or computer wanting to receive settings from a GPO needs to have both **Read** and **Apply Group Policy** permissions on the GPO itself. If those two things do not exist, the GPO is not going to apply successfully to your machine.

GPO Permissions are visible inside the **Delegation** tab of any GPO. Open up GPMC, select the GPO in question, and browse to **Delegation**. Here you can see a very standard **Delegation** permissions output of my **Block USB Drives** GPO:

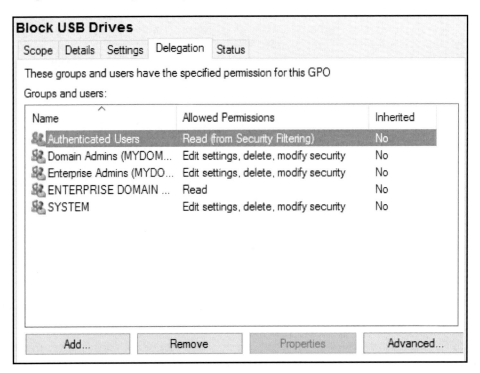

It is also possible that you or someone else created a specific deny permission in a GPO, specifically blocking the permission setting for Apply Group Policy. The deny permissions are not easily visible from inside GPMC; you will need to visit the GPO, head over to the Delegation tab, and then browse inside the **Advanced** button in order to see the lower-level permission details, such as deny access rights. Here you can see that I have denied the **Apply group policy** permission for my LAPTOP2 computer, which means this GPO will fail to apply to LAPTOP2, no matter how I set my links or **Security Filtering**:

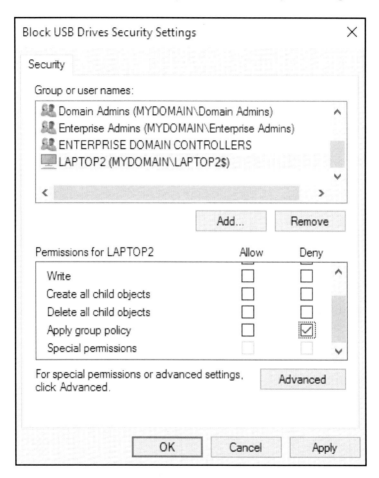

Map out policy settings

If you can remember back in Chapter 1, *Group Policy – The Basics*, we discussed the overall mindset behind Group Policy's application of settings, and that there are multiple tiers within which you can push settings to your user or computer objects. As a quick refresher, Group Policy applies in the following order:

- Local Group Policy
- Site-linked policies
- Domain-linked policies
- OU-linked policies

Always keep this in mind when digging into policies to determine what should or should not be applying. It is often helpful to draw this out on paper. When stuck troubleshooting an issue, try mapping out the flow of a computer account through these four tiers, asking yourself along the way, "Does this computer have any local policy? No, then how about any policies getting applied for the site where it is currently sitting? Yes, there is the printers policy. OK, now how about any policies linked to the root of the Domain?" and so on. Putting quill to parchment, however 17th-century it feels, can benefit your understanding of how Group Policy is ordering its application of settings.

Is the GPO disabled?

This one can be a bit tricky to figure out. Always check to make sure the GPO that you are working with is not disabled in some way. Sometimes GPOs are wholly disabled temporarily for testing purposes, and perhaps you forgot to turn it back on. It's more common that only half of the GPO has been disabled, and you are now wracking your brain trying to figure out why the new drive mapping you plugged in to your computer security policy is not working.

When creating a GPO, you will be inputting **User Configuration** settings, **Computer Configuration** settings, or a combination of both. If the GPO only contains one type of settings, you can easily disable the other side of the GPO so that when this GPO processes on the client computers, it does so more efficiently because the computer does not even have to look inside the unnecessary part of the GPO settings.

Whenever troubleshooting a GPO, remember to visit the **Details** tab and make sure you haven't set yourself up for failure by disabling **Computer Configuration**, **User Configuration**, or both:

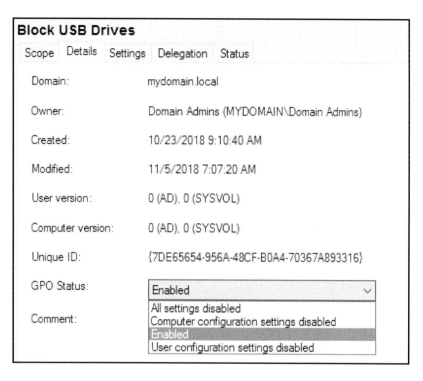

Also remember that this **GPO Status** field follows the GPO wherever it goes. If you change a GPO to be **Computer configuration settings disabled**, all of the associated GPO links will also be set to **Computer configuration settings disabled**. Different links to the same GPO do not have individual filtering or status settings. If you make a change to one link, you are really making the change to the GPO itself. Therefore, your change affects every link associated with that GPO.

Watching for inheritance blocking

Blocking of inheritance is a powerful capability, and very useful for specialized users or systems. Useful, that is, until it causes you problems. Then it quickly becomes a nuisance. When you find yourself staring at GPO settings that you just cannot seem to get to apply to a particular computer, navigate your way up the OU structure from where that computer resides up to the very top of the domain, watching out for those little blue exclamation marks along the way. If **Block Inheritance** is enabled on an OU that is four tiers up from where your computer resides, that block is still affecting your computer! Take a look at the following screenshot. If my laptop was sitting inside the highlighted OU called Dell, even though that OU is way down the chain away from IT Department, my laptop would still be blocked from inheriting GPO settings because I have **Block Inheritance** configured on that IT Department OU. This block affects everything nested inside of it:

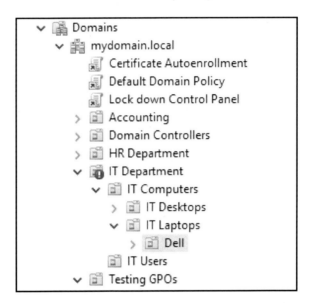

Looking out for Enforced GPOs

The flip side of inheritance blocking, Enforced GPOs, can cause GPO settings to apply that you were not expecting. When a GPO is marked as **Enforced**, the settings inside that GPO will blow past inheritance blocking and will apply anyway. If ever there is a situation where inheritance blocking and GPO enforcement are in conflict, Enforce wins!

You can view enforcement settings either by right-clicking on any GPO or a link to that GPO, and look to see whether **Enforced** is checked. Alternatively, you can click on the OU that you are investigating and take a look at the **Linked Group Policy Objects** tab. Here you will find a quick summary of all GPOs that are linked to this OU, and can see whether each of them is enforced:

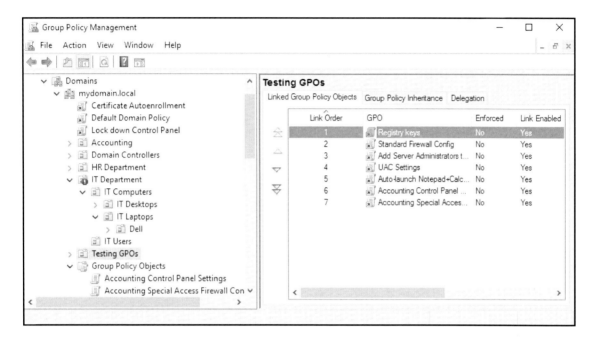

Conflicting settings

You already know that GPOs get applied in order of the tiers at which they are linked, **Local** | **Site** | **Domain** | **OU**. Occasionally, GPOs linked at the different tiers could conflict with each other or contradict each other, and the last settings applied win. OU-linked policies will trump Domain-linked policies, Domain-linked beat out Site-linked, and so on.

A great resource for discovering these potential conflicts is the **Group Policy Inheritance** tab inside GPMC. This tab will show you all of the GPOs that are going to attempt to apply to the particular location you have selected, not only for the selected OU but for all tiers above it. For example, in the following screenshot, I have clicked on my Testing GPOs OU and can quickly see all GPOs that are going to attempt to apply to any workstations or users inside this testing OU. Some of these GPOs are linked straight to my OU, and some are linked at the root of the domain:

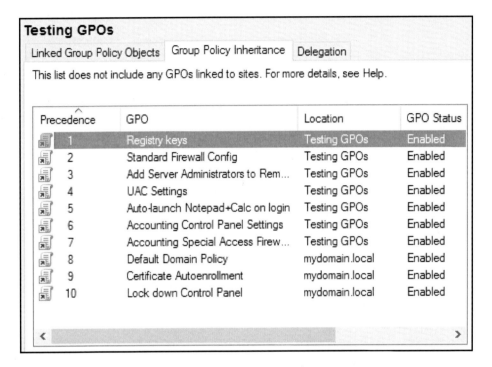

Site-level links are not included in the Inheritance information. This is because client computers will process site links only when inside the applicable site, and so GPMC realizes that displaying them here could be inconsistent or inaccurate.

You might wonder why I keep using the word *attempt*. When a GPO is linked, it is linked, right? Aren't all of the GPOs listed in the inheritance tab going to apply to my machine? Not necessarily. Group Policy Inheritance is showing you what policies will apply based upon their links, but does not consider other factors. Some of these GPOs may still fail to apply to you based on Security Filtering, WMI Filters, or any other GPO-specific filtering criteria.

Occasionally, multiple GPOs will be linked at the same tier, and also conflict with each other. Once again, the Group Policy Inheritance tab can help resolve this issue. Looking back at the preceding screenshot, look closer at the **Precedence** column. These numbers indicate the priority of the GPOs, which are linked to this location. If you notice something out of whack here, you can pop back over to the **Linked Group Policy Objects** tab and use the arrows to adjust GPO precedence order, thereby adjusting the order in which the GPOs are applied, which affects the winning settings at the end of the Group Policy processing cycle.

Is your operating system supported?

Let's pretend for a minute that you are working on an issue where some GPO settings are not applying to the workstation next to you. You have tried to figure this out, including working your way through all of the troubleshooting steps we have discussed so far. In fact, you can successfully verify via Inheritance and from GPResult itself that the GPO is successfully applying to your machine, and yet the settings do not exist!

One other variable that is often overlooked is that certain settings inside Group Policy are only applicable to particular versions of the Windows Operating System. If new security settings introduced in Windows 10 are pushed down to a Windows 7 client, they will likely be ignored. If those settings are for a technology that did not exist in Win7, the settings will definitely be ignored, even though the GPO finishes processing successfully on that Win7 machine.

While this issue is admittedly difficult to track down, you can make sure you never get into this situation by fully understanding the settings that you plug in to your GPOs in the first place, and by making good notes and comments inside your policies. If a setting only pertains to Windows 10 Enterprise systems, make a comment about that inside the GPO. This will at least shorten the amount of time it takes Joe Admin to diagnose this disturbing behavior.

When adding any setting to any GPO, read over the notes and comments provided by Microsoft inside the setting. The GPO settings screen has a section entitled **Supported on**. If the setting you are viewing is limited to working only with certain versions of Windows, you should see it defined here:

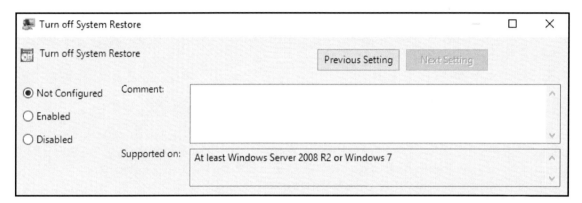

Windows Event Logs

If you are at your wit's end with the common-sense approach to troubleshooting Group Policy and are afraid something is actually going wrong under the hood, it's time to turn to the Windows Event Logs. If you suspect Group Policy is failing to process when the client reaches out and asks for applicable settings, the Windows System event log will generally have some information related to successes or failures in the Group Policy process. Open EVENTVWR.MSC on the client computer, and browse to **Event Viewer | Windows Logs | System**. This is the logging location for many aspects of the Windows operating system, so you may have to filter this log in order to view only events related to Group Policy. Right-clicking on **System** and selecting **Filter Current Log...** will give you some filtering options. Look inside the drop-down list for **Event sources** – there are numerous sources here related to Group Policy. Checking these boxes will filter the System event log down to display only Group-Policy-related events:

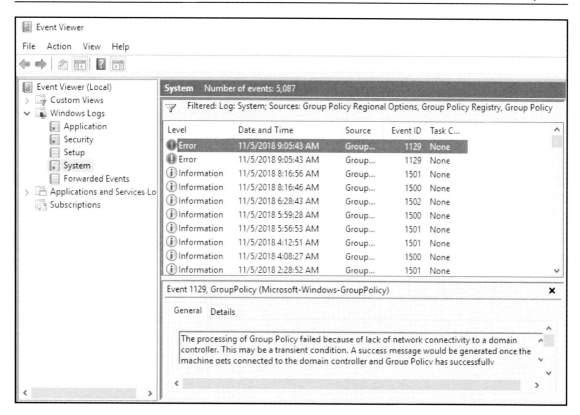

In the previous screenshot, you can see informational events that are indicating successful runs of Group Policy processing. You can also see some errors. This happened because I unplugged the NIC of my LAPTOP1 computer, and then I tried to do a gpupdate /force in order to refresh Group Policy settings. This obviously failed because I did not have any communication to a Domain Controller at the time, and that failure was reported inside the Windows System event logs.

There are additional Group-Policy-specific logs in a slightly different location inside the Windows Event Viewer. Open up the same EVENTVWR.MSC, and navigate to **Event Viewer | Applications and Services Logs | Microsoft | Windows | Group Policy | Operational**.

GPO version numbers

Troubleshooting Group Policy is often a matter of investigation on the client side, then making corresponding changes inside the server infrastructure (GPMC). Occasionally, you may suspect that something goofy is going on at the server level, perhaps that updates or changes that you make to GPOs are not being properly put into place. Group Policy has a bit of a change-management procedure built in, where it keeps track of version numbers for each GPO inside Active Directory.

These GPO version numbers are visible by selecting any GPO inside GPMC, and then visiting the **Details** tab. Here, I have created a brand-new GPO that does not yet contain any settings, and navigated my way into the **Details** tab immediately after GPO creation:

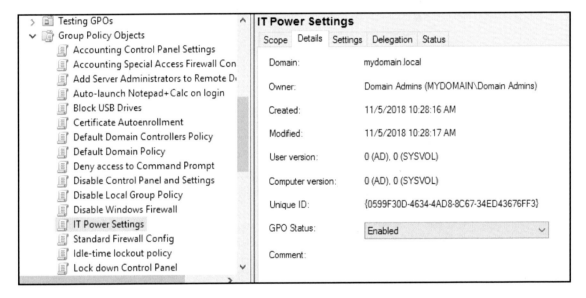

You can see that there are separate version numbers for **User** and **Computer**. These numbers are tracking changes made inside the **User Configuration** and **Computer Configuration** sections of the GPO. Everything is currently reporting zero, because I have not yet made any changes to this GPO. Let's do that now. These numbers will increment following any change, and so if I edit the GPO and make any change inside **Computer Configuration**, I would then see the **Computer version** number increase inside **Details**.

Version numbers track any change, not the overall number of settings inside the policy. For example, if I were to edit that GPO again and remove the settings that I previously put into place, my version number would increase again. It would never return to zero. Even though there are no settings inside my policy at all, my Computer version number now reports a version number of 6. I have also made a few small changes inside **User Configuration**, so you can see some version numbers populated there as well:

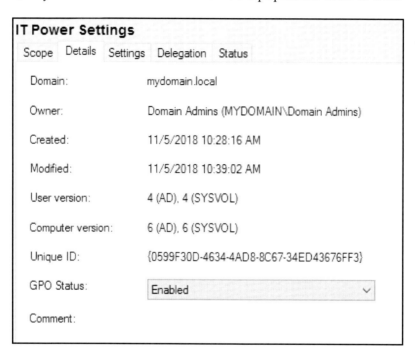

You can utilize GPO version numbers to ensure that changes made to GPOs are updating properly, and that the two pieces of GPOs (the object inside AD as well as the files inside SYSVOL) are remaining in sync. Furthermore, you can check the **Modified** timestamp on this screen to review the last time that changes were made to this GPO, perhaps shedding light on changes made by another administrator that could have caused the trouble that you are experiencing.

Checking Domain Controller synchronization

GPO version numbers are an important part of the change-tracking process in any Active Directory environment, but are exponentially more useful in domains with multiple Domain Controllers. Any time that changes are made inside Active Directory, including any changes made inside Group Policy, Active Directory replicates those changes around the network to all Domain Controller servers. This replication process can take a few minutes, or a few hours, depending on the size and scope of your network and your DC configuration.

When you are making changes inside Group Policy and immediately testing those changes, you run the risk of pushing the changes to one Domain Controller, while your test client computer is pulling GPO information from a different DC. In this case, you certainly could not expect to have immediate results on that client workstation, because you have to wait for replication to finish before the new GPO information exists on all of the DCs.

All that is to say that checking these GPO version numbers across your multiple Domain Controllers can be a practice worthy of your time while troubleshooting potential synchronization problems. Your GPO version numbers should be the same among all DCs in the environment. If they are not, you are either still waiting for replication to finish, or something has gone wrong during the replication process and you now need to turn to Active Directory itself to figure out why.

Version numbers triggering the client

You know that domain clients only pull Group Policy information if they have noticed a change in policy; otherwise, for the sake of efficiency, they skip over GPOs when they realize that nothing has changed inside that GPO since the last Group Policy refresh cycle. Part of the way that clients determine whether a GPO has changed is the version number. If the version numbers have not changed since the last GP refresh, the clients do not process GPOs during the refresh. But if they find a GPO that has updated version numbers since the last refresh, the GP refresh will reprocess the GPOs that apply to that workstation.

Checking the replication status via GPMC

When discussing GPO version numbers, we mentioned Active Directory replication a couple of times. While checking up on the status and health of the replication process itself is generally a topic outside the scope of Group Policy, AD and GP are so intertwined that it's good to know how to check the status of the replication process.

There is some functionality built right into the GPMC for checking on the overall health of the AD replication process. After opening up GPMC, click on the name of your domain, and then look at the **Status** tab:

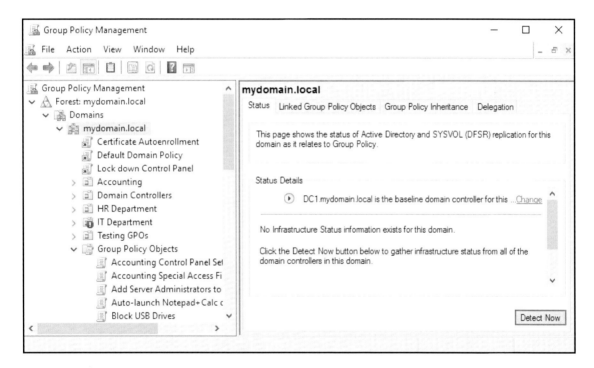

There is not a lot of information listed here by default. You can see the name of my DC1 domain controller listed, indicating that I am currently communicating with DC1 in order to pull information. The real results come when you click on that **Detect Now** button. This will query your Domain Controllers and the replication status between them:

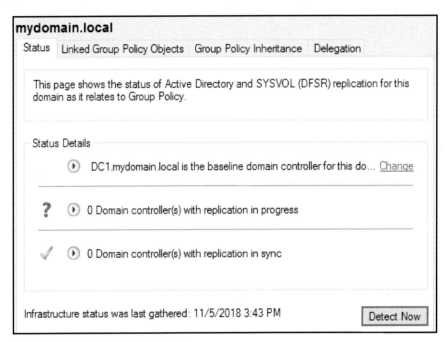

My report is pretty boring. Since this is a simple test lab, there is only one Domain Controller and so we have no replication errors because there is no replication happening. This report will become much more interesting in your own environments, where (hopefully) you are running more than one directory server. This **Status** tab gives you peace of mind that replication between your DCs is behaving properly.

You can also find a **Status** tab on any GPO in the domain. Click on the GPO, visit the **Status** tab, and use the **Detect Now** button to check replication information specific to the GPO that you have selected.

Detecting slow links

LAN connections are fast. Usually, when plugged in to the network in your office, you are connected back to the servers (including Domain Controllers) at a 1 GB link speed, give or take. This kind of speed means that you can interact with Group Policy very quickly, and any GPOs that need to come down the pipe to your computer will process ultra fast.

What about slower connections? Can you really expect a 700 MB application-installation package to successfully install over a VPN connection? This package is going to attempt to install during login, and that installation could take a long time. I hope you had plans to go outside and run a half marathon after typing in your password, because your computer may not get to the desktop for a while.

Domain-joined computers that are reaching into Group Policy self-determine when they are on a fast link or a slow link. Slow links are often detected when users are connected remotely, via VPN or `DirectAccess` connections. Additionally, slow-link detection may be triggered for branch office computers that are connecting back to the corporate data center through MPLS circuits, or site-to-site VPNs.

When your computer communicates to a Domain Controller, the **Network Location Awareness** (**NLA**) mechanism built into the Windows operating system determines the current link speed between you and that DC. When NLA decides it is a fast link, Group Policy processes normally. When NLA determines you to be connected via a slow link, however, GP processing changes and some types of GPO settings will be ignored.

Some GPO settings are always processed. Most security-related policy settings, as well as registry settings, are considered mandatory and will process the same whether the client is connected via fast link or slow link. Other items, however, are deemed less important by Microsoft. When your client computer self-determines to be on a slow link, the following items will be ignored for the sake of login speed:

- Disk Quota
- Scripts
- Folder Redirection
- Software Installation
- Wireless and Wired Network Policies
- Internet Explorer Maintenance

While it might appear super lame that Microsoft would disallow certain policies from running simply for being connected at a slower speed, there is actually great benefit to slow-link detection. Without throttling down the amount of work that Group Policy is doing over these poor connections, the login process could seriously take minutes and minutes to finish when the user tries to log in. Slow-link detection exists for a very good reason.

Changing slow-link detection behavior

The default threshold for determining a slow link is when the connection between your client and your Domain Controller drops below 500 kbps. If you ever need to adjust this threshold number, it is possible to do so on all of your client computers. What is the mechanism for pushing this change out to your users and computers? Group Policy, of course:

User or Computer Configuration | Policies | Administrative Templates | System | Group Policy | Configure Group Policy slow link detection

Take note that this policy setting is available inside either User Configuration or Computer Configuration. If you need to adjust slow link settings for one side or the other, or both, keep that in mind when you adjust this setting.

One final note here: if you think slow-link detection is lame and want to disable it completely, configuring **Group Policy Slow Link Detection** = 0 (zero) will force the client to treat all connections as fast links.

The trouble with FRS

Active Directory has some serious replication capabilities built into it. When adding a new user or group into AD, you certainly want that change to quickly flow to all of your Domain Controller servers, so that the new users can successfully log in to a computer from anywhere in the domain. The automated spreading of this directory information is kind of the whole point of running AD in the first place, right?

The same is true for Group Policy information, as you already know. Create a new GPO on DC1, and within minutes (usually) that new GPO shows up on DC2 and DC3. What if another administrator made some changes to an existing GPO on DC2 at the same time? No worries; replication is fully prepared to handle the synchronization of settings in all directions and those changes will show up successfully on DC1 and DC3, even while the new GPO changes from DC1 are also being sorted.

The mechanisms used to replicate this data have changed over the years, and this is important to be familiar with when troubleshooting Group Policy. Part of the replication process for Group Policy information is the copying of the files that we find inside SYSVOL. On older platforms, this file synchronization was handled by a technology called **File Replication Service (FRS)**. FRS was a solid replication technology and quite stable, back in the Server 2003 and earlier days. However, realizing some changes were needed, Microsoft gave us a newer file-replication technology – releasing for the first time in Server 2003R2, I believe. This new mechanism for distributing files among Domain Controllers is known as **Distributed File System with Replication (DFSR)**.

What's wrong with FRS?

First of all, there was obviously a reason (probably many reasons) why Microsoft released DFSR, so there should be some level of trust that newer is better. I don't pretend to be an expert on FRS or DFSR, but I can relay to you the issues I have experienced when working with customers who are still using FRS.

Yes, I do mean even today as we have just started rolling out Windows Server 2019, that there are still companies out there utilizing FRS in their networks. And the biggest problem with this is that they probably have no idea. We'll talk a little bit more about that in the *Which one am I running* section of this chapter.

FRS is like a magician who only ever learned half of a trick. He's great at making things disappear (watch the crowd ooh and aah over the disappearing data), but not always so great at bringing it back. From what I have experienced, if a domain environment is still running all older Domain Controllers (Server 2008-ish), and you only ever make GPO changes on these older DCs, you'll probably never experience the cool new feature called disappearing data (maybe this is a weird cousin to data deduplication...?). The trouble with FRS comes into play once you start manipulating Group Policy from newer systems inside the FRS-replication environment. They don't necessarily even have to be Domain Controller systems.

More specifically, the trouble shows up when you start making changes or updates to Group Policy data from an operating system newer than Server 2008R2. This might be from the first Server 2012 Domain Controller you install, or it might be from some other Server 2012 or newer box where you happen to have the Group Policy Management tools installed. When you use this new platform to open up a GPO and make some changes to it, there is the possibility that all of the settings inside that GPO might disappear.

Yikes. I'm not making this up; I have helped numerous customers out of this boat after losing GPO settings. Not only is there the potential that when you, with your own hands, make a change to a GPO that the GPO might be deleted, there is also potential that the GPOs might be deleted without you directly touching the GPO. This is because the newer Server Manager starting in Server 2012 does so much for us. There are some management consoles now where you only ever interact with a GUI interface, but what that GUI is really doing is throwing PowerShell commands at Active Directory in the background. You click on a setting, and PowerShell issues the relevant command to the closest Domain Controller to make that change happen. While this is really cool and is the core reason that today's Server Manager is hundreds of times more powerful than the Server Manager of old, it also means that your GPOs are sometimes being updated without you ever touching GPMC.

If this all seems a little confusing and far-reaching, let me give you a real example. When configuring Microsoft `DirectAccess` (remote access technology) inside an environment, we are introducing a Server 2012 (or newer) system to the environment. Chances are that this new server is not the first Server 2012 box that the customer is running, but it could be the case that this is the first Server 2012 or newer that is going to be doing automated manipulation of Group Policy. After prepping the server and installing the role, we head into the `DirectAccess` configuration wizards. At the end of the wizards, after selecting all of our options, the wizard then reaches into Group Policy and creates some new GPOs for us. Those GPOs are then filled with settings, GPO links are established, and even Security Filtering is populated based on the information that we plugged in during the wizard. All of these things are done inside Group Policy without us ever having to touch a Domain Controller or GPMC in any way.

Sometimes even this initial rollout of the GPOs goes sideways, but let's pretend that it went smoothly and `DirectAccess` is up and running. Now it's a couple of days later, and we realize that something needs to be tweaked in our configuration. We simply re launch the `DirectAccess` configuration wizards, make the changes, and click the **Apply** button. This tiny little change is pushed into our GPOs, and from there it rolls down to the client computers, right? Except that, when FRS is still being used for replication, what often happens is that `DirectAccess` completely breaks for everybody. When we look a little closer at what happened, we find that the GPOs related to `DirectAccess` are completely empty. All of the settings have been cleared out of them! The GPOs still exist, their links still exist, and they are still filtered appropriately, but all settings have been forgotten.

`DirectAccess` is not the only technology where this happens, but it's one that I deploy a lot, so it's the best example I have. The point is that FRS is no longer a reliable mechanism for replicating Group Policy data! The only way to fix this behavior is to update your Domain Controllers to replicate using DFSR instead.

Which one am I running?

Most of the companies where we encounter this behavior have no idea that they are still using FRS. In fact, after seeing symptoms such as this, I cautiously ask them the question, "So... do you think it's possible that you guys are still running FRS instead of DFSR?" and they always answer, "No way! We ditched FRS long ago!" But... so far I have a 100% success rate for being right; when we query Active Directory, we find that, sure enough, they are still using FRS.

You can only utilize one or the other to sync data between Domain Controllers. You have either cut your environment over to DFSR, or you are still running FRS. Don't automatically assume that just because you have Server 2016 Domain Controllers running in the environment that you are cut over to DFSR. Thankfully, there is a quick way to test and discover which replication technology is being used in your domain.

Log into a newer (2008+) Domain Controller server in your environment, and open up a Command Prompt. Then issue the `dfsrmig /getmigrationstate` command:

If it reports a Global state of **Start**, this means you are still running FRS. I say again: Start=Bad news!

If you see **Eliminated** listed, this is an indication that you are running the newer DFSR.

There are two additional possible outcomes to this command. If you see either Prepared or Redirected listed here, then it appears someone has started the migration to DFSR but never finished it.

If you discover that you are still running FRS, change it! Guidance on updating your `SYSVOL` replication scheme to DFSR is outside the scope of a Group Policy book, but here is a good starting point: `https://www.microsoft.com/en-us/download/details.aspx?id=4843`.

Group Policy results wizard

Resultant Set of Policy (**RSOP**) data is often critical to the Group Policy troubleshooting process. Usually when working a support ticket, you are trying to correct some behavior by identifying the GPOs applying to a machine or user, and then digging into those policies to figure out what settings contained within are the ones causing your problems.

If you happen to be sitting in the cubicle next to the user having trouble, getting the RSOP data is very easy: just walk over there and do it! Unfortunately, this is rarely the case. Usually the IT staff are in their own section of the building, perhaps on another floor, or in many cases in an entirely different ZIP code. While you certainly could use some kind of remote-assistance technology to screen-share with the user and plunk out the commands right there on the local system, a capability exists inside GPMC that allows us to query Group Policy Result data remotely, initiating this information request right from GPMC and never having to log in to the remote computer.

This capability is called the Group Policy Results Wizard. Down near the bottom of GPMC, you can run this wizard in order to remotely query a particular computer and user to view their current RSOP data. Computer data is readily available on this report, and user data will be also, as long as the user has logged in to that computer at some point. The coolest thing is that the user does not even have to be logged in while you run this wizard. As long as the user in question has logged in to the computer at some point in the past, RSOP data will be pulled from that computer pertaining to both the computer and user account (RSOP information as of the last time the user logged in there).

The Group Policy Results Wizard queries the remote computer using WMI/RPC network protocols. It uses TCP ports 135 and 445, so you need to ensure that these ports are allowed Inbound on your client computers. If the local firewall on the client's side is denying these ports by default, the wizard will fail to retrieve any information until you open them up. It's a good thing you now know how to create Inbound firewall rules via GPO!

Running the report

Open up GPMC and take a look at the bottom of the left-hand tree. You should see an icon called **Group Policy Results**. Right-click on this and choose **Group Policy Results Wizard...**:

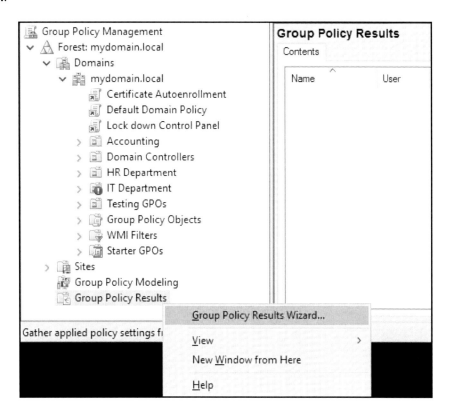

The first decision you get to make in the wizard is which computer to display policy settings for. You could, of course, show data for this computer, but unless you are troubleshooting the Domain Controller or management workstation that you are currently using, you would never select that option. Instead, choose **Another computer**, and specify the name of the system that you want to query. You'll also notice a checkbox that allows you to only query user policies, if you don't have any interest in the computer policies. For our example, I want to see everything that this wizard can get for me, so I am leaving that box unchecked:

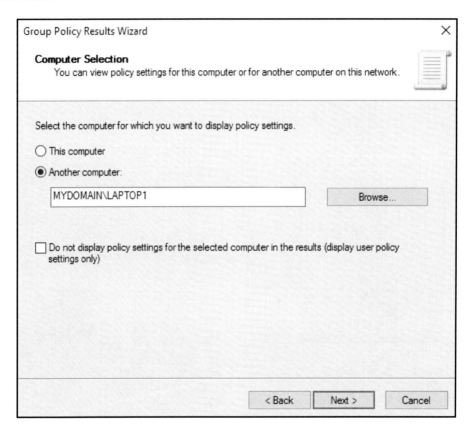

Click **Next**, and the computer is then polled to figure out which user accounts have available data. Any user who has logged in to this computer in the past will be displayed. For my `LAPTOP1` machine, you can see that it started off life with a local user called `jkrause`, and also has options for two domain logins. In the past, I have logged in to this system as both Administrator and Jordan, and so they are both shown to me as available options.

The user who most often utilizes this computer is `Jordan`, so I will select him. In fact, I am going to test and make sure this wizard works properly even when `Jordan` is not logged in to this computer. I just verified that my `LAPTOP1` computer is turned on, but is currently sitting at the login screen.

Also available on this screen of the wizard is an option to only display the computer policy settings, if that is your desire. Again, I am interested in seeing both user and computer information, so I will continue with the options selected in the following screenshot:

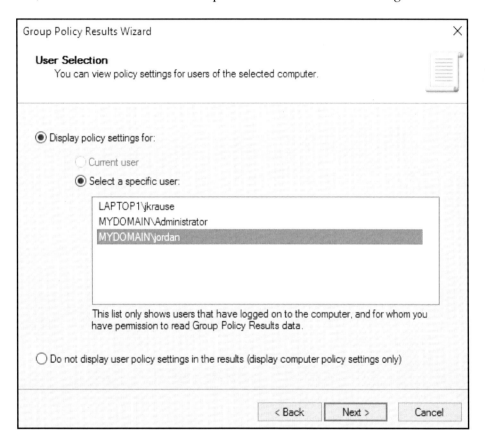

On the final screen of the wizard, simply verify the settings that you have chosen so far. Finishing out the Group Policy Results Wizard then generates a new report that is displayed inside GPMC, underneath the `Group Policy Results` folder. You are free to name this new report however you wish, but you can see the default naming scheme is username on computer name, or in my instance, `jordan on LAPTOP1`:

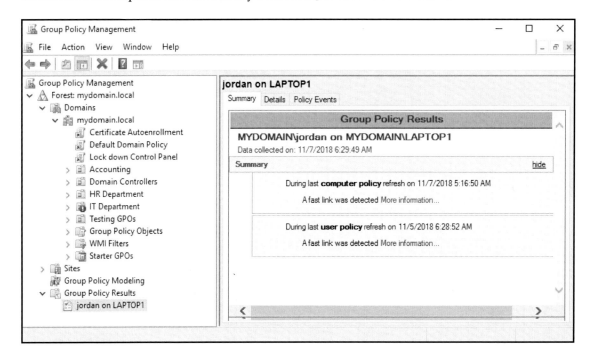

Looking at our new report inside GPMC, you immediately notice that it has some helpful information. Without even clicking on any buttons or tabs, I can already see that both my **computer policy** and **user policy** were last refreshed about 20 minutes before I am writing these words, and that, when processed, the computer had self-identified as being connected via **fast link**.

Moving over to the **Details** tab shows us pretty much everything about what is going on with Group Policy on `LAPTOP1`. Here, I can see information about my computer and user accounts, what site and OU they are part of, and a status of the Group Policy components on those objects. It shows me all of the settings that are coming down from Group Policy, and lists out all of the GPOs that have been applied that gave me those settings. Every GPO that has been applied to `LAPTOP1` and to my Jordan user account is displayed here. When I expand some of the fields, I can even see information about the GPOs themselves, such as where they are linked, what kinds of settings are contained inside, whether they are enforced, and their version numbers:

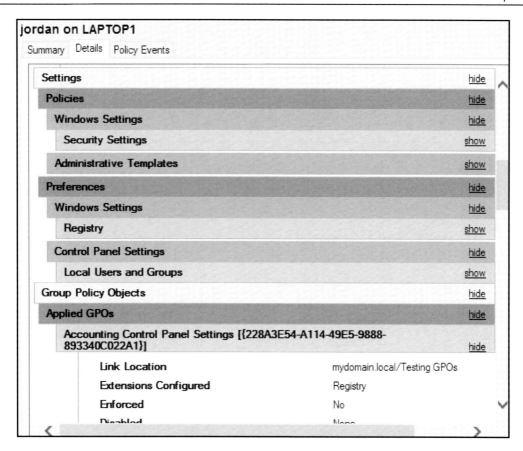

When closing GPMC and re opening, your report still appears to be saved under Group Policy Results, but really all that is saved is your query criteria. Clicking on that report again will tell you that you need to Rerun Query in order to poll for the information again. Rerunning the query is as simple as right-clicking on the report and choosing **Rerun Query**, but I point this out so that you know all of the results are not saved inside GPMC.

In the future, if you ever want to come back and view this information again, you would be best served to save a copy of this report. To do that, right-click on the name of the report and choose the **Save Report...** option. This function will allow you to export and save the report file as an HTML or XML file, which you can then save to another location for safekeeping, or send over to another administrator if you have the need.

The third tab available inside this report is called **Policy Events**. This is essentially the Windows Event Log information from LAPTOP1, but only the events that pertain to Group Policy! If you are troubleshooting a Group Policy issue on LAPTOP1, viewing the event log information this way (automatically filtered to the Group-Policy-related events) would be much faster and easier than poking through Event Viewer on the LAPTOP1 workstation, which would show events from all systems and services inside Windows:

jordan on LAPTOP1

Summary | Details | Policy Events

Type	Date	Time	Source	Category	Event ID	User	Computer
Information	11/7/...	3:28:5...	SceCli	None	1704	N/A	LAPTOP1.my...
Information	11/6/...	11:16:...	SceCli	None	1704	N/A	LAPTOP1.my...
Information	11/5/...	7:04:5...	SceCli	None	1704	N/A	LAPTOP1.my...
Information	11/5/...	2:17:3...	SceCli	None	1704	N/A	LAPTOP1.my...
Information	11/4/...	9:38:3...	SceCli	None	1704	N/A	LAPTOP1.my...
Information	11/3/...	4:59:3...	SceCli	None	1704	N/A	LAPTOP1.my...
Information	11/3/...	12:20:...	SceCli	None	1704	N/A	LAPTOP1.my...
Information	11/2/...	7:41:3...	SceCli	None	1704	N/A	LAPTOP1.my...
Information	11/1/...	3:02:3...	SceCli	None	1704	N/A	LAPTOP1.my...
Information	10/31...	10:23:...	SceCli	None	1704	N/A	LAPTOP1.my...
Information	10/31...	5:44:3...	SceCli	None	1704	N/A	LAPTOP1.my...
Information	10/30...	1:05:3...	SceCli	None	1704	N/A	LAPTOP1.my...
Information	11/7/...	5:46:5...	GroupPoli...	None	1501	MYDOMA...	LAPTOP1.my...
Information	11/7/...	5:16:5...	GroupPoli...	None	1500	NT AUTH...	LAPTOP1.my...
Information	11/7/...	4:01:5...	GroupPoli...	None	1501	MYDOMA...	LAPTOP1.my...
Information	11/7/...	3:28:5...	GroupPoli...	None	1500	NT AUTH...	LAPTOP1.my...
Information	11/7/...	2:16:5...	GroupPoli...	None	1501	MYDOMA...	LAPTOP1.my...
Information	11/7/...	1:40:4...	GroupPoli...	None	1500	NT AUTH...	LAPTOP1.my...
Information	11/7/...	12:31:...	GroupPoli...	None	1501	MYDOMA...	LAPTOP1.my...
Information	11/6/...	11:52:...	GroupPoli...	None	1500	NT AUTH...	LAPTOP1.my...
Information	11/6/...	10:46:...	GroupPoli...	None	1501	MYDOMA...	LAPTOP1.my...
Information	11/6/...	10:04:...	GroupPoli...	None	1500	NT AUTH...	LAPTOP1.my...

Group Policy Modeling

You probably noticed another folder listed near the bottom of GPMC, labeled **Group Policy Modeling**. This is another wizard-driven interface that allows you to configure some fictitious options and create a model of what might happen to a user and computer, should the options that you select during the wizard become true. Basically, you can use this wizard to pretend that you are making changes to a user, a computer, an OU membership, a group membership, and so on, and then take a look at all of the GPO settings that would be put into place in the event that you actually made these changes in production.

While this modeling wizard won't give you a perfect answer that you can 100% rely upon, it is an interesting feature. After running through one of these models, the results presented will be similar to those of the Group Policy Results wizard.

Begin creating a model by right-clicking on **Group Policy Modeling** and choosing the **Group Policy Modeling Wizard...**.

Choose the Domain Controller where you want to run this model, and on the next screen you get to identify the user and computer for which you want to create this model. I have never logged in to any system with the `Laura` user account, so I am going to try to answer the question "What would happen if Laura logged in to `LAPTOP1`?"

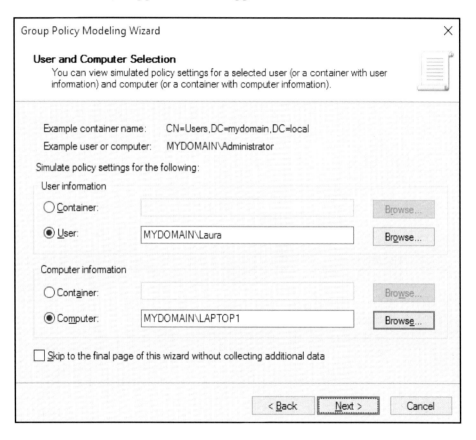

If you simply want to run a quick test for this user+computer combination, you may select the checkbox to skip providing the rest of the optional information and take a look at your results. Proceeding without that checkbox, however, brings you some additional interesting options to add to your model. There are a few more screens where you can create additional pretend information about what the user and computer accounts could look like:

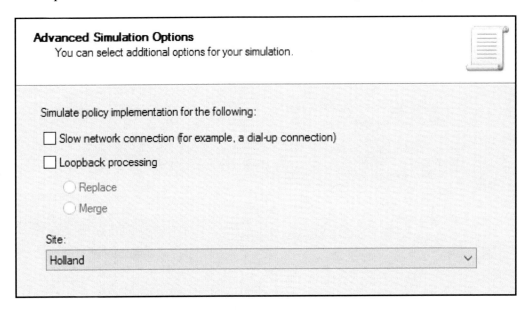

On the **Advanced Simulation Options** screen, you can do any of the following:

- **Slow network connection**: Select this option to cause the model to pretend the computer is connected via a slow link
- **Loopback processing**: Model what RSOP would look like if loopback processing were enabled
- **Site**: Pretend that the computer is sitting in a specific Active Directory site

After making these selections, you come to the **Alternate Active Directory Paths** option. This one is particularly interesting. Here, you get to model what would happen if the user and/or computer accounts resided in a different OU inside Active Directory. Remember that we are providing all fictitious information here; we are just creating a possible scenario. In production, moving computers or users from one OU to another is always a little bit scary. This is because any AD administrator knows that changing OU membership will affect the processing of Group Policy, possibly changing the GPOs that are being applied to the user and computer. By using Group Policy Modeling, we can take the guesswork out of that move, and create a model of what exactly would happen in the event that we moved those objects:

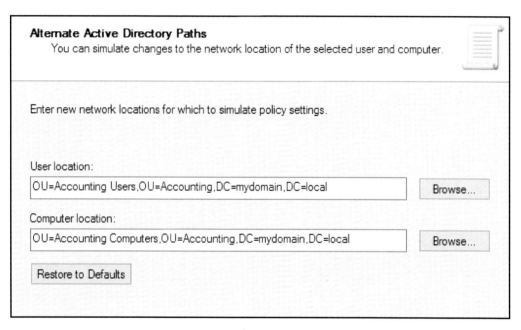

Next, you choose to add the user and/or computer to new Active Directory **Security Groups**, or remove them from existing groups. Remember that this isn't actually changing anything; we are still just pretending that we are going to make these changes.

The last option to select is whether to apply **WMI Filters**. After making all of the selections about your modeling scenario, the wizard will then generate a modeling report. This modeling report is presented in the same format as the Group Policy Results RSOP data, so you can sift through it and then decide whether you want to pursue turning the pretend settings into reality in your production environment. Group Policy Modeling is such a great feature:

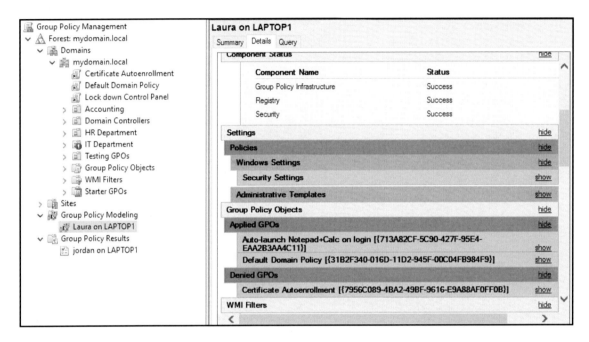

Summary

There are numerous angles to consider when discussing troubleshooting inside Group Policy. Most of the time troubleshooting is specific to a client or a group of users, as you investigate settings gone askew or GPOs who aren't playing nicely with your workstations. To that end, we explored a number of common troubleshooting tools and procedures, including various ways to look at RSOP data. Another form of troubleshooting comes into play when inspecting server-side, or infrastructure, issues. GPO version numbers can help validate successful synchronization and replication among Domain Controllers, as can tools buried inside GPMC. We also talked about the importance of understanding those underlying replication technologies, and external variables that may affect client behavior, such as slow-link detection. Finally, we took a look at two intelligent, but often overlooked, tools inside GPMC: the Group Policy Results and Group Policy Modeling wizards. I hope you log in and start testing them out today!

This chapter on Group Policy Troubleshooting wraps up our core content for Mastering Windows Group Policy. Even if you started this book not knowing what GPO stands for, you now have the knowledge and capability to configure, manage, support, and maintain an Active Directory Group Policy environment in any company you work for.

One topic that has been missing from all of our chapters so far is Group Policy's interaction with PowerShell. We will cover that information in the next chapter. We will explore the commands, `cmdlets`, and syntax needed to accomplish many of the tasks and procedures that we have already covered in this book, but this time ignoring GPMC and instead turning to a PowerShell interface.

10
PowerShell for Group Policy Administration

If you have ever worked with PowerShell, you probably already know that basically anything about the Windows operating system can be manipulated from this fancy blue command-line interface. The same is true for client operating systems as well as servers. Most roles that we implement in Windows Server can be manipulated via GUI or via PowerShell. You are able to tap into the same settings and functionality either way. Active Directory and Group Policy are no different; there are all kinds of PowerShell commands and cmdlets available for interacting with your domain's directory technologies.

In this chapter, we will cover many examples of those cmdlets. The settings, GPOs, links, and permissions that we configure will be things that we have done in this book already, formerly by utilizing GPMC. Now we turn to PowerShell to showcase the capability to perform all of these same tasks from that interface. This allows you to easily save and script common tasks, or to replicate the same task numerous times. Perhaps you have a need to tweak some permission setting on all of the GPOs in your environment, granting or denying a specific user or group to that GPO. If you have hundreds of GPOs, that feels like a daunting task. With some creative PowerShell, this can be scripted and accomplished in an automated fashion while you sip your latte and pretend to be working.

While you could launch PowerShell and utilize it right on a Domain Controller server, there is a lot of inherent risk with taking that approach. Any command-line interface run directly from a server opens up doors into areas of the operating system that you may not want opened. Instead, we are going to use my Windows 10 management workstation where the RSAT tools are installed. I mention this because, once again, using a newer operating system gives us the most functionality. PowerShell has existed inside Windows for many years, but it has been enhanced over those years, and so capabilities of PowerShell in Windows 7 are not on par with capabilities of PowerShell in Windows 10. We will assume that you are going to take the recommended approach and utilize an updated workstation for Group Policy management via PowerShell.

The following topics will be covered in this chapter:

- Importing PowerShell Group Policy modules
- PowerShell for GPOs and Links
- GPO Information and Reporting
- GPO Permissions via PowerShell
- PowerShell to back up and restore GPOs
- Remotely running GPUpdate
- Using PowerShell Help
- Summary

Importing PowerShell Group Policy modules

Since I am using a fresh Windows 10 workstation with the RSAT tools installed, my Group Policy PowerShell cmdlets are all going to work without any special considerations. If you attempt to run the commands in this chapter and are receiving errors that your PowerShell doesn't seem to know what to do with those commands, then it sounds like you are running a version of PowerShell old enough that you need to manually import the Group Policy module before you can expect any results.

The command for importing that module is `Import-Module GroupPolicy`.

If you are unsure about whether or not you already have the Group Policy-specific PowerShell cmdlets available to use, there is a helpful command you can run that lists all of the commands available within the GroupPolicy Module:

```
Get-Command -module grouppolicy | select name
```

Running this command inside a PowerShell prompt will spit out a list of cmdlets that are available inside the Group Policy module, as seen in the following screenshot:

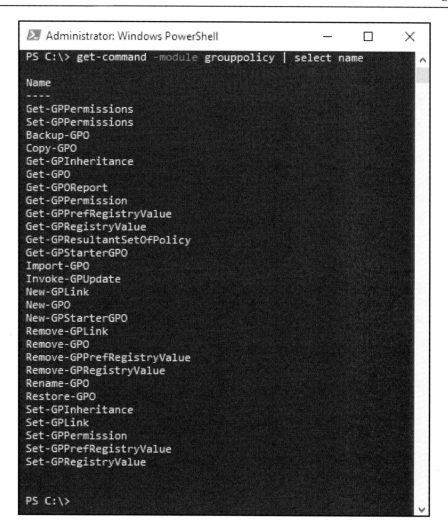

Many of these commands are the ones that we will be experimenting with throughout this chapter.

You may notice that I often interchange the words `command` and `cmdlet` (pronounced command-let). Technically, a `cmdlet` is more like a culmination of multiple commands that work together to do something, but for the most part it doesn't matter what lingo is used. Either way, we are talking about the thing you type into PowerShell to make something happen.

PowerShell for GPOs and Links

We will start using PowerShell to interact with Group Policy by accomplishing some of the most commonly performed actions, working directly with GPOs and their Links. You can utilize PowerShell cmdlets to create GPOs, delete GPOs, create and destroy GPO Links, Security Filters, WMI Filters, and just about anything else that you would normally do via GPMC.

Once again, I will be running PowerShell from my LAPTOP1 computer, to prove that you do not need to be logged into a Domain Controller for anything inside this chapter. PowerShell can be launched via any standard methods for launching an application inside the Windows operating system. You can find it inside the Start Menu, or type in the word PowerShell from either **Start** | **Run** or into an already-open Command Prompt. Probably the easiest and quickest way to open a PowerShell window is to right-click on the **Start** button, which invokes the quick admin menu. On newer versions of Windows 10, you will see a link to open PowerShell right from this menu:

Creating new GPOs

There isn't much to do inside Group Policy without first having some Group Policy Objects to play around with. New GPOs are created from PowerShell with a simple `New-GPO` cmdlet. Let's create a new GPO, and verify that it exists inside GPMC. For the sake of consistency throughout these commands and so that you can easily pluck any of these commands from the chapter and use them directly, I am going to call my new GPO `MyNewGPO`. I had to think pretty hard about that one. This is obviously a terrible name for a GPO, as it does not tell me anything about what this GPO is designed to do, so I wanted to provide an explanation as to why I am naming it as such:

```
New-GPO -name MyNewGPO
```

That's it! The new GPO is now created inside Group Policy. Opening GPMC, we can see our new GPO listed under the `Group Policy Objects` folder:

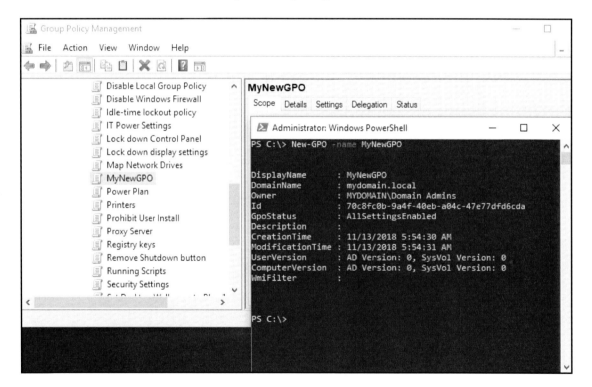

You noticed that when we were ready to specify the name of our new GPO, we used a switch to modify the cmdlet. In this case, we simply used `-name` to specify for the cmdlet that we were about to provide the name of the GPO. Each cmdlet has the potential to work with multiple different switches in order to provide extra information while running the command. Make sure to check out the section of this chapter entitled *Using PowerShell Help* to see the details on discovering all of these cmdlet switches.

Deleting GPOs

Removing a GPO from existence is even faster. There is a simple `Remove-GPO` cmdlet that will completely delete whichever GPO name you specify. Keep in mind that if your GPO name consists of multiple words, you will need to encase the name of the GPO in quotes:

```
Remove-GPO MyNewGPO
```

Or, here is another example:

```
Remove-GPO "This is my other new GPO"
```

Linking a GPO

New GPOs do not do anything until they are linked to a location inside Active Directory. I have now recreated the MyNewGPO object, and we are going to link it to the OU called `IT Department` via the following command:

```
New-GPLink -name MyNewGPO -target "ou=IT Department,dc=mydomain,dc=local"
```

You can see that I had to specify not only the name of the OU, but also its location inside the directory. This ensures that the cmdlet can correctly identify the OU to which we are linking. Checking inside GPMC again, the `IT Department` OU now has a link to `MyNewGPO`:

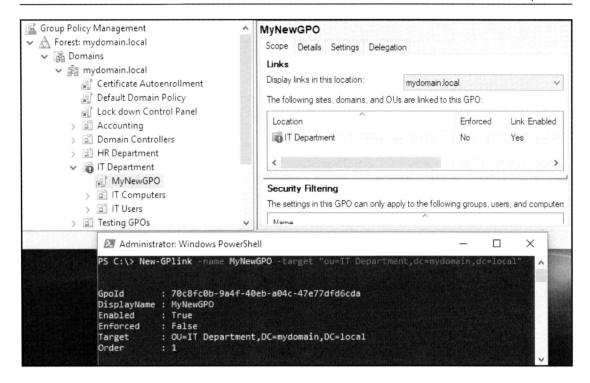

Disabling a GPO Link

Let's pretend that we need to disable that GPO link that was just established to the IT Department OU. We don't want to fully delete the link, because we plan to re-enable it again later, so we will simply issue a command to disable the link and make it inactive:

```
Set-GPLink "MyNewGPO" -target "ou=IT Department,dc=mydomain,dc=local" -
LinkEnabled No
```

As you can guess, re-enabling this link is as simple as running the exact same command, but changing No to **Yes** at the end, as such:

```
Set-GPLink "MyNewGPO" -target "ou=IT Department,dc=mydomain,dc=local" -
LinkEnabled Yes
```

Deleting a GPO Link

But what if we decide that we really don't need MyNewGPO linked to an IT department at all, and now we want to completely remove that link? This is accomplished just as easily as disabling a GPO link; removal is a one-line command inside PowerShell:

```
Remove-GPLink -Name MyNewGPO -Target "ou=IT
Department,dc=mydomain,dc=local"
```

Creating a new Starter GPO

Creating new Starter GPOs is extremely similar to creating a regular GPO, changing only the name of the cmdlet itself. To create a new GPO that is inserted into the Starter GPOs folder, use the following command:

```
New-GPStarterGPO -Name "My New Starter GPO"
```

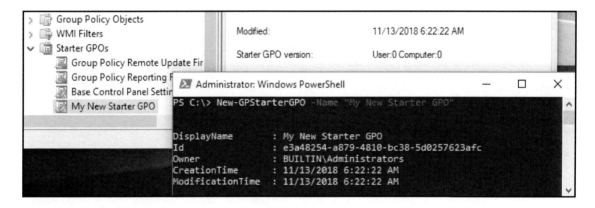

Enforcing a GPO

You already understand what it means to enforce a GPO, and how to do it inside GPMC. Now let's turn to PowerShell to enforce the link between MyNewGPO and the IT Department OU, in order to override the inherency blocking that is currently in place on that IT Department OU:

```
Set-GPLink -Name "MyNewGPO" -Target "ou=IT Department,dc=mydomain,dc=local"
-Enforced Yes
```

Disabling GPO enforcement

Now we back away our previous change, leaving the link in place at the `IT Department`, but changing it back so that `Enforced` is no longer enabled:

```
Set-GPLink -Name "MyNewGPO" -Target "ou=IT Department,dc=mydomain,dc=local"
-Enforced No
```

Setting inheritance blocking on an OU

You can see in some of the previous screenshots that my `IT Department` OU has inheritance blocking enabled. This is showcased by the little blue exclamation mark that sits on top of the OU. How can we use PowerShell to go about setting inheritance blocking for an OU? Let's issue the command to enable inheritance blocking on the `HR Department` OU:

```
Set-GPInheritance -Target "ou=HR Department,dc=mydomain,dc=local" -
IsBlocked Yes
```

After refreshing GPMC, we can see that blue exclamation marks now exist on both `IT Department` as well as `HR Department`:

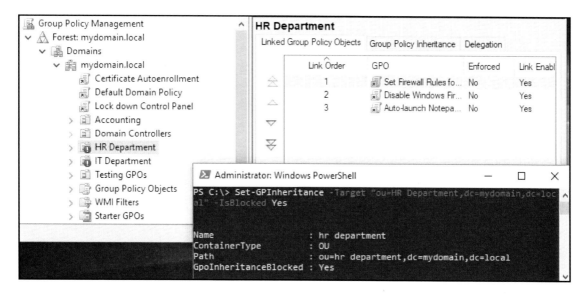

Configuring security filtering on a GPO

Remember that one of the most powerful ways to filter your GPOs so that they only apply to specific users or devices is by using the Security Filtering section of a GPO's properties. Setting up Security Filtering inside the GPMC is quite fast and easy, requiring just a few mouse clicks. We must first remove Authenticated Users from Security Filtering so that the GPO no longer applies to everyone and everything, and instead specify a more selective group or even individual user or computer accounts to which the GPO should apply. In PowerShell, we need to use multiple commands for this to happen.

First, we must remove the Authenticated Users permission that exists by default inside any new GPO:

```
Set-GPPermissions -Name "MyNewGPO" -Replace -PermissionLevel None -
TargetName 'Authenticated Users' -TargetType group
```

Now that the GPO is cleared of Security Filtering settings, it is not applying to anyone at the present time. Step 2 is to plug information back into Security Filtering. I am going to issue a command that sets up Security Filtering for my Server Administrators group:

```
Set-GPPermissions -Name "MyNewGPO" -PermissionLevel gpoapply -TargetName
"Server Administrators" -TargetType group
```

After running both commands, GPMC now shows me correctly that MyNewGPO is filtered to only the Server Administrators group:

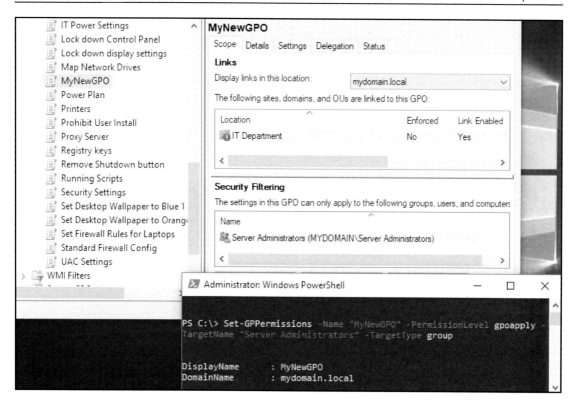

Modifying Security Filtering is really modifying permissions inside Group Policy, which is a topic that we will discuss more thoroughly in a few pages. This example is presented here to give you a quick taste of permissions-related cmdlets, but also because modifying Security Filtering is a very common task for any Group Policy administrator.

GPO information and reporting

PowerShell can also be handy for pulling information about GPOs, or from inside GPOs. This can be used as a powerful tool for documenting and reporting on your Group Policy environment. Remember that since we are using PowerShell for this data, all of the PowerShell rules for manipulating data output by object still apply. While this is not a book about PowerShell itself, I will say that oftentimes when issuing commands that output large amounts of data, the data is able to be formatted in various ways by using a pipe (|) and some syntax behind the pipe. We'll point out an example of that data formatting in our first cmdlet, but know that these object formatting capabilities are present whenever querying information with pretty much any PowerShell cmdlet, Group Policy-related or not.

Viewing information about a GPO

Information about the GPOs themselves is visible inside the **Details** tab of GPMC. This same information is also available by using the `Get-GPO` cmdlet in PowerShell. In the following screenshot, I have issued a simple `Get-GPO MyNewGPO` command which displays for me the same information that would be present if we opened GPMC and visited the `Details` tab of `MyNewGPO`:

```
Administrator: Windows PowerShell                          —    □    ×
PS C:\> Get-GPO MyNewGPO


DisplayName       : MyNewGPO
DomainName        : mydomain.local
Owner             : MYDOMAIN\Domain Admins
Id                : 70c8fc0b-9a4f-40eb-a04c-47e77dfd6cda
GpoStatus         : AllSettingsEnabled
Description       :
CreationTime      : 11/13/2018 5:54:30 AM
ModificationTime  : 11/13/2018 6:45:18 AM
UserVersion       : AD Version: 0, SysVol Version: 0
ComputerVersion   : AD Version: 0, SysVol Version: 0
WmiFilter         :


PS C:\>
```

While it's cool to be able to query this information inside PowerShell, it becomes powerful when you realize that you can just as easily pull this same information for ALL of the GPOs in your domain:

```
Get-GPO -ALL
```

This command presents me with pages and pages and pages of information, because even in this simple test lab environment, I have created quite a number of GPOs as we progressed through these chapters. While this command gave me some good data output, it's a bit overwhelming. Perhaps instead of spitting out all of the information about each GPO, I would rather just see a quick list of all the GPOs in my domain. Here, we will use a pipe in order to format the output of the `Get-GPO` command, and filter it down to showing us only the `DisplayName` field for each GPO. Now that's some data that I can get excited about:

```
Get-GPO -ALL | select DisplayName
```

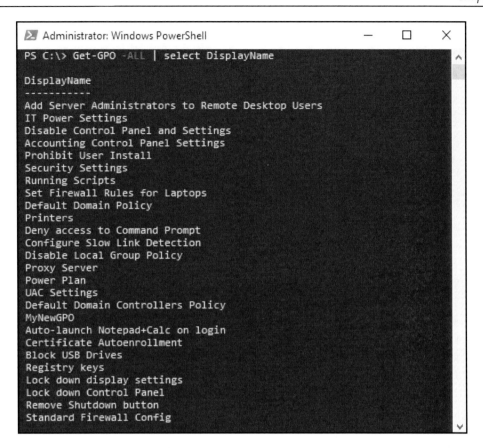

GPO Reports

We know that a nice HTML or XML report can be generated for each GPO from inside GPMC, simply by right-clicking on the GPO. Is there a way to get that same report via PowerShell? Of course! Here is a command to generate the HTML report from MyNewGPO:

```
Get-GPOReport -Name MyNewGPO -ReportType HTML -Path
C:\GPO_Reports\MyNewGPO.html
```

Looking inside the `C:\GPO_Reports` folder on my workstation, I can see and double-click on this new HTML report to view information about `MyNewGPO` inside a browser window:

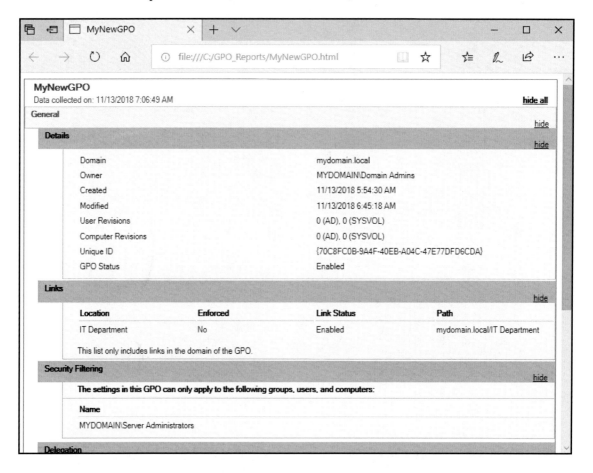

Now, what if we combine what we know about `Get-GPOReport` with our previous examples of the `Get-GPO` cmdlet? Would it perhaps be possible to generate a GPO report of all GPOs that exist in my environment? Sure enough, that is also easily done by adding one simple switch to `Get-GPOReport`, as seen here:

```
Get-GPOReport -ALL -ReportType HTML -Path C:\GPO_Reports\AllGPOs.html
```

What a quick and easy way to document everything about your Group Policy objects, with one simple PowerShell command!

RSOP data via PowerShell

The Resultant Set of Policy information is available in a myriad of different ways, as we have already discovered. One additional way to get a quick bearing on what is going to be applied to a particular user or computer is by using `Get-GPResultantSetOfPolicy` inside PowerShell. This cmdlet can also generate some HTML or XML reports for you, but rather than containing information about the insides of the GPOs, these reports will show you RSOP data for the object specified.

As an example, let's query my `Jordan` user account and the `LAPTOP1` computer account at the same time, to find out what is going to be applied when I log into that machine. You can use this command with separate `-user` or `-computer` switches as well, if you have the need to query only one or the other:

```
Get-GPResultantSetOfPolicy -user MyDomain\Jordan -computer LAPTOP1 -
ReportType HTML -Path C:\RSOP_Reports\Jordan_LAPTOP1.html
```

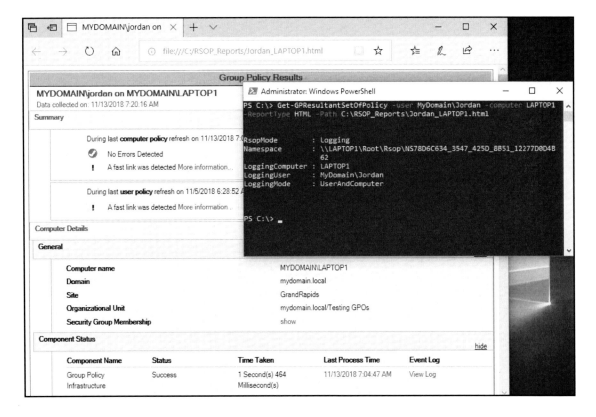

GPO permissions via PowerShell

The application of GPOs is all about permissions. When Group Policy processes on a computer or a user, it basically tries to apply everything all the time, and the only reason you don't receive every setting from every GPO on your machine is because the permissions surrounding that GPO have been stacked in a way that you only receive the items that your Group Policy admins have deemed necessary to your user account or your workstation. We have already worked with a myriad of different permission tiers through the GPMC, now let's take a peek into the `GPPermissions` cmdlets that are available inside PowerShell in order to modify GPO permissions from a command-line interface.

Viewing current GPO permissions

Inside GPMC, you can view the current permission settings for any GPO by clicking on the GPO and then visiting the Delegation tab. To see the same information in text format from PowerShell, we can use the `Get-GPPermissions` cmdlet as shown in the following command. The `-all` specification at the end of the command tells Group Policy that we want to see all permissions that are listed inside the **Delegation** tab:

```
Get-GPPermissions -name "MyNewGPO" -all
```

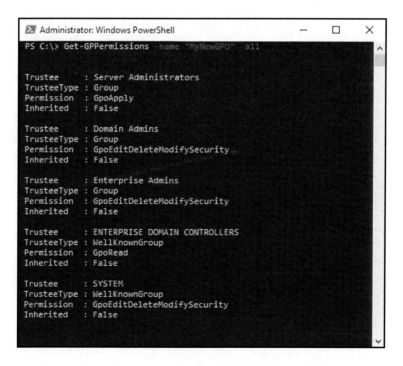

This is a pretty normal listing of default permissions on a GPO, except that you can see our definition for Server Administrators that shows up as a result of Security Filtering being specified for that individual group.

In addition to viewing all of the permissions for a GPO, you can filter that output down to selectively view GPO permissions that are related to a single user or group. Earlier, when we covered the topic of modifying Security Filtering via PowerShell, we used a switch called -TargetType and we set it to group, because we were injecting a group into those Security Filtering permissions. The -TargetType switch can also be set to user to query or set information for a specific user, which we will accomplish here.

I am currently working with the GPO called Map Network Drives. My user named Jackson needs to have permissions to be able to edit this particular GPO. I am going to use PowerShell to query this GPO specifically for Jackson's user account to quickly check his level of permissions:

```
Get-GPPermissions -name "Map Network Drives" -TargetType User -TargetName
"Jackson"
```

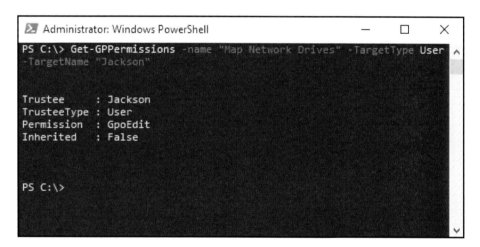

Sure enough, here we can see that Jackson has the Permission called GpoEdit, which means he has sufficient rights to edit this GPO if he should have the need to do so.

Setting GPO permissions

If you can view permissions via PowerShell, you should be able to configure new GPO permissions via PowerShell as well, correct? Absolutely right. While this is slightly more difficult than viewing permissions because you need to know the special syntax for which permission type is going to accomplish what you are looking for, permissions are added into GPO Delegation by simple, single PowerShell cmdlets. This is akin to configuring permissions for users or groups via the **Delegation** tab inside GPMC.

Before jumping into a sample command, let's discuss what the various `PermissionLevel` settings are when working with Group Policy permissions inside PowerShell:

- `None`: No permissions. As we experienced earlier when removing Authenticated Users from the Security Filtering section of our GPO, we can utilize `PermissionLevel=None` to remove a user or group from having permissions inside `GPO Delegation`.
- `GpoRead`: Grants a user or group `Read` access to the GPO.
- `GpoApply`: Grants the **Apply group policy** rights. Remember that this one is necessary for a user, group, or computer to successfully apply the GPO.
- `GpoEdit`: Grants permission to edit a GPO.
- `GpoEditDeleteModifySecurity`: This one is kind of a mouthful. It grants someone access to do pretty much whatever they want with a GPO, including editing as well as deleting it or configuring permissions on it later. Keep in mind that this delegation does *not* include `GpoApply` rights. This is a nice way to grant an administrator access to tweak or modify a GPO, without causing the GPO to automatically start applying to their user account when they log into a computer.

If you were to add a new permission to the Delegation tab inside GPMC, you'll notice that three of these permissions are more or less exactly the same as the options provided to you in the drop-down box:

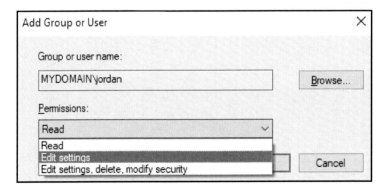

Let's try modifying permissions from PowerShell. I want to grant a user named Grace the ability to edit, delete, or in any other way modify my GPO called `MyNewGPO`. Here is the command for accomplishing such a task:

```
Set-GPPermissions -Name MyNewGPO -PermissionLevel
GpoEditDeleteModifySecurity -TargetType User -TargetName "Grace"
```

Removing GPO permissions

I mentioned using `None` as a `PermissionLevel` to remove someone's rights from `GPO Delegation`, but let's spin out a sample command to make sure you can do it on your own. When deleting a GPO or a GPO Link, you are utilizing entirely different PowerShell cmdlets (one starting with the word `Remove`) from what you use for building those objects, but for GPO permission removal you do not use a `Remove-type` command. Instead, you continue to use `Set-GPPermissions`, but flag them for configuring a `PermissionLevel` called None. Here is a command that reverses the rights that we just handed to our user called Grace. We have now decided she does not require permission to modify `MyNewGPO`, and so we are going to take those rights away from her:

```
Set-GPPermissions -Name MyNewGPO -PermissionLevel None -TargetType User -
TargetName "Grace"
```

Maybe even more useful is a sample command to remove `Authenticated Users` from a GPO, as we did when setting Security Filtering earlier. This is a common thing to do whenever you want to filter a GPO down to particular users or groups. The following command will remove `Authenticated Users` from `Delegation` on `MyNewGPO`:

```
Set-GPPermissions -Name "MyNewGPO" -TargetName "Authenticated Users" -
TargetType Group -PermissionLevel None
```

You probably noticed by now that in these commands I am sometimes changing around the order of the different switches. Sometimes -`PermissionLevel` comes first followed by -`TargetType`, then -`TargetName`. Sometimes, it's completely the opposite! The order of these switches does not matter, as long as they are all specified within the command when you press *Enter*.

Using PowerShell to back up and restore GPOs

PowerShell is so powerful because it has access to do anything on a system, but also because normal mundane tasks can be saved off as scripts and run at scheduled intervals without any administrative input. One of those regular mundane tasks for you could be the backing up of GPOs in your domain. Wouldn't it be nice if I could create a scheduled task that backed up all of my GPOs once a day, every day? There is no accommodation for that inside GPMC (though it's not too difficult to log in there and back them all up—but then you have to remember to do that every day). If we turn to PowerShell, we can come up with a simple one-liner command that backs up all of the GPOs in our domain in a single action. Then we can use a plethora of task-scheduling or scripting tools to simply make sure that our command gets run every 24 hours.

Backing up a single GPO

Let's start with backing up a single GPO, if that is ever a needed item for you. The following is the PowerShell command to backup `MyNewGPO` to a folder on my system called `C:\GPO_Backups`:

```
Backup-GPO -name MyNewGPO -Path C:\GPO_Backups
```

Backing up all of the GPOs

Backing up a single GPO is fine and dandy, but using one single command to back them all up? Now that's what I'm talking about! Here is a command that will immediately back up every GPO in our domain:

```
Backup-Gpo -All -Path C:\GPO_Backups -Comment "This is the regular nightly
backup of all GPOs"
```

Cool! You can even add comments to the backup jobs! After allowing this command to run, if we take a look inside `C:\GPO_Backups` we will see many folders with crazy names. Backing up GPOs via PowerShell accomplishes the same thing that it does via GPMC – where each GPO backup will be stored using a unique, random GUID so that you can back up time and time again into this same folder, and the backups will never step on each other's toes or overwrite each other:

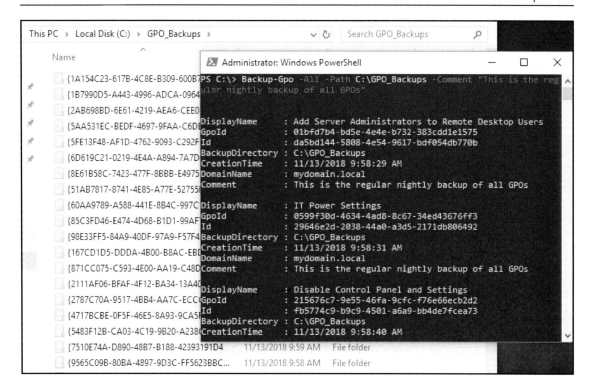

Restoring a GPO

We know that there are two different ways to restore a GPO inside GPMC—one to overwrite a current GPO with an older version (rolling it back), and another restoration process that brings back a GPO that has been completely deleted from Group Policy. Weirdly, you can only use PowerShell's Restore-GPO to do the rollback version, recovering a GPO back to a previous version if the GPO still exists. This is because the PowerShell cmdlet to restore GPOs is going to look for the name of the GPO to perform the restoration, and if that name is missing it won't know what to do.

So, if you do have the need to restore a fully deleted GPO using PowerShell, you would have to first create a new GPO with the exact same name as the GPO that got deleted, and then perform the restoration command. Just a heads-up on that.

Regardless, it's good to cover the bases and make sure you have the information needed in order to restore a GPO from PowerShell, in the event that you're ever asked to do so. Here is a command to restore `MyNewGPO` from a previous copy that is stored inside `C:\GPO_Backups`:

```
Restore-GPO -Name "MyNewGPO" -Path C:\GPO_Backups
```

 You see in the command that I did not specify anything about a particular backup file from which to restore. The `Restore-GPO` cmdlet automatically assumes that you want to recover the GPO to the newest backup file, so it goes ahead and does that. If you had multiple backup copies inside that folder and wanted to specify a particular one, you could additionally provide the `-BackupID` parameter in your command to specify a particular version of the backup.

Remotely running GPUpdate

Whenever troubleshooting Group Policy on a client computer, the first step is almost always connect to the computer and do a `GPUpdate`. Support personnel want to try this first because there are many cases where missing or incorrect GPO settings are simply the result of a timing issue, and manually issuing a `GPUpdate` command will resolve the situation.

This scenario means that you as the support person have to find a way to remotely connect to that user's workstation, simply for the purpose of typing this command. You could try to talk the user through it over the phone, but we all know how easy it is to spell out commands (not easy), let alone explain to the user how to get the command prompt open in the first place.

Starting with Windows 7 clients, there is a way to remotely invoke a `GPUpdate` command. Nice! All that is needed to do this is a PowerShell window open on your own computer.

 Well, the receiving client computer also needs to allow your remote command through its firewall on the inbound. The same ports are required here as when GPMC reaches into a computer for Group Policy Results data. TCP ports `135` and `445` will need to be allowed between your computer and the endpoint computer.

As an example, I am currently logged into my `LAPTOP1` workstation. A user is having trouble on `LAPTOP2`, and I want to try a `GPUpdate` as a first troubleshooting step. Without ever talking to the user or connecting to their computer, I simply open up my local PowerShell prompt and issue the following command:

```
Invoke-GPUpdate –Computer LAPTOP2
```

That's it! A command has been issued over the network to `LAPTOP2`, asking it to perform a background Group Policy refresh. Now I can ask the user to test again, and see if that corrected the problem.

Using PowerShell Help

All PowerShell cmdlets have a particular syntax that the command must follow to work properly. Additionally, many of the cmdlets have many different switches, or variables, that you can configure in order to tweak the command to do something specific. We have walked through many examples of this already. What if you want to discover more about any particular PowerShell cmdlet? You could certainly turn to the internet and type the name of the command into your search engine, and that would likely steer you toward a Microsoft Technet page with all of the information you are looking for. If you don't feel like searching the internet, there is help information stored right inside PowerShell. For any cmdlet inside PowerShell for which you want to query up all of its related options and information, you simply open PowerShell and type the word `help` followed by the name of the cmdlet.

Let's take a look at one together. We have already used the `New-GPO` cmdlet, but we did so in a very simple way. There are additional options you can flag onto a `New-GPO` command in order to set up more things about the GPO when it is first created. For example, you can create a new GPO and require it to be built from a Starter GPO, just like we can do inside GPMC. If I want to learn more about how to build out that more complex command, I would open PowerShell and type `Help New-GPO`:

```
Administrator: Windows PowerShell                          —    □    ✕

PS C:\> Help New-GPO

NAME
    New-GPO

SYNTAX
    New-GPO [-Name] <string> [-Comment <string>] [-Domain <string>]
    [-Server <string>] [-WhatIf] [-Confirm]  [<CommonParameters>]

    New-GPO [-Name] <string> -StarterGpoGuid <guid> [-Comment
    <string>] [-Domain <string>] [-Server <string>] [-WhatIf]
    [-Confirm]  [<CommonParameters>]

    New-GPO [-Name] <string> -StarterGpoName <string> [-Comment
    <string>] [-Domain <string>] [-Server <string>] [-WhatIf]
    [-Confirm]  [<CommonParameters>]


ALIASES
    None
```

Depending on your machine's internet connection, the results displayed may be static data that is stored inside PowerShell, or it may be more comprehensive. If there is updated information available online, and if PowerShell has access to the internet to pull the newest Help data from Microsoft's server, you may see even better results. You will see a message regarding this near the end of the command output, so you know whether or not you still need to visit Technet in order to find the latest/newest information.

Summary

PowerShell is the ultimate Windows administration tool, capable of reaching into even the deepest, darkest parts of our computer and server operating systems. Group Policy administration can be made more efficient by defining your common, everyday tasks, and building out PowerShell commands in order to perform those actions. This enables you to do the daily chores without having to log into a Domain Controller, and without having to open GPMC in any way. These cmdlets can then be saved to be run very quickly in the future, or even set to run automatically at scheduled intervals, such as with GPO Backups.

There are many ways to dig deeper into GPOs by using the PowerShell cmdlets inside the Group Policy module, allowing you to accomplish anything via PowerShell that you would otherwise be able to do with GPMC, including modifying the settings inside GPOs.

Do I expect all of you to immediately jump ship and start using PowerShell for all Group Policy-related tasks? No way. Until you take the time to really learn and experiment with these cmdlets, they will take longer than popping open GPMC and doing it the normal way. But, if you put in the time, you won't regret it. Not only is PowerShell useful for Group Policy administration, knowledge of PowerShell can be advantageous to all aspects of your IT career.

Thank you for sticking with me on this jungle safari ride through Microsoft Group Policy. If you use Active Directory as your directory services technology (and almost every business in the world does), you already have Group Policy sitting, waiting at your fingertips. I hope this book has encouraged you to get out there and start using it! If you're already well-versed in all things GPO, then my goal is to whet your whistle for getting back in there at a deeper level to discover new security features that get introduced with every iteration of the Windows operating system. If you haven't re-visited your security policies and posture in the last year, you are almost certainly missing out on some features in your environment!

Other Books You May Enjoy

If you enjoyed this book, you may be interested in these other books by Packt:

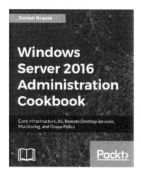

Windows Server 2016 Administration Cookbook
Jordan Krause

ISBN: 978-1-78913-593-0

- Become skilled in the navigation of Windows Server 2016, and explore the technologies and options that it provides
- Build the infrastructure required for a successful Windows Server network
- Move away from those open-source web server platforms and start migrating your websites to Server 2016's Internet Information Services today
- Provide a centralized point for users to access applications and data by configuring Remote Desktop Services
- Compose optimal Group Policies

Learn PowerShell Core 6.0

David das Neves, Jan-Hendrik Peters

ISBN: 978-1-78883-898-6

- Get to grips with Powershell Core 6.0
- Explore basic and advanced PowerShell scripting techniques
- Get to grips with Windows PowerShell Security
- Work with centralization and DevOps with PowerShell
- Implement PowerShell in your organization through real-life examples
- Learn to create GUIs and use DSC in production

Leave a review - let other readers know what you think

Please share your thoughts on this book with others by leaving a review on the site that you bought it from. If you purchased the book from Amazon, please leave us an honest review on this book's Amazon page. This is vital so that other potential readers can see and use your unbiased opinion to make purchasing decisions, we can understand what our customers think about our products, and our authors can see your feedback on the title that they have worked with Packt to create. It will only take a few minutes of your time, but is valuable to other potential customers, our authors, and Packt. Thank you!

Index